CHICAGO HOME BOOK

"YOU USE A GLASS MIRROR TO SEE YOUR FACE; YOU USE WORKS OF ART TO SEE YOUR SOUL."

George Bernard Shaw

CHICAGO HOME BOOK

A COMPREHENSIVE HANDS-ON DESIGN SOURCEBOOK TO BUILDING, REMODELING, DECORATING, FURNISHING AND LANDSCAPING A LUXURY HOME IN CHICAGO AND ITS SUBURBS

Photo courtesy of:
Susan Fredman

PUBLISHED BY

The

Ashley

Group

Chicago   New York   Los Angeles

Las Vegas   Philadelphia   Atlanta   Detroit

Phoenix   South Florida   Washington D.C.   Denver

San Francisco   Raleigh   Dallas

Published By
The Ashley Group
1350 E. Touhy Avenue
Des Plaines, Illinois 60018
847-390-2882 FAX 847-390-2903
www.chicagohomebook.com

Cahners
Cahners Business Information
A Division of Reed Elsevier Inc

ISBN 1-58862-001-8

CHICAGO HOME BOOK

Publisher *David Julian*

Editor-in-Chief *Dana Felmly*

Managing Editor *David Jackson*

Writers *Barb McHatton, Cathy Kallas*

Senior Account Executive *Lori Dub*

Account Executives *Andy Rees, Jim Carroll, Jeff Carnes*

Group Production Director *Steve Perlstein*

Production Director *Catherine Wajer*

Creative Director *Maura Gonsalves*

Production Managers *Anna Dronjak, Cory Ottenwess, Amie Smith*

Production Assistants *Jola Krysztopa, Karen Mages,
Kent Giacomozzi, Kirsten Hansen*

Graphic Designers *Sheri Bolliger, Ronda Farina, Kent Giacomozzi, Theodore
Hahn, Kirsten Hansen, Dona Kight, Dorit Paryzerband, Scott Piers*

Director of Marketing *Maria Bronzovich*

Public Relations Manager *Adam Miezio*

Prepress *Cahners Prepress, Lehigh Press Colortronics*

Printed in Hong Kong by *Dai Nippon Printing Company*

THE ASHLEY GROUP

Group Publisher *Paul A. Casper*

Director of Publications *N. David Shiba*

Regional Director *Jospeh M. Lattimer*

Director of Finance *Patricia Lavigne*

Group Administration *Nicole Port, Kimberly Spizzirri*

CAHNERS BUSINESS INFORMATION

Chief Executive Officer *Marc Teren*

Chief Financial Officer *John Poulin*

Executive Vice President *Ronald C. Andriani*

Vice President, Finance *David Lench*

Front Cover *Architects Wheeler Kearns
Photo by Steve Hall/Hedrich-Blessing*

Back Cover *Landscape Architects Mariani Landscape*

Editor's Note

The Chicago Home Book, the premier volume of the *Home Book* network, was created like most other successful products and brands—out of need. The *Home Book* concept was originally conceived by Paul Casper, currently Group Publisher of the Ashley Group. Paul, a resident of the North Shore, at one time was planning the renovation of his home. However, he quickly discovered problems locating credible professionals to help his dream become a reality. Well, Paul's dream did become a reality—it just happens to be a different dream now! Instead of Paul simply finishing his new home, he foresaw the need by consumers nationwide to have a complete home resource guide at their disposal. Thus, Paul created the distinct *Home Book* to fulfill the consumer need for reliable and accessible home improvement information.

After three years of successful publishing, the *Home Book* gained exposure and credibility, and drew the attention of Cahners Business Information. The *Home Book* proved to be attractive enough for Cahners, and in April of 1999, Cahners purchased it. Since then, the *Home Book* network has grown rapidly. Today, *Home Books* are available in three new markets: South Florida, Washington D.C. and Los Angeles. Before the end of 2001, the *Home Book* will also be published in New York, Dallas, Denver, Detroit, and Atlanta.

Public demand for high quality, home improvement services is still increasing. The Ashley Group recognizes this trend, and continues the challenging task of providing the finest and most experienced professionals to consumers. We exact the same amount of dedication and hard work out of ourselves as we expect from our *Home Book* clients. As a result, we are able to offer you the credible and reliable family of *Home Books*. We sincerely hope our hard work rewards you with the quality craftsmanship you deserve, turning that dream house of yours into reality. Congratulations on purchasing a *Home Book*, and enjoy the inspiring ideas within, as much as the actual work!

Thank you very much, from myself and The Ashley Group.

Dana Felmly *Editor-in-Chief*

Why
You Should
Use This
Book

Why You'll Want to Use the Chicago Home Book

At times, in this high-speed information-driven culture, we can easily become lost and disoriented. Where we find information, how we find it, and how credible this information is, has become critical to consumers everywhere.

The *Chicago Home Book* recognizes and addresses these concerns, and provides ease of use and comfort to consumers looking to build, renovate or enhance their home. As a consumer, the anxiety of searching for trustworthy, experienced housing professionals can be overwhelming.

Relief is in Sight

The *Chicago Home Book* puts an end to this stress. It offers you, the reader, a comprehensive, hands-on guide to building, remodeling, decorating, furnishing and landscaping a home in Chicago and its suburbs. The book also offers readers convenience and comfort.

Convenience

The **Chicago Home Book** compiles the area's top home service providers with easy-to-read listings by trade. It also dissuades readers' fears of unreliable service providers by featuring many of the finest professionals available, specialists who rank among the top 10 of their respective fields in the Chicago area. Their outstanding work has netted them many awards in their fields. The other listings are recommendations made by these advertisers.

The goal of the **Chicago Home Book** creators is to provide a high quality product that goes well beyond the scope of mere Yellow Pages. Its focus is to provide consumers with credible, reliable, and experienced professionals, accompanied by photographic examples of their work.

This crucial resource was unavailable to the founders of the **Chicago Home Book** when they were working on their own home improvement projects. This lack of information spurred them on to create the book, and to assist other consumers in finding the proper professionals that suit their specific needs. Now, thanks to the team's entrepreneurial spirit, you have the **Chicago Home Book** at your fingertips, to guide you on your home enhancement journey.

Comfort

Embrace this book, enjoy it and relish it, because at one time it didn't exist; but now, someone has done your homework for you. Instead of running all over town, you'll find in these pages:

* More than 700 listings of professionals, specializing in 40 different trades.

* Instructional information for choosing and working with architects, contractors, landscapers and interior designers.

* More than 1,000 photos inspiring innovative interior and exterior modeling ideas.

*A compilation of the area's top home enhancement service providers with easy-to-read listings by trade.

Excitement... The **Chicago Home Book** can turn your dream into a reality!

David Julian

David Julian, *Publisher*

The premier resource provider for the luxury home market

Chicago Home Book

About the Front Cover:
An elegant setting created by architects Wheeler Kearns.

Contents

Continued

407

124

139

22

538

237

Chicago Home Book

Contents

459

338

71

639

665

How To Use

TABLE OF CONTENTS

Start here for an at-a-glance guide to the 12 tabbed categories and numerous subcategories. The book is organized for quick, easy access to the information you want, when you want it. The Table of Contents provides an introduction to the comprehensive selection of information.

HOT DISTRICTS

An easy guide to a day of shopping in seven of our city's hottest districts - Lincoln Park, The Merchandise Mart's 13th Floor, River North, Winnetka, Barrington, Geneva and Evanston. Use the Hot District maps and information to plan weekend shopping sprees to some of the liveliest centers for furniture, fabrics, accessories, art, antiques and more.

"HOW-TO" ARTICLES

Each tabbed section begins with a locally researched article on how to achieve the best possible result in your home building, remodeling, decorating or landscape project. These pages help take the fear and trepidation out of the process by giving you the kind of information you need to communicate effectively with professionals and how to be prepared for the nature of the process. You'll have a step by step guide, aiding you in finding the materials you need in the order you'll need them.

DESIGN UPDATE

Read what top home industry professionals think are the most exciting new styles, future trends and best ideas in their fields as we begin the new century. See even more inspiring photos of some of the Chicago area's most beautiful, up-to-date luxury homes and landscapes. It's a visual feast, full of great ideas.

FOCUS ON...

What's it like to live in Chicago, the North Shore or the Western Suburbs? These pages are filled with beautiful visuals that showcase the special atmosphere of these three well-known residential areas and their current design trends.

This Book

DIVIDER TABS

Use the sturdy tabs to go directly to the section of the book you're interested in. A table of contents for each section's sub-categories is printed on the front of each tab. Quick, easy, convenient.

LISTINGS

Culled from current, comprehensive data and qualified through careful local research, the listings are a valuable resource as you assemble the team of experts and top quality suppliers for your home project. We have included references to their ad pages throughout the book.

NEW FEATURES!

From Interior Design Spotlight to New in the Showroom, we've devoted more attention to specific areas within the various sections. We've also gone in-depth, with feature articles in the Architects and Custom Builders sections.

ESSAYS

When home design, builders and landscape professionals get the chance to speak directly to their future clients, what do they have to say? Find out by reading the Chicago Home Book's Professional Essay Series. Their knowledge and unique viewpoints will entertain, enlighten and educate you. See the Table of Contents for the Essay pages.

BEAUTIFUL VISUALS

The most beautiful, inspiring and comprehensive collections of homes and materials of distinction in the Chicagoland area. On these pages, our advertisers present exceptional examples of their finest work. Use these visuals for ideas as well as resources.

INDEXES

This extensive cross reference system allows easy access to the information on the pages of the book. You can check by alphabetical order or individual profession.

The A
Grou

RESOURCE COLLECTION

sual resource images, and strives to provide the highest
esources available, to upscale consumers and professionals.
roup, visit our website at www.ashleygroup@cahners.com.
member of the Reed Elsevier plc group, is a leading
ertical markets, including entertainment,
ncompasses more than 140 Web sites as well as *Variety*,
arket-leading business-to-business magazines

Design

22

GREGORY MAIRE
ARCHITECTS, LTD.,

Gregory Maire: "Today's clients are waking up to
'green architecture,' in which building form and
siting evolve organically out of issues such as sun
and shade, natural ventilation, day lighting, non-toxic
building materials and energy management. With a
sensitive use of native stone, wood and glass, these
homes can offer all the warmth, textures and scale
of traditional styles while honoring the ecological
imperatives of the 21st Century."

...teriors and landscapes in Chicago and its suburbs? Read ...w in their businesses, and what's coming in the future.

"Discriminating designers are creating furniture-style vanities"

DREAM KITCHENS,

Rick Glickman: "Following the trend of the 'unfitted kitchen,' discriminating designers are creating furniture-style vanities for powder rooms and master baths. Some utilize antique dining room buffets as a sink base, others create their own design from customized modular cabinetry."

STONECUTTERS, INC.,

Howard Goldstein: "Natural stone in neutral colors is timeless, not like other trends that come and go. Using natural stone has grown in popularity because the machinery used for quarrying and fabricating has become faster and better, making it cost competitive with synthetic solid surfaces. Designers are moving away from simple edges and want unique, detailed edges, sometimes incorporating more than one edge profile or a variety of stone in the same room. For example, a kitchen may have different stones or edges on the island, table or backsplash. Until now, highly reflective polished surfaces have been favored for nearly all interior granite applications. New trends are leaning toward a honed, flat finish or velvet finish. All are cared for in the same manner."

"Combining several neutral colors gives the room a clean, classic and comfortable feel."

O'BARAN, INC.,

Douglas and Susan Barnes:
"Designers and architects are turning toward timeless traditional woods and finishes. People are beginning to realize that they would rather have quality that will last for years to come."

timeless

"...timeless traditional woods and finishes."

PERIHELION, LTD. ARCHITECTURE AND DESIGN,

Eric Pepa: "An interesting concept we have seen in higher end homes is the design of essentially two master bedroom suites — one upstairs and one on the main floor. Each suite would be complete with full bath, walk-in closet and even wet bar. This allows for a number of family situations that respond to changes in the way people live today. For example, a 'squeezed generation' couple with children could have aging grandparents living in the lower suite. Alternatively, an 'empty nest' couple could have young married children live with them for a time while saving for their own home, or they could use it as a guest suite for out of town relatives or for an au pair. Finally, as a couple grows older in the same house, they can move to the main level bedroom for ease of use. As always, housing must change to reflect the way people live."

WYNSTONE REALTY,

Ron Sever: "In the custom homes being built, we see an emphasis on quality finishes, custom woodwork, cabinets and built-ins. In addition, new materials or finishes that are becoming popular are tumbled marble, multi-colored wrought iron balusters, Mexican limestone columns and fireplace mantels, more use of granite for kitchen and bath tops, and natural finishes of woods, including cherry, mahogany, Brazilian cherry, Australian cypress and many others. Tastes are always changing or rotating through the vast choices."

MONTAUK,

Stacy Zimmerman: "More and more people are using slipcovers to add versatility to the look of their sofa. Slipcovers offer variety, character and piece of mind. You can leave your slipcover on for a more casual, relaxed look, or take it off and you will have a more formal, tailored look. Another popular combination is the summer and winter look. A slipcover is the perfect way to update a room. With the comfort of down, the support of kilned maple and a state-of-the-art spring system, we create a perfect seating system with your personal flair."

26

LEMONT KITCHEN & BATH, INC.,

Gary A. Lichlyter: "We are seeing a real push toward multi-step color and finish cabinetry. Our clients are excited when we tell them the sky's the limit when selecting the color and finish of their cabinetry. This gives the client a real opportunity to reflect their true personal style with no limitations. A client can select cabinetry to match the color of a favorite unique plate, crackle the finish or choose one of a hundred exotic veneers. There are simply no limitations."

SANDRA SALTZMAN INTERIORS,

Sandra Saltzman, "When asked if I follow a certain trend my response is, 'I adhere to the continuum of classical elements, utilizing the percept of good taste, elegant stylings and intellectualized theory substantiated by historic reference and guided by the integrity of the architecture.'"

27

Photo by Photofields

MANDY BROWN ARCHITECTS,

Mandy Brown: "We find that our clients are moving toward sophisticated informal living combined with the latest technological advances. Among some of the most requested items are master suite on the first floor, large steam showers replacing whirlpool baths, home offices, homes wired for the Internet and home computing, laundry rooms near the bedroom, and in-law suites on the ground floor."

ANI
INCORPORATED,

Ann Neumann:
"People are looking for ways to simplify their life. Some look for companies that can provide what they need in design, architecture and construction within one organization."

KEMPER CAZZETTA LTD, ARCHITECTS,

Cheryl Ferguson: "Many homeowners struggle with the 'when to renovate and when to vacate' dilemma. In every case, the issues are the same, but the solutions are different. Those who decide to renovate are typically attached to their neighborhood, schools or home, but their home no longer fits their lifestyle. When these people consider renovating their existing conditions, the key question is resale. People who stay in their home for at least five years readily recover their renovation dollars. For those who relocate within two years, we recommend updating what is necessary or what may be detrimental to a sale. Homeowners who decide to move do so for other reasons. The underlying desire is freedom — the freedom to live in a home that is tailored to their lifestyle — then it is time to move on. This is a family who should design an affordable custom home. We enjoy the challenge of incorporating new space into a present home and the freedom associated with designing custom space for a new home."

Ⓐ

30

LICHTENBERGER DEVELOPMENT CORP.,

Ⓐ *Joe Lichtenberger:* "Luxury home buyers are looking for spacious living areas with traditional architecture. The homes are being built with an overwhelming attention to detail, blending Old World materials with today's latest construction techniques and the latest technology. These homes will never become outdated."

"Container plantings, changed seasonally and watered by micro-irrigation systems hidden beneath railings and deckwork, have been very popular of late. New polymers, resins and fiberglass have been adopted by manufacturers for their low cost, cold resistance and ease of use to form very detailed moldings and inlays. Concrete and limestone planters are also still big."

ⓑ LIGHTSCAPE, INC.,

Deborah Schmitt: "Interest in landscape lighting in the Chicagoland area has increased dramatically in the past few years. The increased interest is a combination of factors: the need for security, exposure to quality lighting, extending the use of outdoor areas into the night and increasing the property value. With more exposure to the effects and beauty of outdoor lighting, homeowners and business owners are making lighting an integral part of the landscape. Landscape lighting transforms outdoor space into a beautiful new 'room' to be used for intimate and large gatherings. From indoors, it creates a night scene that is like an evolving piece of artwork to be enjoyed throughout all seasons."

31

ⓒ TERRAZZO & MARBLE SUPPLY COMPANIES,

Terri Sparks: "The use of natural stone has always been a favorite of homeowners. Not only does it add value and beauty, but it also allows the owner to bring a certain uniqueness into their home. No two stones are exactly alike, so every installation is one of a kind. Consumers are also starting to request stone accessories to compliment their installations. More and more pre-fabricated mosaic borders are being used for backsplashes; mosaic medallions used for great entryways and stone moldings are adding to the overall design."

"Solid bronze extrusions for window and door systems appeal to the architect and homeowner…"

ASSURED CORPORATION,

Mark J. Sala: "Steel, stainless, bronze and fine hardwood window and door systems are growing in popularity. Using these materials allows the architect the flexibility to create vast areas of light and space, which in turn brings the outside environment inward for the homeowner to enjoy. These systems are also available in combinations of fine materials, including mixed pieces of hardwoods, steel and hardwood, or bronze and hardwood. Solid bronze extrusions for window and door systems appeal to the architect and homeowner because of the beauty of raw materials. Custom fabrications can also include skylights, window walls, bi-folding assemblies, and pivot window and doors."

Photo by Peter Wodarz

AQUAWORKS,

Annette Carnow: "The explosion of new products and designs available within the bath industry gives clients more options in more styles. We've come to a point where anything goes, and there is no one look that dominates the market. Industrial, minimalist cabinetry and exposed plumbing co-exist in the marketplace with ornate rococo vanities and gilded faucets. Items such as traditional china console tables, art glass vessels and sleek, contemporary Italian vanities are finding their way into American bathrooms. Designers have helped influence the new, unexpected mix of products we show today. Plus, we're always searching for the unusual and unique from all over the world. An extensive collection of varied styles helps each client strike the perfect balance and achieve a harmony of style and function."

STYCZYNSKI WALKER & ASSOCIATES,

Kim Haig: "Despite the fact that more people are eating out than ever before, the demand continues to be very strong for well-appointed kitchens. Even if we don't cook, we all want that 'trophy kitchen', either to impress our friends and neighbors or because we love the idea of home-cooked gourmet meals. And, for those times when we do cook, we want to have the latest conveniences at our fingertips, plus a cozy environment in which to work our culinary feats. All the features available to customers for their kitchens underscore an increasing desire for homeowners to individualize their homes, to make them unique and to reflect their own personal tastes."

MILIEU DESIGN, INC.,
Peter Wodarz: "Well worn and weathered — designers are looking to incorporate materials that bespeak history and durability through the passage of time. Moss- and lichen-covered boulders, paving materials softened and tumbled as if generations have tread across them, and materials with a patina of time lend an air of comfort and belonging. Our contemplative moments are fleeting, and landscapes with a sense of the past and lasting quality dimensionally expand the experience of our milieu."

33

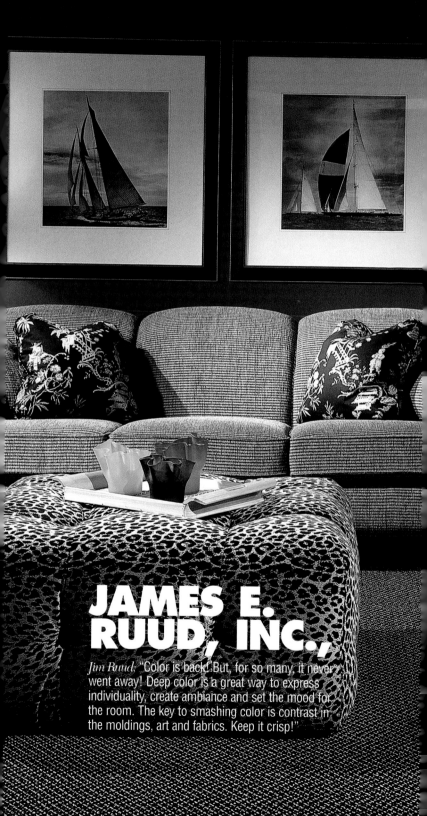

"Deep color is a great way to express individuality..."

JAMES E. RUUD, INC.,

Jim Ruud: "Color is back! But, for so many, it never went away! Deep color is a great way to express individuality, create ambiance and set the mood for the room. The key to smashing color is contrast in the moldings, art and fabrics. Keep it crisp!"

35

OSCAR ISBERIAN RUGS,

"Traditional colors and design are having a resurgence in Oriental rugs. Many of our designers are requesting classic patterns in navy blue and burgundy. Another color palette that has been desired are eggplant and aubergene. For those who desire a unique look, these shades work nicely. They are available in both contemporary and traditional patterns. Black background rugs remain popular. A black background is not only beautiful, but because of its neutrality, it can work well with existing colors."

KAISER GUTHAM PARTNERSHIP, INC.,

Jean Kaiser: "With the advent of the vast array of choices for luxury bathrooms, the use of glass takes on new meaning. No longer is it only for showers and mirrors, but glass mosaic tiles, bowls and insets in cabinetry allow the architect to create an environment that is contemporary, yet classic."

Ⓐ OUT-FRONT DESIGN,

Marty Heller: "Homeowners are starting to realize that the mailbox can be a weak link in their design chain. With all the effort, time and money invested in landscaping and home design, many people don't realize that the mailbox is often the first thing visitors see on the property, yet it is so commonly overlooked as to be almost comedic. People who display impeccable taste in all other aspects will often completely ignore the design and quality of their mailbox and how it reflects on its owner. 'Curb appeal' begins at the curb!"

Ⓐ

Photo by Photo Group

CLOSET WORKS,

Mike Carson: "The hot trend in new homes today is dressing suites. Comprised of a large closet and dressing area off the master bathroom, it allows you to get ready for the day without running from a dresser to a closet and back to an armoire. Dressing suites decrease the amount of time it takes to get dressed and expands wardrobe possibilities. By having all your garments in one location, all your clothes are worn more frequently, and new clothing combinations are created."

GEUDTNER & MELICHAR ARCHITECTS,

Diana Melicahr: "In the 1980's and 1990's, master bathrooms were large, opulent 'destination' spaces. In the year 2000, we are designing master bathrooms that are more practical, supporting our clients' daily lifestyles. The whirlpool tub has taken a backseat to the shower, which typically includes multiple showerheads, a seat and occasionally a steam unit. Beauty and maintenance are key factors in selecting bathroom finishes."

THE POULTON GROUP, LTD.,

Sharon Harvey:

"Something new is old again. Characteristic of the historic nature of our design/build projects and in the tradition of timeless design, many details on both the interior and exterior of our homes are made from authentic, traditional materials and then distressed, usually by hand. These techniques lend an overall warm patina and slightly rustic look to the project's quality and feel. Examples of this developing trend would be to specify rift-sawn wood, such as oak, that has a more vertical grain and then distress the timbers, beams, columns and brackets by sandblasting. This results in a consistent weathered appearance. The timbers also may be chamfered, which is a hand-axed technique completed by an experienced craftsman, along with exposed edges. The result is a rich, warm, ageless patina texture and over-all quality using authentic, durable, long-lasting materials."

MARIANI LANDSCAPE,

Carrie Woleben-Meade: "There is a huge trend in garden ornament and outdoor decorating. We like to encourage people to put those finishing touches in their outdoor rooms just like they do on their interior spaces. The right furniture or pot arrangement can add the personal touch that really finishes a space. Pots can add height, color or even signal the change in seasons with rotating arrangements. They can even be functional, add a little basil or sage to a pot to use in the kitchen."

UNIQUE DECK BUILDERS,

Joel Boyer: "Many decks have built in BBQ work areas with stainless steel grills that look like they came out of *Better Homes and Gardens.* Some people even add fire pits and waterfall treatments to the deck areas. Another great feature is the addition of a custom three- or four-season screen room. These can also be added to current decks or designed into new deck areas. Most decks are finished with Western red cedar that is specifically hand selected. Other wood types are Pau Lope and other hardwoods that are used on many of the select decks that we build."

VISBEEN ASSOCIATES, INC.,

Wayne E. Visbeen: "Old is new. Our clientele from the east to the west coast continue to have a desire for authenticity and a recollection of the past. Whether it is an English manor house, shingle style, French country or European cottage, there is a desire to create that feeling of the past while designing a home that fits the current lifestyle of each client. We focus on capturing the beauty and appreciating the architectural details of the past in our designs. This gives the client the excitement of creating a house that is their home the moment they move in."

BALTIS ARCHITECTS, INC., *Joanne Mascaro-Baltis:* "A graceful habitat is a beautiful and functional environment for living that stimulates good living within the environment and satisfies the homeowner's desire to uniquely express individual family identity. With this understanding, clients are open to create environments that exceed pre-determined style. They are seeking clear, simple environments designed with enduring character that can change with them as their lives grow and their individuality is expressed differently over time."

41

**RUDOLPH
ARCHITECTS,**
*Christopher
Rudolph:*
"We are seeing
a strengthened
connection
between the
world outside and
a home's design.
When combined
with the integrity
of natural
materials like
natural stones —
both polished and
unpolished —
hardwood floors,
wood details, and
custom-designed
art glass
elements, this
connection is
reinforced. The
current desire for
harmony between
natural and built
environments has
a profound effect
on one's spiritual
and psychological
health."

42

Photo by Kip Jacobs

44

Ⓐ

Ⓐ CHAMPAGNE FURNITURE GALLERY, INC.,

Patricia A. Champagne: "The look of elegance is definitely continuing with silks being used more frequently for upholstery and draperies. Furniture has more carvings and often is embellished with gold or silver in both the French and Italian designs, and lots of intricate marquetry in the English pieces. The bedding ensembles are positively opulent in silks and cut velvets trimmed with fringe, beading, pearls and sometimes ostrich feathers."

DALE CAROL ANDERSON LTD.,

Dale Carol Anderson: "Good design should be timeless and be able to stand scrutiny 20 years later. When attention to the finest details, subtle layering of textures, incorporation of art pieces and art collections, and blending of colors and nuances of light are combined to create a mood suitable for each room, a personality and couture design is created that transcends fleeting trends."

A. SPRINGER INTERIORS, LTD.,

Annette Springer: "With our increasingly global economy, the influence of many other cultures and styles can be seen reflected in the interiors of today. Asian, Mexican, Mediterranean, Island, and many other cultures can be seen in the furnishings, art and accessories available in today's market. In addition, a wide diversity of architectural styles can be seen in new construction and renovation. Anything from Victorian through sixties pop revival is in demand."

Ⓑ
PETRINA SCLAFINI,

Vesma Vera: "With more and more of my clients working from home, there has been a trend toward high-end furnishings that are functional as well as elegant. As shown in this home office, furnishings include hand-carved mahogany Chippendale partners desk with brown leather top and a hand-carved gold regency armchair with embossed ostrich leather seats that are offset with an oil painting."

Ⓑ

KEYSTONE BUILDERS, *Joanna Szymel:* "More often than not, people are staying in their current homes. They like their neighborhoods, schools and most of all their homes. These homes have individual charm and Old World elegance. However, they lack modern amenities. Home expansion addresses these issues. The most common solutions are bathroom renovations and master suite additions that include luxury items such as natural stone finishes, whirlpool baths, body spa showers and steamers. The prevalent request is for great rooms, which create dramatic architectural focal points to the clients' homes. The great rooms incorporate creative window arrangements, vaulted ceilings and beautiful fireplaces. Great rooms would not be complete without an adjacent gourmet kitchen, which reflects today's family lifestyle and casual entertaining. All new home construction addresses these issues and tries to recapture the Old World charm."

46

SUSAN FREDMAN
& ASSOCIATES, LTD

Susan Fredman: "There seems to be a renewed passion for nature, which I appreciate, for I believe it allows us to have a better quality of life. We can create peaceful and harmonious surroundings from the colors, patterns and textures found in nature. People are drawing from it to create "retreats" in their homes. They are now looking for spaces that will nurture their spirits and souls."

Photo by Linda Oyama Bryan

VAN ZELST, INC.,
David Van Zelst:
"Landscape design and construction excellence seems to be achieving a greater appreciation from our clients. Now, people are more knowledgeable about their home's landscape and want more use of their gardens. Clients want their home's landscape to not only look great but to function as an outdoor living space."

CHARLES PAGE ARCHITECT,

Charles Page: "Many empty nesters are planning for the future by incorporating more handicapped-accessible features in their homes. At least one first-floor bathroom is equipped with grip bars and wider doorways to accommodate a wheelchair. Ramping, so wheelchairs can gain access through the garage and at least one entrance of the home, is being designed into floorplans. Elevators also have become big. More and more buyers are adding an elevator to plan for any future necessity. Clients also are adding on screened porches for summer space where people can entertain, dine and visit with the family. The added advantage is people can enjoy the outdoors in a space that is rain-resistant, shady and insect-free."

S & B INTERIORS, INC.,

Sandi Samole: "The audio/visual room is fast becoming one of the most important places in the home. Not only is it imperative that the sound and viewing be perfect, but the ambiance created by the furnishings is extremely important. We have seen media rooms go from being the smallest room in the house to becoming the largest, most important room. While theatre style seating has become popular, the more traditional leather sectional sofa is still one of our favorites."

UNILOCK,

Brad Punke: "The newest look in paving is incorporating two or more colors, styles, textures or sizes of paving stones. With the recent manufacturing advances in surface texturing and the development of innovative paving systems, the ability to create one-of-a-kind installations is at the customer's fingertips."

ARVIN DESIGNS,

Sandra Arvin: "I find the tendency today is toward quiet, comfortable, elegant design with the desire to treat home furnishings as investments. There is a great emphasis on European tastes, rich fabrics and custom work. Clients today want their homes to reflect their own uniqueness within the guidelines of good design, encompassing the functional with the art."

JOHN MARSHALL CONSTRUCTION, INC.,

John Marshall: "One of the recent trends in the remodeling industry is the design/build concept that has gained favor among many homeowners. Although the majority of the remodeling industry continues to be comprised of smaller firms, the trend is for a remodeling contractor to join forces with an architectural group to provide a full-service team venture to clients."

49

NUHAUS,

Doug Durbin: "Flexibility is what people are seeing as value these days. A more neutral look in cabinetry and millwork is becoming more and more popular. Classic but simple detailing coupled with warm wood tones or paint allows for a 'supporting cast' of materials and furnishings. This could include stools, window treatments, furniture, hoods, decorative hardware, potracks and backsplashes. This gives one the ability to take the feel of a room to the degree of contemporary or traditional that one desires."

50

IDEA COMPANIES,

Frank Quintero:
"Detail. It's all in the details. In fact, the kitchen can
be one of the most exciting rooms for consumers
to design and express their own personal style.
With all the innovative appliances and accessories to
choose from, clients can create their own look,
whether that be classic elegance or sleek, clean lines."

FRAERMAN ASSOCIATES ARCHITECTURE, INC.,

James Fraerman: "Our clients desire an environment which reflects their everyday family and personal needs. I believe that casual, free-flowing and flexible spaces will be emphasized in the 21st Century home to accommodate daily activities and informal entertaining. The house will also need to balance unique personal spaces with the informal living spaces in an aesthetically pleasing whole."

APEX WOOD FLOORS,

Lou Borden: "We have experienced a renewed interest in borders and accents that will add creative appeal in any area of the home. Demand has risen for the exotic hardwoods with custom hand-scrapping techniques that add softer and more luxurious elements to the floor."

Ⓐ NORTH STAR SURFACES, LLC,

Chuck Geerdes: "The products offered for counters and wall cladding are expanding at an amazing rate. White is no longer the majority color choice. Innovation is the norm. With so much competition to differentiate one product from another, the consumer has a vast palette of product choices in color and texture. They are the ultimate beneficiaries of this evolution."

GARY & WALTER, LTD.,
Kenneth Walter:
"I see home design becoming 'the calm after the storm' now more than ever. All of us exist at such a frenetic pace. It is crucial that our home becomes a haven that gives us the safe harbor we all need when we've had enough. Our homes must become the place where we can do more than ever before. The technology at the average person's fingertips is staggering compared to five years ago. It is very exciting. Each one of us has a different idea of what the perfect space is. When it is all said and done, we all need a space that gives us happiness, comfort and peace."

53

Ⓐ

WOOD-MODE, INC.,

"There's a whole new renaissance happening in the world of cabinetry design. This latest trend focuses on adapting the best in furniture design and finishes throughout the ages, adding a new elegance that spans country and traditional to a softer-edged contemporary. Greater attention to turnings, moldings and trim detail brings in another note of authenticity to period styling."

FLORIAN ARCHITECTS,
Paul Florian:

"Multi-functioning rooms, mobility, miniaturization, and integration of new technologies for efficiency, comfort and convenience — that's our focus right now."

KIRSCH,

Linda Busch: "In decorative drapery hardware, materials have grown from the original metal and wood, to both natural materials and materials that can simulate anything. Real or authentic materials such as stone, rattan, terra-cotta, leather, horns, shells, skins, feathers, leaves, hemp and seeds are showing up on products in all home areas. At the same time, synthetic resins can be used as a base for finishes that can simulate any material desired and provide tremendous flexibility for design. Mixed media is very important. In decorative hardware, this means mixed metal and wood, wood and rattan, metal and glass, wicker and wire — the list is endless."

Photo by Nugent Wenckus

CHARDONNAY DESIGNS,

Charmaine Donnay: "Stained Glass as an art form and statement of personal expression has been well developed over hundreds of years. Today's tastes, however, require more detail, greater selection of colors and textures, as well as the security of single unit construction. We are seeing an exciting burst of interest in art glass that reflects our client's personality, style and sophistication. Although decorative glass was primarily seen in traditional settings, now the styles of Art Deco and Contemporary are being reflected in entryways, cabinets, ceiling panels and mirrors. Homeowners with architecturally challenging windows are turning to art glass rather than window treatments to enhance their beauty."

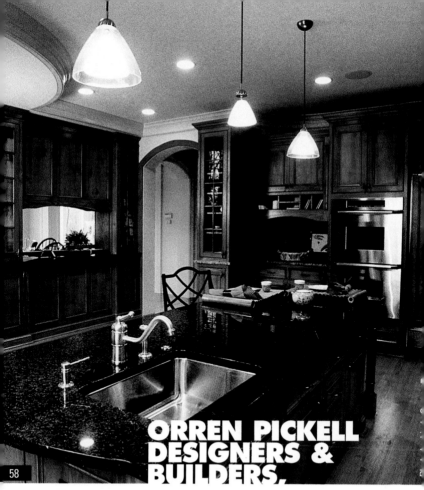

ORREN PICKELL DESIGNERS & BUILDERS,

PENNY & GENTLE FINE ART STUDIO, *Mary Jane Maher:* "Replicas of the old masters are increasing in popularity to complement fine furniture reproductions, as well as beautiful antiques, oriental rugs, ornamental details and accessories. Art can be an integral part of every room and an expression of individuality in design and decor. Art is personal. Art is subjective. Art evokes nostalgia and memories from the past, and provides pleasure and enjoyment for the present and future."

Tony Perry: "Architectural trends in custom homes are client driven. Changing lifestyles are a heavy influence right now. As the population ages, clients are requesting smaller yet higher quality homes with dramatic detailing, so every moment in the home is an aesthetic joy. This is the jewel box trend. Every room in these homes is used every week, and 'quarterly' rooms, used once every few months like formal living and dining rooms, are being eliminated in favor of great rooms, formal/informal dining areas, and sun rooms that double as reading and informal eating areas. Also, people are preparing for the second half of their lives, including possible extended stays by their parents, returning college children, and even returning adult children and grandchildren. Many clients are building master bedroom suites on the first floor with bedrooms, closets, baths, and kitchens on first floor, second floor and basement. Thus, three families could live in the same home for lengthy periods of time. Finally, with modems and high-speed cable lines making home offices and entertainment systems more common, families are 'cocooning', spending more time in their homes together. This makes for a safer, warmer, closer family relationship, especially between parents and children."

DARLEEN'S INTERIORS,

Bill Marler: "This season, classic looks tailored for the 21st Century allow clients to add their personal touch. Intricately hand-carved designs in upholstery, bedrooms and occasional furniture distinguish an ever-changing world. Window coverings flow with elegance in natural fibers and silks, with more sheers adding a touch of warmth and seductiveness. The result is exquisite!"

Photo by Scavolini SPA

SUNBURST SHUTTERS,

Lory Thelander: "Customers are requesting polywood shutters over the traditional shutters. The benefits of polywood (no wearing, cracking, fading or splitting) as well as the flawless finish are extremely attractive to our clientele. Polywood, an engineered wood substitute, looks like real wood but costs typically 15 to 20 percent less than wood. Nationwide we've seen polywood grow in popularity."

ANN SACKS TILE & STONE,

Debbie Winton: "As we enter the information age, it is important to have places of retreat and rejuvenation. Airy, streamlined, logical designs with minimal distraction is a key feature of this modern living."

CABINET WORKS,

Ed Sucherman:

"Everything old is new again! The latest trends in kitchen design include worn and distressed finishes, as well as 'unfitted' furniture pieces incorporated into a cabinetry run. Consumers appreciate the look of 'Old World' charm and are unafraid to depict it through the use of several finishes, doorstyles, and dimensions in a single room. Often, we accent a vintage-looking cream kitchen with a dark, glazed cherry island, for example. Inset doors emphasize the furniture appeal of hutch-like pieces, as do varied heights and depths. This is an exciting time for kitchen design as consumers are making their kitchens as unique as their owners."

59

Photo by Kohler Photography Studio

BECKER ARCHITECTS, LTD.,

Richard Becker: "We continue to see rising construction costs here in Chicago. Due to a strong economy and a lack of skilled labor, there continues to be a disparity in costs between rehab (more expensive) and new construction (less expensive). This has led to a bias toward new construction that has resulted in teardowns that continue to dot many North Shore blocks to the horror of preservationists and longtime residents. Some replacement homes are improvements in the streetscape, while many others are destructive. We try to save homes when economically feasible, but infrastructure issues sometimes compel the owner to build new for less money than rehabbing."

LEWIS CARPET ONE,

Bruce Stender: "Beautiful flooring is available in a number of forms and styles such as carpet, tile, stones and wood. Each has its place and application. Color, texture and durability are major concerns for most of our clients. Area rugs have become a major decorative accessory for many hard surfaces."

Ⓐ ALCHEMIST WOODWORKS, *David Broncroft:* "The philosophy and design aesthetics of the arts and crafts movement have withstood the test of time and remain relevant in our increasingly technological society. In an age where planned obsolescence and disposable consumer items are the norm, the enduring qualities of straight-forward design and traditional joinery offer a welcomed sense of permanence and stability. Variations of dimensions, trim details, and upholstery treatments offer an easy means of customizing these timeless designs to fit clients' individual tastes and environments."

PAGE ONE INTERIORS,

Adele Lampert: "Things that are always 'in' include proportion, moldings, detail, workmanship and your own style. Wood and stone floors also are hot this year, along with earthy colors."

CHICAGO PLASTERING INSTITUTE,

Gerald Holdway: "Once thought to have disappeared, plaster is making a strong comeback. Veneer Plaster is a viable alternative to drywall as an interior finish for walls and ceilings for quality conscious homebuyers. Although it is considered an upgrade by some contractors, it is always recouped in resale and the occupants reap the benefits while they live there."

L. A. DESIGN,

Randolph Liebelt: "We understand that proper detail and construction work hand-in-hand. This will allow the final design to stand alone. The client's own personal feeling and touch is felt within the design solution."

CRIEZIS ARCHITECTS, INC.,

 *Susan Schneider-Criezis:*

"There has been a return to placing gazebos in the landscape. Gazebos and terraces are a way to create outdoor living rooms and use a garden more fully. Along with extensive renovation and additions to older homes, homeowners are now interested in renovating their yards into usable spaces."

HESTER DECORATING,

Tom Hester: "Earth tones are currently fashionable in home painting. Quite often, our clients request a faux finish, such as marbled stone, polished Venetian plaster or a textured-trawled finish, using two or three very natural colors. Combining several neutral colors gives the room a clean, classic and comfortable feel. In many cases, colorful touches are added to the room through furniture and artwork."

CONCEPT DESIGN CONSTRUCTION, INC.,

Ted Cohn: "In kitchens, there is a preference for dark cabinets and countertops, i.e., islands with cherry wood and block granite. Stainless steel appliances are also popular. Dark colors are the trend in bathrooms as well. In Chicago, housing is reverting back to the very traditional. This includes design elements like crown molding, chair rails and wainscoting."

65

POWELL/KLEINSCHMIDT,

Robert Kleinschmidt: "People today are expressing greater interest and appreciation of modern furniture from the fifties and sixties. With all the chaos in the world and the complex and swift pace of business and technology, the simplicity and minimal concept of less is more is more appealing today than ever. It cleanses the mind and soul to live with clean, classic design rather than clutter. It really shows that a lot of thought went into designing this furniture for the way people live that 50 years later it is still the choice for sophisticated clients seeking refuge from a busy world."

ChicagoHome

Tour Guide to Your Dream Home

Tired of being lost? Feel that you don't know
where you're going without a map? Can't find useful information
regarding home improvement? The **Chicago Home Book**
Web site (www.chicagohomebook.com) provides you
with a full-color atlas of information to
map out the home of your dreams.

www.chicagohomebook.com

Book.com

YOU WANT IT, WE'LL FIND IT

The **Chicago Home Book** Web site (www.chicagohomebook.com) was officially launched in July of 2000. It covers a full area range of resources for building, remodeling, decorating, furnishing and landscaping projects. Just log on at (www.chicagohomebook.com). It also provides the user with unique, functional features designed to locate all of the necessary information regarding the interior and exterior design of your luxury home.

YOUR RESEARCH SOURCE

The site enables the user to research the latest trends in luxury design and home enhancement through its current editorial segments and interviews with industry experts. Users can also search for professionals under a wide variety of criteria, including by location.

THE PERFECT PAIR

The **Chicago Home Book** Web site is best used when complemented by a copy of the *Chicago Home Book*. The Web site picks up where the book leaves off, providing regular updates to ensure that consumers have the most well timed and detailed information possible. Together, the two work in unison to provide consumers the most up-to-date and timely information regarding their most prized investment—their home.

WE'RE ONLY A FEW CLICKS AWAY

If you are planning to design or renovate your home, please don't hesitate to consult (www.chicagohomebook.com) today. Allow us to be your road map, and we will gladly lead you to your final destination. There is only one premier resource provider for the luxury design and home enhancement market—the **Chicago Home Book.** Thank you from everyone at the **Chicago Home Book,** and we all hope to see you online!

The Internet domain seems as vast as outer space at times, especially when searching for home improvement, renovation, and remodeling information. The **Chicago Home Book** minimizes this complexity by acting as your guide to the stars. There is no doubt that consumer's will find the **Chicago Home Book** to be star packed.

There is only one premier resource provider for the luxury design and home enhancement market—the Chicago Home Book!

AND THE LIVIN' IS EASY

CHARMING OLDER COMMUNITIES AND NEW CONSTRUCTION GREET THOSE MOVING TO THE BURBS

Western Suburbia brings thoughts of winding tree-lined streets, children playing baseball in an open field, white picket fences, brick storefronts with family-owned diners and people who know each other by name. Family values draw young couples and new families from the city to rear their children. They are looking for a family atmosphere where neighborhoods offer activities like soccer leagues and fishing holes.

The southeast section DuPage County is an ever-growing area which is luring city dwellers westward. It has a settled and prosperous atmosphere in the midst of burgeoning growth. Commercial and residential development have mixed harmoniously with the area's old-time charm. Towns in this area include Darien, Downer's Grove, Hinsdale, Oak Brook, Westmont, Clarendon Hills, Burr Ridge and Willowbrook.

These hometown styled villages offer a nice mix of vintage and new housing. Residential streets display restored Victorians, Prairie design homes, bungalows, Georgians, Cape Cods and ranches mixed with contemporary styles of housing. Townhomes, condos and apartments

The wealthy suburb of Oak Brook, located in DuPage County, offers a mix of vintage and new housing, such as this relatively recent home that updates a traditional design with a modern look. Photo courtesy of Stoneridge Custom Homes

are scattered throughout. A blend of old and new construction gives the area a unique attractiveness.

Many of these communities were established as the railroad lines moved west into the area. Some were originally designed as refuges for elite Chicago commuters, while other neighborhoods were settled by families displaced by 1871's great Chicago fire, and still others have emerged as recently as 30 years ago. Each neighborhood was established at a different time, providing each community a distinctly individual feel.

The neighborhoods with downtown districts retain their turn-of-the-century atmospheres. Picturesque brick-fronted shops have been carefully maintained and are being renovated. These locales convey a warm hometown feel, where one can still find family owned barbershops and meat markets among the Starbucks and McDonalds.

Today, the area provides a wealth of entertainment, cultural and educational opportunities. Theater and restaurant choices are almost limitless, with some of the trendiest luring Chicagoans out of the city to the suburbs. Suburbanites can wander the small town boutiques or shop at the upscale Oakbrook and Yorktown Malls. A wide variety of museums and cultural centers enrich the area. Historic landmarks, like the Graue Mill in Hinsdale, provide a sense of heritage. ■

BURR RIDGE

In the early 1950s, the area southwest of Chicago was sparsely settled. However, the gently rolling hills, woodlands and grassy prairie expanses began to lure home buyers. Slowly, the area was annexed into what is now known as Burr Ridge. Today, Burr Ridge retains the wetlands, ponds and burr oak trees that appealed to the founders.

Compared with its neighbors, Burr Ridge is a young community. Established in 1962, the town has grown into a community with character that is distinct from its neighbors. The peaceful, natural surroundings attract busy professionals with young families who like being close to all that Chicago has to offer.

While nearby communities lean more toward a preference for traditional architecture, Burr Ridge has become a potpourri of contemporary and traditional, with homes that have made their mark with very personal touches reflecting the owners' personalities. Joe Lichtenberger, of LGD Construction in Carol Stream, believes there's more traditional than contemporary, though, and he is fine with that.

"I'd rather stick to traditional; that's where I do my best work," he said. "There's a sense of accomplishment when a new traditional style I build in an older, existing neighborhood blends into the community.

In the case of a recent, Old English-style home he built in Burr Ridge, the home not only blended in well, but became a trendsetter for other, similar styles nearby. Set on four acres, the house looks deceptively small and quaint from the street, but boasts a 14,000 square foot expanse, and expands into three wings in the back. The builder plans the home around the natural settings, incorporating as much of the original landscaping and trees as possible. In the case of this home, he planned around an 18-inch base Linden tree.

The structure incorporates much natural stone work throughout. Even the interior floors are stone, and are warmed by radiant heat, so that they are warm all the time. The library, a two-story room, features white oak flooring, and solid knotty pine beams stretch across the ceiling of the family room. Similar to the diverse exterior styles in Burr Ridge, this spacious interior rooms of this home also reflect diverse styles, from a comfortable country to sophisticated elegance.

"Many people think that traditional equals small rooms," Lichtenberger said, "but it doesn't have to be that way. They can have the look of traditional on the outside, and rooms big enough to accompany to their needs and desires."

Burr Ridge is conveniently located about 23 miles southwest of the Loop, right off I-55. ■

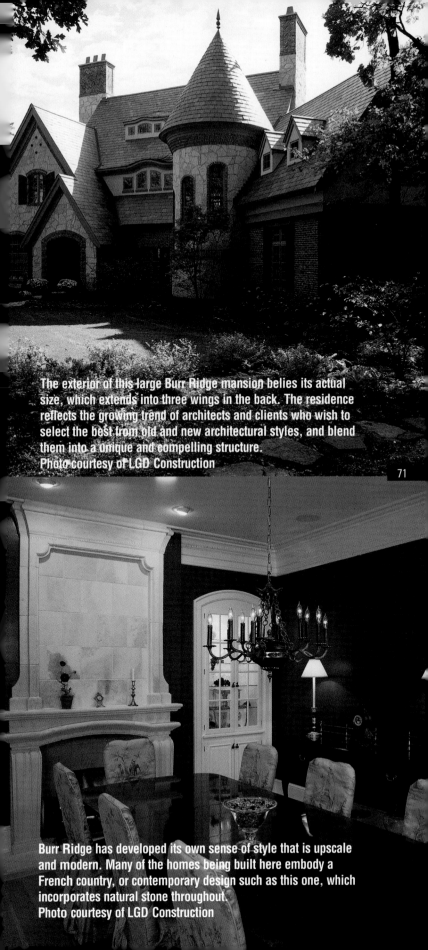

The exterior of this large Burr Ridge mansion belies its actual size, which extends into three wings in the back. The residence reflects the growing trend of architects and clients who wish to select the best from old and new architectural styles, and blend them into a unique and compelling structure.
Photo courtesy of LGD Construction

Burr Ridge has developed its own sense of style that is upscale and modern. Many of the homes being built here embody a French country, or contemporary design such as this one, which incorporates natural stone throughout.
Photo courtesy of LGD Construction

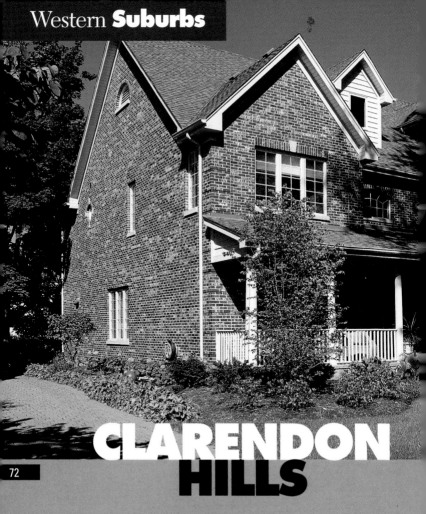

CLARENDON HILLS

In the 1850's, Charles Middaugh purchased 270 acres of land north of the railroad tracks in what is today known as Clarendon Hills. He planted 11 miles of trees, largely white ash and elm, which he hoped would soon line the new town's landscape. Rising from its rustic heritage, Clarendon Hills, 21 miles west of the Loop, has evolved into a uniquely structured village with historic tree-lined streets.

Middaugh built a magnificent 20-room mansion, still standing today, anticipating that other wealthy persons would soon follow. This dream of growth, however, did not come true until after his death. His heritage to the community was daisies, which were mistakenly planted in his fields instead of grass seed.

Today, this picturesque village offers excellent schools and elegant, tree-lined streets amidst gently rolling hills, providing a beautiful backdrop for both the old and the new. The downtown business district has a landscaped, colonial motif. There is a wide variety of housing available, including older Colonials, Georgians and Cape Cods mixed with newer ranches and split-level homes.

Sue Boparai of Stoneridge Custom Homes, Burr Ridge, Ill., has just completed a tear-down in one of the established neighborhoods. "We designed this home specifically to blend into the existing neighbor-

The traditional design of this tear-down replacement with its dark red brick exterior, dormer windows, front porch and roomy modern kitchen is a perfect blend of old and new.

hood," says Boparai, "We wanted the home to look as if it had been there forever."

The design, including a dark red brick exterior, dormer windows and a front porch, lends a traditional look. They were able to maintain most of the original landscaping.

Inside, an open floor plan features such distinctive elements as vaulted and volume ceilings, with crown molding and transoms throughout the house. The front door opens into a spacious two-story foyer. The roomy kitchen offers a more modern touch with maple cabinets, granite countertops and stainless steel appliances. Living and dining areas are separated with an arch and columns. The large master suite incorporates a tray ceiling and his and hers walk-in closets. The master bath boasts a double vanity with double whirlpool tub and skylights.

Since lack of space was a problem, they decided to build up. Stoneridge designed a third floor with bedroom, full bath and walk-in closet utilizing the attic and roof space.

Clarendon Hills is conveniently located near the Tri-State Tollway (I-294), and the East-West Tollway (I-88). The Loop, and Midway and O'Hare airports are all a 45-minute drive. Near the train station, express commuters reach the Loop in about 30 minutes. ■

74

CLASSIC ELEGANCE

Abounds near the Shore

One of the nation's most affluent residential areas lies just north of Chicago. The North Shore has a reputation for classic homes and appealing, well-manicured neighborhoods. These affluent neighborhoods include Evanston, Lake Forest, Glencoe, Highland Park, Kenilworth, Lake Bluff and Winnetka.

These picture-perfect suburbs are among the oldest and most exclusive in the Chicago area. Classic, stately Georgian and Colonial estates grace Lake Michigan's shoreline. The area's mature, tree-lined streets are scattered with vintage homes. You can find regal Victorians and renovated farmhouses blending nicely with newer ranches, bungalows and split-levels. Apartments and condominiums have added to the diversity of the neighborhoods.

Imbued with history, many of these communities are painstakingly restoring the classic architecture of those who originally settled in the area.

These magnificent neighborhoods have been used as a backdrop for many films. Robert Redford filmed "Ordinary People" here, while John Hughes used the area for "Sixteen Candles," "Ferris Bueller's Day Off," "Risky Business" and "Home Alone."

The tree-filled North Shore offers traditional houses, many designed with a French architectural flair.

75

These communities have developed and maintained an historic feel. Green areas add an important part of the area's appeal. Great pride is taken in preserving the native flora of the area. These villages were carefully designed with parks, homes and streets following the natural topography of the land. Each community maintains its own parks, forest preserves and recreation areas. The picturesque lakeshore is well preserved. Strict zoning helps to maintain the individuality of each community.

The historic downtown areas combine Old World charm with suburban convenience. Many have been renovated and offer modern amenities, while keeping a nostalgic feel. Brick storefronts offer a laid back appeal. Here you will find major department stores alongside one-of-a-kind specialty stores, boutiques and trendy cafes.

People come from all around the nation to share some of the treasures the North Shore has to offer. One can enjoy visiting the beautiful Chicago Botanical Gardens, listening to the Chicago Symphony Orchestra at Ravinia Festival (a concert series with daily performances from June through September), boating at Wilmette Harbor, or spending the day at one of the many well-maintained beaches.

The North Shore suburbs are just a few minutes to Chicago by car or by public transportation. This convenient location makes it a wonderful place to enjoy all that Chicago has to offer. ■

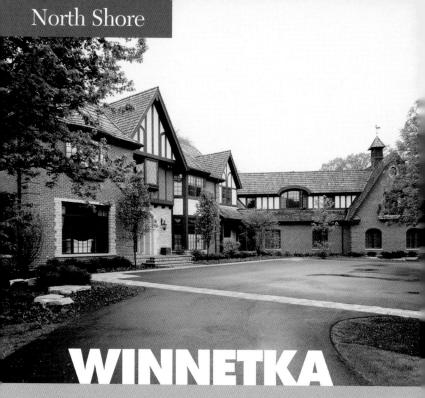

WINNETKA

W innetka is part of the prestigious North Shore of Chicago. It has a reputation as a solid, stable community reflecting a comfortable blend of both the present and the past. It appeals to newly successful professionals with young families, as well as empty nesters, offering charming tree-lined streets, decorative brickwork, Old World architecture and meticulous landscaping.

Winnetka is a unique community. Only four square miles in area, it's an unusually beautiful town with many stately, turn-of-the-century lakefront mansions. Named after a Native American phrase meaning "beautiful land," it has a natural attractiveness rivaled by few communities. Its picturesque lake front property, mature landscaping and top-notch schools have established Winnetka's reputation as one of the most desirable communities in the Chicago area.

The home style is diverse, including everything from Colonial, Tudor, Georgian and Victorian to unusual contemporary homes and charming cottages. Many of Winnetka's homes are large, some over 12,000 square feet, and often have spacious lots up to one acre. Most homes are 50 to 100 years old.

Charles Page Architects/Designers of Winnetka, Illinois, designs and builds luxury homes on the North Shore. Charles Page, owner, has been building homes on land that he's developed over the past 30 years. He has just completed several homes in the Thorntree subdivision of Winnetka.

Thorntree is the first new Winnetka community in 25 years. "The subdivision is located right in the heart of the nicest area of Winnetka," says Page. This tree-filled neighborhood offers very traditional houses, each on one-half to three-quarter acre lots. Mostly designed with a French architectural flair, houses range from 5,500 square feet to over 12,000 square feet.

In Winnetka, the home style is diverse but the city's architectural commission works closely with builders to assure that new construction is aesthetically compatible within the village.

Location and pristine views are a big draw for this area, bringing families and empty nesters together. Houses were planned around the existing natural settings, with bluffs of trees and winding roads giving the area an even more country-like atmosphere. Most homes in the community have a large screened porch, adding to the rustic feel of the area.

One of his projects was a 5,500 square foot English Tudor home in Thorntree. With a trend in empty nester housing, this home boasts wider hallways and doorways, and is handicapped accessible. The master suite is located on the first floor for convenience, although this trend is seen in many newer homes.

The kitchen is the focal point for family living. This 'gathering room' abundantly provides for seating, and incorporates the great room atmosphere with a natural stone fireplace. The house also has a separate living room and dining room for formal affairs.

The city's architectural commission works closely with builders to assure the new construction is aesthetically compatible within the village.

Only a 30-minute drive from the Loop, Winnetka offers excellent schools and a wide range of recreation. ■

Located in the heart of the nicest area of Winnetka, this elegant, luxury home exhibits an aesthetic commitment to Old World architecture. Meticulously landscaped, it sits on a spacious lot.

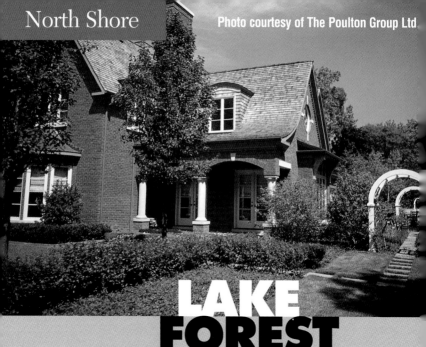

LAKE FOREST

Lake Forest, located 32 miles north of downtown Chicago, is the northernmost community of the exclusive North Shore. It is a quiet, residential, lake front community with a reputation for prominent and expansive architecture.

Lake Forest was originally settled in 1856 by a group of Presbyterian clergymen. They chose this spot for the site of their new college, now called Lake Forest College. By 1870, Lake Forest had become a resort for Chicago's elite. Around 1900, wealthy Chicagoans began building summer homes and mansions on the shores of Lake Michigan.

Lake Forest's strict zoning ordinances help to retain the area's charm and integrity. The original town plan contained many European influences. Careful planning and designing helped Lake Forest retain a largely rural character. Its winding roads twist past the beautifully landscaped and maintained Lake Forest and Barat Colleges. Today, they take pride in carefully mixing the old with the new.

Downtown Lake Forest contains Market Square, one of the nation's oldest planned shopping centers. Built in 1916, it is listed on the National Register of Historic Places. The square retains a nostalgic turn-of-the century ambiance, while offering upscale and trendy amenities.

Lake Forest places high value on retaining the historical value of its properties. Many old estates are being gutted and brought up-to-date with modern conveniences, while keeping the historical significance.

The Poulton Group Ltd., a design/build firm headquartered in Lake Forest, is currently renovating a 16,000 square foot turn-of-the-century estate. One of the first farmhouses built in Lake Forest, they are trying to retain the English shingle revival style.

"Our major goal is to keep with the city's historical preservation effort by adapting the architectural style of this 1880's farmhouse," says Sharon Harvey of The Poulton Group Ltd. "Initially, we walked through the home and cataloged all the existing pieces that are reusable," continues Harvey.

They plan to recycle many original fixtures, including the antique marble fireplace surround, stained glass windows, Art Deco black-leg

Lake Forest residents take pride in their ability to seamlessly mix the old with the new. This charming new residence is an example of the town's commitment to retaining its unique historical flavor, while providing residents with a range of options from which to choose.

pedestal sink and the cast iron tubs. Each item is being restored or refinished and reused.

Bringing the building up to code can be a challenging job. "Depending on the age of the house, it's quite often very difficult to determine what's behind the plaster walls unless we tear parts of the walls down," says Harvey, "yet, we often need to update the electrical, heating and air conditioning systems."

Incorporating modern appliances to make it usable is very important to homeowners. "People want the historical character of these older homes, yet they want the modern amenities," continues Harvey, "we find they want timeless looking appliances. You won't find glass." Instead, built-in appliances with hidden vents are installed to look like pantry cabinets.

Though the house is being updated with newer amenities, the restored pieces will be incorporated into the newer design. The project will take about a year to complete. In the end, the homeowner will have a feeling of accomplishment and pride in the heritage he or she has helped to retain.

The west side of Lake Forest has seen tremendous growth in new construction. Some large estates have been broken up in the last 20 or 30 years to develop new communities. These newer neighborhoods are carefully designed to maintain the historical integrity of the community. There is also an emerging trend to recreate estates and combine lots.

The charm and nostalgia of Lake Forest are unmatchable. A convenient location, solid schools and a family atmosphere make it an extraordinary draw. ■

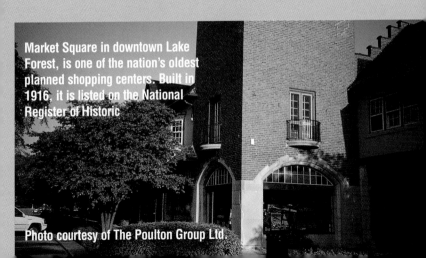

Market Square in downtown Lake Forest, is one of the nation's oldest planned shopping centers. Built in 1916, it is listed on the National Register of Historic

A REVIVAL SWEEPS THIS "CITY OF NEIGHBORHOODS" CHICAGO

When Mrs. O'Leary's cow kicked over that lantern, Chicago was devastated. From the smoldering ruins, a richly colorful Chicago rose up.

Located on the western shores of Lake Michigan, Chicago is a beautiful city, claiming a lakefront and skyline with breathtaking grandeur, complete with the Sears Tower, the Hancock Building and the Tribune Tower. Major parks run along the 29-mile shoreline, from Lincoln Park to Navy Pier to Grant Park.

Chicago has been called the "city of neighborhoods." No distinctive housing style defines the city, making each community individual and varied. Many different types of homes are found here, from the Victorian homes of Lincoln Park, to upscale loft living in River North, to brick bungalows on the South side to the historic, mansion-esque homes of the far south side. Although recently there has been a change in demographics, ethnic neighborhoods still abound from Chinatown to Greektown to Marquette Park.

Housing options are abundant in Chicago. A rehab and renovation movement is sweeping the north, northwest, south and southwest corners of the city. Many young professionals and empty nesters are being

Empty nesters and young professionals can enjoy the best of the old and the new in Chicago. Residences such as this one offer upscale, elegant spaces with breathtaking views of the Chicago skyline, as well as access to Chicago's diverse mix of culture, entertainment, and nightlife.

81

lured to the city with housing bargains in older neighborhoods, several of which have been landmarked. Classic styled brick cottages and bungalows are abundant in Bucktown, Ravenswood, Irving Park and Andersonville. Renovated loft condos and newer townhouses in near-downtown locations are attracting new residents to the South Loop/Burnham Park, Near West Side and River North neighborhoods. The neighborhood surrounding the University of Chicago exhibits a renewed interest in renovation.

Chicago offers culture, entertainment, theater, nightlife, history and sports fans. Whether interested in one of its famous blues clubs like Buddy Guy's or a jazz club like the Green Mill, or the internationally renowned Chicago Symphony Orchestra or the Lyric Opera, music fans have a score of options. Sports fans likewise enjoy a field of choices from the Cubs and White Sox baseball, Bears football, Blackhawk hockey to the Fire soccer and the Chicago Bulls.

From the shiny buildings in the financial district, to the elegance of the theater district, to shopping the Magnificent Mile, Chicagoans enjoy the best of the old and the new. It's easy to see why Chicagoans say, "It's my kind of town." ■

LAKESIDE

Lakeview is a bustling section near the north side of Chicago. Bounded by Diversey Avenue, Irving Park Road, Damen Avenue and Lake Michigan, the neighborhood borders Lincoln Park to the south and Uptown to the north.

Lakeview began in the mid-1800's as a small suburban farming community and summer vacation spot. After the Chicago Fire in 1871, people swarmed to the area to rebuild. In 1916, a new stadium, now known as Wrigley Field, was built, which was home to the Chicago Cubs and the Chicago Bears. By 1940, residential growth in the area had slowed. In the 1960s, residents successfully contested the urban renewal projects.

The intersection of Lincoln, Belmont and Ashland Avenues contains many locally owned retail shops, restaurants and theatres. Twenty-five years ago this area was one of the largest shopping districts in Chicago. Today it is seeing renewed life with major retailers coming into the area, including Crate & Barrel and Starbucks.

The Lakeview area is filled with many smaller neighborhoods. Wrigleyville boasts brick and graystone two- and three-flats, and is home to the Chicago Cubs baseball team. The southeast portion, called New Town, boasts some of the community's more valuable real estate. Roscoe Village, with its many antique shops, is known locally as "Antiques Row." One block, graced with 40 Victorian townhouses constructed between 1900 and 1904, was designated as a Chicago landmark in 1971.

More than half of the homes in Lakeview were built before 1940. Developers are tearing down these aging frame houses and replacing them with condos, townhomes and new single-family homes. Commercial buildings are being turned into lofts and condos. Housing consists mainly of brick and frame two- and three- flats, and a few brick courtyard buildings. Affordable single-family homes are still available, but values have risen steadily in recent years. A great deal of rehabbing is underway in the community.

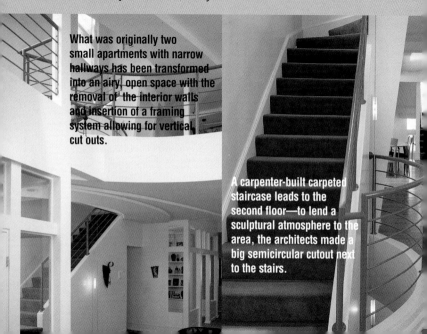

What was originally two small apartments with narrow hallways has been transformed into an airy, open space with the removal of the interior walls and insertion of a framing system allowing for vertical, cut outs.

A carpenter-built carpeted staircase leads to the second floor—to lend a sculptural atmosphere to the area, the architects made a big semicircular cutout next to the stairs.

Elissa Morgante of Morgante Wilson Architects, Chicago, works with many young professionals who are rehabbing existing buildings. "The trend is toward families who want to be in the city," says Morgante. "I think they like it here because it's close to downtown, and within walking distance to shopping, entertainment and the theater district on Belmont," she says.

One project Morgante Wilson completed began as a two-flat that was converted to a modern single-family home. "The client wanted a very open, contemporary floor plan," she says, "they have a very extensive contemporary art collection that we had to plan blocks of walls for and niches for sculpture. They wanted it to be very sculptural and contemporary to house all of their artwork."

The structure originally had been two small apartments with narrow hallways and little rooms throughout. "We had to remove all the interior walls and insert a framing system that would allow for vertical cut outs."

The first floor accommodates the living room and library/art gallery with a sitting room. The living room's double volume ceiling is open to second floor, giving an open, airy feeling. The stairway leading to the second floor is a carpenter-built carpeted stair. "We made a big semicircular cutout next to the stair to lend a sculptural atmosphere to the area," continues Morgante.

The second floor houses the dining room and kitchen. The dining area overlooks the living room. The third floor contains the master bedroom with gracious master bath and two smaller bedrooms. White walls throughout the house add to the contemporary feel. Outside, gray stucco and plate-glass windows lend a very modern feel.

The trend in Lakeview's growth seems to be young professional singles, many who work in the city. With a low crime rate and good public schools, Lakeview also attracts families who prefer city life to the suburbs. Lakeview is a very desirable community, offering a multitude of great restaurants and entertainment. It is easily accessible to downtown Chicago by bus or train. ■

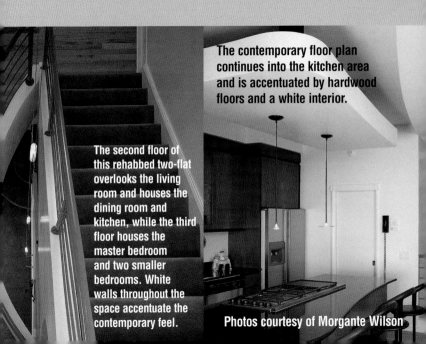

The contemporary floor plan continues into the kitchen area and is accentuated by hardwood floors and a white interior.

The second floor of this rehabbed two-flat overlooks the living room and houses the dining room and kitchen, while the third floor houses the master bedroom and two smaller bedrooms. White walls throughout the space accentuate the contemporary feel.

Photos courtesy of Morgante Wilson

This two-story brick town-home, located in the River North area, is one of the many housing options offered in this burgeoning community. The building's architectural design was designed to blend into the existing neighborhood, which offers a blend of the old and the new.

84

The design of this remodeled townhome maintains the area's historic charm, but also brings a modern aesthetic feel to the structure, with the unique design and detailing on the windows, and other 21st century architectural touches

RIVER NORTH

River North is the fastest growing urban community in the country. Though only one square mile, it boasts the largest concentration of art galleries outside of the Soho District in Manhattan. The area, bordered by Superior, Chicago, Orleans and Wells Streets, offers unique shops, world famous restaurants, and night clubs as well as jazz and blues clubs, including the House of Blues. These businesses add to the vitality of the growing community.

The economic climate of the 1970's left many warehouses and factories in the neighborhood empty. The 1980's found River North the place to be for emerging artists. They grabbed up this inexpensive space and began opening galleries. As the area's popularity increased, other empty buildings were renovated into lofts and condominiums.

High-rises along Clark and Wabash are being built or renovated into newer lofts. The twin towers of Marina City, a condominium rehab, welcomed its first residents 30 years ago. Fulton House, a 16-story condo was once the North American Cold Storage Building. It was renovated into 112 condos and office space. Many area warehouses are still undergoing conversions into lofts and condos.

Steve Rugo, one of the owners of Rugo/Raff in Chicago, is currently adding a glass loft to an existing penthouse. "The owner gained rights to the roof and is adding a second floor living area," says Rugo.

The main level is open with wooden beams, exposed masonry walls and wood floors to lend a natural feel to the space. A sculptural staircase and glass vertical corridor lead upstairs. The bedroom area is on the second floor. Surrounded in glass, this area on the roof draws light into the downstairs living area. The glass is clad on the outside with a type of metal screening reducing the ultraviolet light, as well as heat from the summer sun.

"This structure adds a very strong sense of light while offering views of the Hancock building and surrounding areas," says Rugo. "The screening was strategically designed to block the view of the other buildings." The original 1,900 square foot penthouse will be roughly 3,200 square feet when the project is completed.

River North offers many living options from luxury condominium lofts, to one- or two-bedroom condos, to studios. Average prices per month range from $600 for a studio to $3,200 for a three-bedroom unit.

River North is just a short walk from Navy Pier, Michigan Avenue and the Loop. Once an old manufacturing and warehouse district, today the area booms with large employers and various businesses, including upscale clothing and furniture stores in the recently converted Merchandise Mart. Today, this bustling area with premiere retail, shopping and entertainment is becoming the place to live for young professionals and empty nesters. ■

Finally...
Chicago's Own
Home & Design
Sourcebook

Call Toll Free at 888-458-1750

The Chicago Home Book, www.chicagohomebook.com, is your
final destination when searching for home improvement services.
This comprehensive, hands-on-guide to building, remodeling,
decorating, furnishing, and landscaping a home, is required
reading for the serious and discriminating homeowner. With over
700 full-color, beautiful pages, this hard cover volume is the most
complete and well-organized reference to the home industry. The
Home Book covers all aspects of the process, including listings of
hundreds of industry professionals, accompanied by informative
and valuable editorial discussing the most recent trends. Ordering
your copy of ***The Chicago Home Book,*** now, can ensure that
you have the blueprints to your dream home, in your hand, today.

Order your copy today!

O R D E R   F O R M

THE CHICAGO HOME BOOK

☐ YES, please send me ____ copies of the CHICAGO HOME BOOK at $39.95 per book, plus $3 postage & handling per book.

Total amount sent: $_____   Please charge my: ☐ VISA   ☐ MasterCard   ☐ American Express

Card # _____ Exp. Date_____

Signature _____

Name _____ Phone (   ) _____

Address _____

City _____ State _____ Zip Code _____

Send order to: Attn: Book Sales–Marketing Dept., The Ashley Group, 1350 E. Touhy Ave., Suite 1E, Des Plaines, Illinois 60018
Or Call Toll Free at: 1-888-458-1750   Or E-mail ashleybooksales@cahners.com

All orders must be accompanied by check, money order or credit card # for full amount.

Hot Districts

Where the Unexpected Resides

I magine meeting a leading furniture designer who listens to your dreams and instinctively understands just what you want, or entering an antique shop and finding an elegant one-of-a-kind piece that is the perfect focal point for your foyer. Whether you're building a new residence or redecorating a single room, the search for furnishings and decorative art objects that speak to your spirit can be a joyous experience and one filled with discovery.

Every town boasts elegant shops and "appointment only" showrooms that are "hot" — places only the insiders know. Sometimes located on a popular shopping street, often tucked away in an outlying area, they are beloved shopping venues that leading interior decorators and architects frequent...and treasure.

Whether you're looking for a furniture or glass craftsman to bring your vision to life, custom moldings for a new residence or an exquisite, imported treasure to lend focus to a well-appointed room, these "hot" shopping venues can spark your creativity and shorten your search immeasurably. The problem is just knowing where they are.

We created this special section to help you locate these unique and popular shopping meccas. To make it easier, they have been divided into local areas that include the address and telephone number of each store, even an easy-to-follow map.

In a book designed to inspire you and get your creative juices flowing, this is the place where you can start to make it all become real. Whether quaint or cutting-edge, elegant or funky, in these pages you'll find shops that are the leading lights in today's galaxy of elegance, art and interior design. Peruse this special section and enjoy. Then go out and discover something wonderful!

River North

Shopping for the Fabulous & the Funky

Long before River North became home to theme restaurants and night life, it was the place to shop for furniture, antiques and home accessories. This tradition continues, offering a homeowner the opportunity to visit a wide variety of unique shops and galleries.

A Kreiss Collection
415 N. LaSalle St.
312-527-0907
Mon.-Fri. 9:30 a.m.-5:30 p.m.
Sat. 10 a.m.-5 p.m.
The Kreiss Collection is a home furnishings company that specializes in an international mix of custom, furniture, one-of-a-kind accessories, professional design consultation and exclusive fabrics. The store encompasses "California Casual" as well as European Formal, Spanish Mediterranean and other classic styles.

B Champagne Furniture Gallery
65 W. Illinois St.
312-923-9800
At Champagne, you'll find a selection of hand-crafted pieces from Italy, as well as exquisite French and Italian reproductions. We also offer fine accessories, original oil paintings and full service interior design.

C Tech Lighting
300 W. Superior St.
312-944-1000
Mon.-Fri. 10 a.m.-6 p.m.
Sat. 10 a.m.-5 p.m.
One of the Midwest's finest contemporary lighting showrooms, specializing in the elegant, low-voltage track alternatives Kable Lite, RadiusWire, TwinRail and Monorail. Tech Lighting carries lamps and lighting from Artemide, Koch + Lowy, Kovacs, Luce Plan, Estiluz and Italiana Luce, as well as one-of-kind designs from local artists. Complimentary lighting design assistance; in-home consultation available for a fee.

D Manifesto
755 N. Wells St.
312-664-9582
Tues-Fri. 9 a.m.-5 p.m.
Sat. 11 a.m.-4 p.m.
Owned and operated by an architect and an interior designer, Manifesto features minimal and modern furniture, custom-made or imported from Europe, displayed in a warm contemporary setting.

E Montauk
223 W. Erie
312-951-5688
Mon.-Fri. 10 a.m.-6 p.m.
Sat. 10 a.m.-5 p.m., Sun. 12-5 p.m.
Sofas, loveseats, chairs, and ottomans are handmade to feel the way furniture was meant to. The styles are subtle and traditional. Each piece is upholstered and slipcovered in the fabrics of your choice.

Ann Sacks

The store is managed by a designer to help you plan your selection.

🅕 Material Culture
401 N. LaSalle
312-467-1490
Material Culture is the term folklorists give to the objects, crafts and arts made and used by people. We offer handmade oriental and European carpets, antique furniture and pottery, textiles and a multitude of vintage and contemporary arts and crafts.

🅖 Trowbridge Gallery
703 N. Wells St.
312-587-9575
Tues.-Fri. 10:30 a.m.-5:30 p.m.
Sat. 12-4 p.m.
Also by appointment
Carrying 16th-19th Century prints, the gallery specializes in rare 17th Century botanical, natural history and architectural prints presented in European handmade gilt and lacquered frames.

🅗 Ann Sacks
501 N. Wells St.
312-923-0919
Ann Sacks features a selection of the most exclusive tile, stone and plumbing products in the industry. Whatever environment you want to create—traditional,

Trowbridge Gallery

modern, industrial, sophisticated or just "fun"–we have the elements for your design. Antique stone and terra-cotta, limestone, slate, glass, metal and many handcrafted art tile products are among our offerings, as well as our own line of ceramic tile and custom mosaics. Exquisitely designed plumbing fixtures have also been added to our selection.

🅘 Caspian Oriental Rugs
700 N. LaSalle St.
312-664-7576
Mon.-Wed., Fri.-Sat. 10 a.m.-6 p.m.
Thur. 10 a.m.-8, Sun. 12-5 p.m.

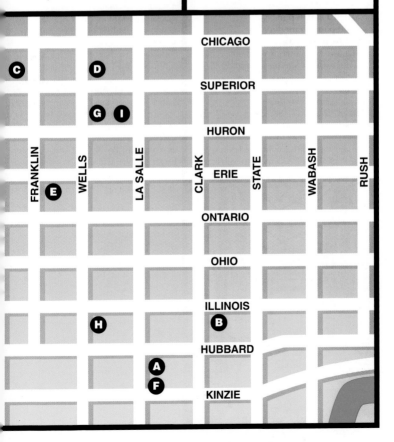

Winnetka/Northfield Kenilworth

Experience North Shore Boutique Shopping

Approximately 20 miles north of the city, these three lovely suburban locations represent a home shoppers paradise. Stately homes and leafy streets are home to sophisticated families and empty nesters alike who share in common the desire for beauty and only the finest qualities in their homes and gardens. Local shops meet their clientele's high expectations by providing unique items of uncompromising quality. A day of shopping along the North Shore will certainly yield many treasures. Parking is readily available and snack shops, coffee bars and restaurants abound. From Chicago, take the Edens north.

Ⓐ Sawbridge Studios
1015 Tower Rd., Winnetka
847-441-2441
Also at:
153 W. Ohio, Chicago
312-828-0055
M-F 10 a.m.-6 p.m.
(5:30 p.m. Winnetka)
Sat.10 a.m.-5 p.m.
Hand-crafted furniture and home accessories made by artisans from across the country in a gallery setting that features biographical information about the craftsman, as well as portfolios of their work. Styles range from 18th Century to Prairie, Shaker, Farmhouse and Contemporary. Each piece is built to order, allowing you to customize dimensions, finish, even design details. Come savor the possibilities!

Ⓑ Caledonian, Inc.
820 Frontage Rd., Northfield
847-446-6566
Tues.-Sat. 9 a.m.-5 p.m.
Mon. by appointment
A leisurely stroll through Caledonian's spacious 10,000-foot galleries is like a visit to 18th and 19th Century England. Here you can experience the joy of discovering treasures of the past: fine antiques of the William and Mary, Georgian and Regency periods in everything from magnificent breakfronts, sideboards and secretaries, to charming occasional pieces. Here, too, you will see the works of the exclusive Caledonian Collection. These extraordinary pieces are custom made for Caledonian in England, and today, represent the best of the furniture craftsman's art. They are, therefore, destined to be the fine period antiques of the next Century. To complete the experience, Caledonian offers an extensive collection of paintings, prints and decorative accessories.

Sawbridge Studios

Caledonian, Inc.

⊙ K&B Galleries, Ltd.
197 Northfield Rd., Northfield
847-446-1519
Mon.-Fri. 8 a.m.-4:30 p.m.
K&B Galleries, Ltd. is a distributor
of fine decorative plumbing products.
The showroom presents a wide range
of kitchen and bath furniture, fixtures,
faucets and accessories. Traditional, contemporary or eclectic, this gallery of ideas
displays and sells some of the best decorative plumbing the world has to offer.
Their lines include Franke, KWC (both
Swiss), Dornbracht, Jado, Hansgrohe

(German), Porcher (French) and many
others.

⊙ Carol Knott Interiors
430 Green Bay Rd., Kenilworth
847-256-6676
Mon.-Fri. 8:30 a.m.-4:30 p.m.
This Kenilworth shop features a most
wonderful selection of decorative home
accessories: unique picture frames, beautiful pillows, planters and a bountiful
collection of seasonal holiday items.

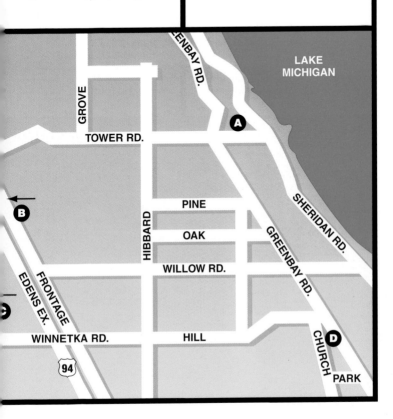

Barrington

Fabulous Shopping in the Countryside

Only 35 minutes northwest of the city, Barrington feels like it's hundreds of miles away. Magnificent countryside residences and new gated communities are home to sophisticated homeowners who love the tranquillity and amenities of this suburban area. Barrington's independent retail shops respond to the residents' expectations for unique, top quality merchandise — from cabinet pulls to Oriental rugs. Cozy restaurants and coffee bars offer perfect spots to relax and admire your purchases! Free parking is readily available all around town. From Chicago, take Highway 90 west to Barrington Road.

Ⓐ Insignia Kitchen & Bath Design
1435 S. Barrington Rd.
847-381-7950
www.insigniakitchenandbath.com
Mon.-Wed., Fri. 10 a.m.-5 p.m.
Thurs. 10 a.m.-8 p.m.; Sat. 10 a.m.-4 p.m.
Appointments encouraged
Insignia's nationally recognized showroom features 6,600 sq. ft. of recently updated kitchen and bath displays. Faucets, showers and appliances are hooked up to give "hands on" experience with products. Complete product specification and installation is performed by experienced company employees. The firm specializes in full service, turnkey projects. Several projects have been featured on HGTV and in both local and national magazines.

Ⓑ Barrington Home Works
102 S. Hager Ave.
847-381-9526
Mon.-Fri. 9 a.m.-5 p.m.
Sat. 9 a.m.-2 p.m.
Appointments encouraged
We feature custom designed kitchens, baths, studies, home offices and entertainment centers.

Insignia Kitchen & Bath Design

Page One Interiors

⊖ Bathhaus
860 S. Northwest Hwy.
847-277-1313
Mon.-Wed., Fri. 9 a.m.-5 p.m.
Thurs. 9 a.m.-8 p.m.
Sat. 9 a.m.-4 p.m.
The Bathhaus puts it all together for you. We are a luxury bathroom store that features the top brands in bathroom products and handmade tile and custom cabinetry. Our store is staffed with professional product consultants that are trained to guide you through your new house or remodeling plumbing and bathroom selections. We display Kallista, Herbeau, Ultra Bath, Dornbracht, Hansgrohe, Perrin and Rowe, KWC, Hado and many more. We pull all facets of your project together for you by specifying everything you need for your dream bath.

⊖ Page One Interiors
320 E. Main St.
847-382-1001
Mon.-Fri. 10 a.m.-5 p.m.
Sat. 10 a.m.-1 p.m.
Also by appointment
You will be charmed and inspired by this beautiful Painted Lady Victorian building, surrounded by gorgeous, award-winning gardens (which attract visitors of their own!). Owner Adele Lampert, converted the 124-year-old farmhouse into what you see today, and she has the architectural expertise to help you realize the same kind of fabulous results. The store features 18th and 19th century Continental antiques, fine reproductions, furniture and accessories.

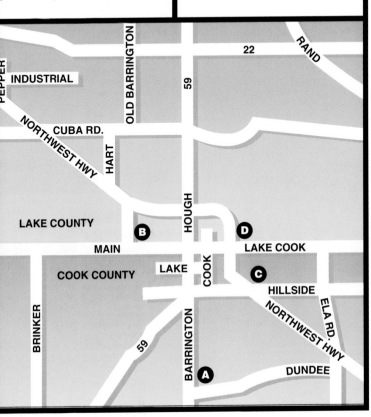

Lincoln Park

Urban Shopping for the Discriminating Homeowne

Chicago's Lincoln Park is one of the city's oldest and most enjoyable neighborhoods to visit for a day of home shopping. Home to both city singles and families, the area combines residential, tree-lined streets with busy, bustling retail districts. Browse through specialty shops offering antique pine furniture, home and garden accessories and contemporary furniture designed with a nod to the past. You can find Oriental rugs and French antiques – more than one location specializes in table top accessories. Parking requires ingenuity – you may want to consider a cab or public transportation. Take an expressway or Lake Shore Drive to Fullerton and Halsted.

Ⓐ Jayson Home & Garden
1885 & 1911 N. Clybourn Ave.
773-525-3100
Mon., Thurs. 9 a.m.-8 p.m.
Tues., Wed., Fri. 9 a.m.-6 p.m.
Sat. 10 a.m.-5 p.m.; Sun. 12-5 p.m.
These adjacent stores feature imported antique, vintage and reproduction home furnishings and an extraordinary selection of garden accessories, exotic plants and fresh flowers. Rugs from Pakistan, India and Afghanistan. Custom upholstered sofas and chairs in luxurious fabrics. Beautiful flower arrangements, vases, urns, benches, chaises, books and dried flowers. Inspiration for your city or country home.

Ⓑ Pine and Design Imports
511 W. North Ave.
312-640-0100
Mon., Thurs. 10 a.m.-8 p.m.
Tues., Wed., Fri., Sat. 10 a.m.-6 p.m.
Sun. 11 a.m.-5 p.m.

Ⓒ Vintage Posters, Ltd.
1551 N. Wells
312-951-6681
Mon.-Sat. 11 a.m.-6 p.m.
Sun. 12-5 p.m.
This shop has one of the largest fine collections of original European and American lithographic posters in the Midwest.

Photo by Graddy Photograph

Closet Work

Ⓓ Granitewerks, Inc.
2218 N. Elston
773-292-1202
Mon.-Fri. 9 a.m.-5 p.m.
Sat. 10 a.m.-2 p.m. — by appointment
Granitewerks specializes in residential, hospitality and commercial interior dimensional stonework.

Ⓔ Closet Works
1001 W. North Ave.
800-273-6511
Also at:
20514 Milwaukee Ave., Deerfield
847-520-5222
Chicago: 312-787-2290
Completed closet systems in a wide range of colors are on display. From basic to hanging shelving, to systems with drawers, hampers and shoe shelves— many different designs can be viewed. System colors range from basic white to decadent mahogany to suit your lifestyle. Stop by today and speak with one of our designers.

Ⓕ Scandinavian Design
501 W. North Ave.
312-337-4200
Mon., Thurs. 10 a.m.-8 p.m.
Tues.-Wed., Fri.-Sat. 10 a.m.-6 p.m.
Sun. 12-5 p.m.

Jayson Home & Garden

Ⓖ Bartlett Shower Door Company
2219 N. Clybourn
773-975-0069
Mon.-Fri. 9 a.m.-12 p.m. and 1-5 p.m.
Sat. 9 a.m.-1 p.m.

Ⓗ Tabula Tua
1015 West Armitage
773-525-3500
Mon.-Wed., Fri. 10 a.m.-7 p.m.
Thurs. 10 a.m.-8 p.m.
Sat. 10 a.m.-6 p.m.
Sun. 11 a.m.-5 p.m.
www.tabulatua.com
Chicago's premier tabletop store features hand-crafted dinnerware, serving pieces, glassware, and linens as well as hand-crafted and custom furniture from American and European studios.

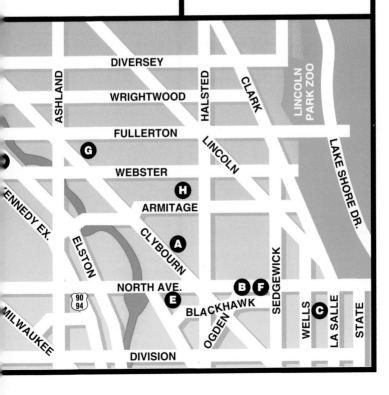

The Merchandise Mart, 13th Floor

One-Stop Shopping for Your Kitchen & Bath

Located in the heart of downtown Chicago, the Merchandise Mart is and has been a world-renowned design center for years. With over 150 residential showrooms displaying the newest in high-end home furnishings, it's where professionals shop for their clients' home needs — from upholstery to tile to paintings. Homeowners are invited to visit the showrooms on the 13th floor, the home of the Mart's kitchen and bath and building products showrooms. Parking is available in a secure lot across the street at 350 N. Orleans.

Ⓐ Designs in Corian by Sproveri
Suite 1306
312-527-2966
Mon.-Fri. 9 a.m.-5 p.m.
This showroom encourages creativity and the expression of personal style using a product, a product excelling not only in aesthetics, but also in function. Corian's design versatility and vast color spectrum are showcased, while reflecting Sproveri superior quality in craftsmanship. As the largest solid surface fabricator in Illinois housing the latest technology in fabricating machinery, Sprovieri can accommodate both residential and commercial project applications, ranging from shower bases and walls, to cabinets and tabletops, from windowsills to furniture. Sprovieri invites you to visit their showroom to experience the unlimited possibilities available in Corian.

Ⓑ K&B Galleries, Ltd.
Suite 1368
312-645-1833
Mon.-Fri. 9 a.m.-4:30 p.m.
Also at:
197 Northfield Road, Northfield, IL
847-446-1519
Mon.-Fri. 8 a.m.-4:30 p.m.
K&B Galleries, Ltd. is a distributor of fine decorative plumbing products. The showroom presents a wide range of kitchen and bath furniture, fixtures, faucets and accessories. Traditional, contemporary or eclectic, this gallery of ideas displays and sells some of the best decorative plumbing the world has to offer. Their lines include Franke, KWC (both Swiss), Dombract, Jado, Hansgrohe (German), Porcher (French) and many others.

Ⓒ Chicago Kitchen Design Group Inc
Suite 1332
312-245-0100
Mon.-Fri. 9:30 a.m.-5 p.m.

Ⓓ Rutt of Chicago
Suite 13-160
312-670-7888
Mon.-Fri. 9 a.m.-5 p.m.
Evening & Sat. by appointment
Rutt of Chicago is one of eight Rutt Flagship Showroom locations in the United States, locally owned and comprised of a kitchen design group capable of servicing the most discriminating clientele. Renowned Chicago chef Charlie Trotter chose this design team to create and implement his residential test kitchen adjacent to his famous restaurant in Lincoln Park.

Smartrooms, Inc.

Ruff of Chicago

E Smartrooms, Inc.
Suite 1356
312-644-4446
The Wood-Mode and Brookhaven cabinetry showroom offers a complete array of cabinetry for all rooms of the home–kitchens, media centers, libraries/home offices and bedrooms. Our Brookhaven cabinetry line is semi-custom, while our Wood-Mode cabinetry line can be completely customized to your specification. We will assist in designing your cabinetry and obtaining the necessary appliances, counter tops and accessories. Come in and let us design the living space you require and deserve.

F Flooring Network
Suite 1346
312-321-1217
Mon.-Fri. 9:30 a.m.-5 p.m.
For all you can imagine in floor covering, such as stone, tile, wood, carpeting, and decorative hand, custom and machine-made area rugs, Flooring Network is the showroom to visit. Information on all of the exciting products this showroom carries is available by visiting with a member of their friendly and professional staff.

G Aquaworks
Suite 1326
312-494-2111
Aquaworks newest showroom is designed as a jewelry store for the bath and kitchen. Aquaworks features the best of European and domestic in vignettes displaying faucets, decorative vanities, console tables and mirrors, unusual kitchen sinks, high fashion lighting, and beautiful door and cabinet hardware.

H Cucine Del Veneto
Suite 1344
312-644-9520
Val Cucine, featuring the newest in innovative Italian kitchen designs, can now be viewed in our beautiful new showroom. From the heart of the Veneto region of Italy, Cucine Del Veneto is bringing you the most stylish and innovative kitchens available today. Truly exciting in their beautiful design as well as their creative and lasting function, Val Cucine kitchens will astonish even the passive observer. Val Cucine offers four dramatic systems for every buyer's taste: the Ricicla for the ecological minded, the Fabula for the romantic, the Artematica for the technological buyer and the Cerasus for contemporary sense of play. We hope to awaken the customer to such issues as the blend of sophisticated design with highest quality materials. Our primary aim is seeking the eco-compatibility of materials to safeguard the health of the environment as well as the kitchen space. It is this aim which has made Val Cucine synonymous with "quality" throughout Europe. Please feel free to visit and enjoy our showroom at your leisure.

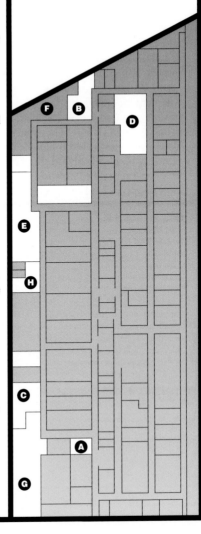

EVANSTON

Artsy to Urbane — Shopping to Suit Your Styl

As one of the most culturally diverse and active North Shore communities, Evanston offers urban ambiance without the hassles of big city life. Whatever your calling card, Evanston is your passport to shopping, dining and leisure pursuits. This is a lively city that brims with excitement. Its fabulous shopping opportunities include unusual boutiques that attract the style savvy shopper. Sophisticated or quirky, elegant or funky, an eclectic mix of wares is there for the taking. From antiques to contemporary furniture, oriental carpets saturated with color, to one-of-a-kind tabletop accessories, you're sure to find pieces to grace your home. In addition to world-class universities, the city boasts fine bookstores, art galleries and museums. When needing a break, take a stroll along the beaches of Lake Michigan or wander lovely residential streets lined with historic homes, including stately mansions, Victorians, and some Frank Lloyd Wright designs thrown in for good measure. Dining aficionados will enjoy sampling the diversity of restaurants—Italian, French, Asian or vegetarian, formal or casual to suit your mood. Year round special events beckon visitors. They range from annual Mother's Day House Walks to art festivals throughout the summer. In addition to the downtown, neighborhood shopping areas include Chicago Avenue's intersections with Main and Dempster Streets, and the stretch of Central Street west of Green Bay Road.

Ⓐ Evanstonia, Inc.
702 Main St.
847-869-0110
Mon.-Sat. 11 a.m.-6 p.m., Sun. 12-5 p.m.
Also at:
4555 N. Ravenswood, Chicago
773-907-0101
Evanstonia, Inc. specializes in 19th and early 20th century fine traditional American and European antiques and decorative accessories. Evanstonia also offers a complete restoration service by skilled European craftsmen.

Ⓑ Rouzati Oriental Rugs, Inc.
1907 Central St.
847-328-0000
Rouzati Oriental Rugs Inc., has extended its inventory of thousands of quality handmade pieces, including a selection of antique, semi-antique and new rugs. We also offer repair, wash and restoration of all types of rugs.

Ⓒ Karlson Kitchens
1815 Central St.
847-491-1300
Mon.-Sat. 9 a.m.-5 p.m.
Also by appointment
Karlson Kitchens has cabinetry for every room in the house. We are kitchen, master bath and closet wardrobe specialists. We have an elaborate showroom with 13 display areas featuring a wide range of cabinetry. We carry traditional products such as Brookhaven and Wood-Mode as well as Studio Becker, imported from England and the Black Forest of

Rouzati Oriental Rugs, Inc.

Aquaworks

Germany. We also offer general construction services and complete packages for construction management, demolition, preparation and installation.

ⓓ Audio Consultants
1014 Davis St.
847-864-9565
Mon., Thurs.-Fri. 10 a.m.-9 p.m.
Tues.-Wed., Sat. 10 a.m.-6 p.m.

ⓔ Aquaworks
2308 Main St.
847-869-2111
Mon.-Wed., Fri. 10 a.m.-6 p.m.
Thurs. 10 a.m.-8 p.m.; Sat. 10 a.m.-5 p.m.
Tucked away in a nondescript strip center in southwest Evanston, Aquaworks is a surprising find. People are amazed to find a large showroom concealed behind the doors of the narrow store frontage. They are even more surprised by the quality and variety of exclusive lines of bath and kitchen fixtures displayed from around the world. Aquaworks is located just a half-hour drive from downtown Chicago with plenty of free parking.

ⓕ Oscar Isberian Rugs
1028 Chicago Ave.
847-475-0000
Mon., Thurs. 8 a.m.-8 p.m.
Tues.-Wed., Fri. 8 a.m.-5 p.m.
Sat. 9:30 a.m.-5 p.m.
Sun 12-4 p.m. (except June-Aug.)
Since 1920, Oscar Isberian Rugs has been traveling the world in search of the finest hand woven carpets. In addition to sales, we have a world class cleaning and repair department.

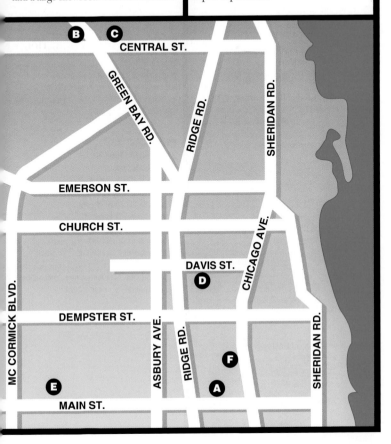

GENEVA

Small Town Charm with Big Time Shopping

Tucked into the Fox River Valley, Geneva charms visitors. Its gaslit, treelined streets are home to over 100 appealing shops with a fabulous array of goods, from antiques and home accessories, to fashions and jewelry. Dining options are as numerous as they are varied. Enjoy cozy cafés, outdoor spots, or more formal dining. Geneva also hosts annual events such as "Geneva on the River," a festival devoted to the home and garden, featuring architectural walking tours, demonstrations and seminars. The "Christmas Walk" is a holiday tradition where visitors and residents alike can spend the day touring charming homes decorated for the season. Merchants, in the spirit of the holiday, graciously serve traditional refreshments, including roasted chestnuts, while carolers fill the air with the sounds of the season. Enjoy complimentary parking within the shopping district. Geneva is located just 40 miles west of Chicago on Route 38.

Ⓐ The Past Basket
310 Campbell St.
630-208-1011
Mon.-Fri. 9 a.m.-5 p.m.
Sat. 11 a.m.-3 p.m.
Other times by appointment
Also at:
765F Woodlake Rd., Kohler, WI
920-459-9976
Established in 1976, the Past Basket has evolved from a resource for fine antiques and home accessories, to a company that also creates custom kitchens. Departure from the ordinary and close attention to detail are hallmarks of our work. Clients throughout the Chicago and Milwaukee areas prefer the personal approach of Past Basket's design team. Custom cabinetry vendors are carefully selected to be compatible with our discriminating approach.

Ⓑ Cocoon
212 South Third St.
630-232-8340
800-842-4352
Mon.-Wed., Fri. 9:30 a.m.-5:30 p.m.
Thurs. 9:30 a.m.-8 p.m.
Sun. 11 a.m.-5 p.m.
Call for holiday hours
Change is good. That's our philosophy. For the hottest in bath and beauty, baubles, illuminations and home furnishings, visit our 12-room shop. Visit us on the web at www.cocoongeneva.com.

The Past Basket

Strawflower Shop

C Strawflower Shop/Rug Merchant
210 W. State St.
630-232-7141
Mon.-Wed., Fri 10 a.m.-5:30 p.m.
Thurs. 10 a.m.-8 p.m.
Sat. 10 a.m.-5 p.m.
Sun. 12-4 p.m.
The Strawflower Shop, Geneva's most popular and complete store for all your design needs. A rare gem of a shop specializing in award winning dried and silk floral arrangements. Showcasing 3½ floors of quality furniture, antiques, framed prints, mirrors, lamps and unique gifts. The Rug Merchant features a vast array of high quality imported and domestic area rugs.

D Les Tissus Colbert
207 W. State St.
630-232-9940
Mon.-Wed., Fri.-Sat. 10 a.m.-5 p.m.
Thurs. 10 a.m.-7 p.m.
Sun. 12-4 p.m.
Les Tissus Colbert is a full service decorating shop located in the heart of Geneva. Staff consultants are able to assist with all of your decorating needs, from drawing up floor plans to helping with drapery and upholstery decisions. Our European style shop specializes in 110-inch widths imported from Europe along with our custom upholstered furniture adding a Euro-touch to your home.

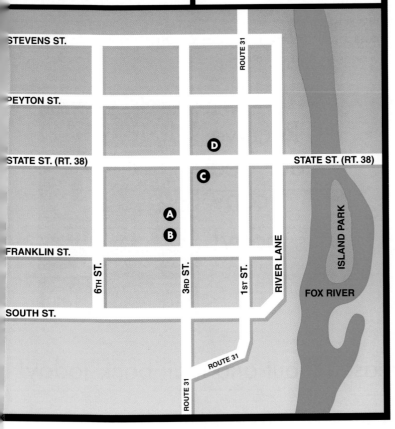

The Home Book

Dear Home Book Reader —

We hope that you have enjoyed our *Home Book*, and found it very resourceful for your dream home.

The following is a simple survey that we ask you fill out to receive your FREE COPY of **Distinguished Home Plans**. After filling out the survey, detach at the perforation and mail back to The Ashley Group.

We thank you for taking the time to fill out this survey; your FREE copy of **Distinguished Home Plans** is on its way!

Sincerely,
Maria Bronzovich, The Ashley Group

Receive your free copy today!

Please fill out and mail back today!

ashleybooksales@cahners.com

Finally...
Chicago's Own
Home & Design
Sourcebook

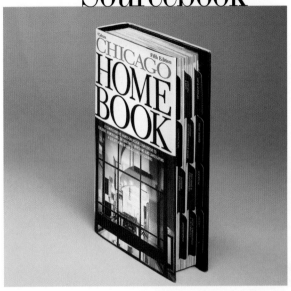

Call Toll Free at 888-458-1750

The Chicago Home Book, www.chicagohomebook.com, is your final destination when searching for home improvement services. This comprehensive, hands-on-guide to building, remodeling, decorating, furnishing, and landscaping a home, is required reading for the serious and discriminating homeowner. With over 700 full-color, beautiful pages, this hard cover volume is the most complete, and well-organized reference to the home industry. The Home Book covers all aspects of the process, including listings of hundreds of industry professionals, accompanied by informative and valuable editorial discussing the most recent trends. Ordering your copy of ***The Chicago Home Book,*** now, can ensure that you have the blueprints to your dream home, in your hand, today.

Order your copy today!

O R D E R   F O R M

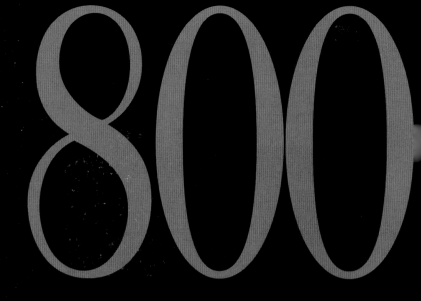

You can call any professional in this book TOLL FREE!

Need to contact a professional from the *Chicago Home Book*...use the Toll Free Number – Just dial **800-492-2708** and just enter the Extension number in their listing.

Sample Listing

THE POULTON GROUP, LTD. ....**(847) 615-1178**
268 Market Square, Lake Forest   Fax: (847) 615-1177
See Add on Page: 190, 253   800 Extension: 6259
<u>Principal/Owner:</u> David J. Poulton, AIA
<u>Description:</u> We are a small exclusive high-end residential Design/Build firm providing both new construction, renovation, preservation and interior design services.

CHICAGO
HOME
BOOK

800-492-2708

Photo courtesy of:
Scott Himmel Architects

ARCHITECTS

Photo: Jon Miller: Hedrich Blessing

MORGANTE · WILSON ARCHITECTS, LTD.
3813 NORTH RAVENSWOOD   CHICAGO, IL 60613
TEL 773 528 1001   FAX 773 528 6946

"To me, a building—
if it is
beautiful
—is the love of
one man;

he's made it out
of his love for

space and
materials. "

Martha Graham

oto courtesy of:
emper-Cazzetta

The First Step

An architect is the first step in realizing your vision for your new or remodeled home. These professionals are not only skilled in the technical areas of space planning, engineering and drafting, but also happen to be experts in materials, finishes, energy efficiency, even landscaping. An architect takes the time to find out how you live, what your needs are, and how you'd like to see your dreams come into fruition, all the while keeping your budget in mind. These creative professionals can assemble seemingly disparate elements into a design that incorporates what you need with what you want, with grace, beauty and efficiency. We have the privilege of featuring the finest of these creative, technically proficient problem solvers to help you bring your ultimate home to life.

- Who lives in the house now?
- Who will live there in the future?
- Who visits and for how long?
- Do you like traditional, contemporary or eclectic design?
- Why are you moving or remodeling?
- What aspects of your current home need to be improved upon?
- Do you like functional, minimalist design, or embellishments and lots of style?
- Do you entertain formally or informally?
- How much time will you spend in the master bedroom? Is it spent reading, watching TV, working or exercising?
- What are the primary functions of the kitchen?
- Do you need a home office?
- Do you like lots of open space or little nooks and crannies?
- What kind of storage do you need?

BRINGING IDEAS TO LIFE

Whether you're building your dream home in the city, a second vacation home, or remodeling your home in the suburbs, it takes a team to design and build a high quality residential project. A team of an architect, builder, interior designer, kitchen and bath designer, and landscape architect/designer, should be assembled very early in the process. When these five professionals have the opportunity to collaborate before ground is broken, you'll reap the rewards for years to come. Their blend of experience and ideas can give you insights into the fabulous possibilities of your home and site you never considered. Their association will surely save you time, money and eventually frustration.

THE ARCHITECT - MAKING THE DREAM REAL

Licensed architects provide three basic, easily defined tasks. First, they design, taking into account budget, site, owner's needs, and existing house style. Second, they produce the necessary technical drawings and specifications to accomplish the desires of their clients, and explain to a contractor in adequate detail what work needs to be done. Lastly, architects participate in the construction process. This straightforward mission requires more than education.

It requires listening. The best architects have gained their status by giving their clients exactly what they want — even when those clients have difficulty articulating what that is. How? By creatively interpreting word pictures into real pictures. By eliciting the spirit of the project and following that spirit responsibly as they develop an unparalleled design.

It requires experience. Significant architects, such as those included in your Home Book, maintain a reputation for superiority because their buildings are stunningly conceived, properly designed and technically sound. If a unique, steeply pitched roof was custom-designed for you by a licensed architect with an established reputation, you can be confident that it is buildable.

Suggestions by an experienced architect can add value and interest to your new home or remodeling project. Because of their exposure to current, thoughtful design, they'll suggest you wire your home for the technology of the future, frame up an attic for future use as a second floor, or build your countertops at varying levels to accommodate people of different heights.

This area is blessed with many talented architects. It's not uncommon for any number of them to be working on a luxury vacation retreat in another country or a unique second home in another state. Their vision and devotion to design set a standard of excellence for dynamic design and uncompromising quality.

WORKING WITH AN ARCHITECT

The best relationships are characterized by close collaborative communication. The architect is the person you're relying on to take your ideas, elevate them to the highest level, and bring them to life in a custom design that's never been built before. So take your time in selecting the architect. It's not unusual for clients to spend two or three months interviewing prospective architects.

In preparation for the interview process, spend time fine-tuning your ideas. Put together an Idea Notebook (See 'Compile an Idea Notebook'). Make a wish list that includes every absolute requirement and every wild fantasy you've ever wanted in a home. Visit builder's models to discover what 3,000 square feet feels like in comparison to 6,000 square feet, how volume ceilings feel, or what loft living feels like. Look at established and new neighborhoods to get ideas about the relationship between landscaping and homes, and what level of landscaping you want.

GOOD COMMUNICATION SETS THE TONE

The first meeting is the time to communicate all of your desires for your new home or remodeling project, from the abstract to the concrete. You're creating something new, so be creative in imprinting your spirit and personality on the project. Be bold in expressing your ideas, even if they are not fully developed or seem unrealistic. Share your Idea Notebook and allow the architect to keep it as plans are being developed. Be prepared to talk about your lifestyle, because the architect will be trying to soak up as much information about you and your wishes as possible.

• Be frank about your budget. Although some clients are unrestricted by budgetary concerns, most must put some control on costs, and good architects expect and respect this. Great ideas can be achieved on a budget and the architect will tell you what can be achieved for your budget.

• However, sticking to your budget requires tremendous self-discipline. If there's a luxury you really want, (a second laundry room, a built-in aquarium) it's probably just as practical to build it into your design from the outset, instead of paying for it in a change order once building has begun.

COMPILE AN IDEA NOTEBOOK

It's hard to put an idea into words, but so easy to show with a picture. Fill a good-sized notebook with plain white paper, tuck a roll of clear tape and a pair of scissors into the front flap, and you've got an Idea Notebook. Fill it with pictures, snapshots of homes you like, sketches of your own, little bits of paper that show a color you love, notes to yourself on your priorities and wishes. Circle the parts of the pictures and make spontaneous notes. "Love the finish on the cabinets," "Great rug," "Don't want windows this big." Show this to your architect, and other team members. Not only will it help keep ideas in the front of your mind, but will spark the creativity and increase understanding within the entire team.

BUILT TO LAST

Custom home clients in the Chicago area are abandoning the quest for the big house in favor of designing a home of high quality, integrity and harmonious balance. When the emphasis is on using top quality materials and custom design to create a comfortable home, the result is truly built to last.

TOO BIG, TOO SMALL, JUST RIGHT?

If you're designing rooms with dimensions different from what you're used to, get out the tape measure. If you're down-sizing, can you fit the furniture into this space? Is the new, larger size big enough – or too big? Ask your architect, builder, or interior designer if there's a similar project you can visit to get a good feel for size.

• Ask lots of questions. Architects of luxury homes in the area are committed to providing their clients with information up front about the design process, the building process and their fees. These architects respect the sophistication and intelligence of their clientele, but do not necessarily expect them to have a high level of design experience or architectural expertise. Educating you is on their agenda.

• What is the breadth of services? Although this information is in your contract, it's important to know the level of services a firm will provide. There is no set standard and you need to be sure if an architect will provide the kind of services you want – from basic "no-frills" through "full service."

• Find out who you will be working with. Will you be working with one person or a team? Who will execute your drawings?

• Ask for references. Speak to past and current clients who built projects similar to yours. Ask for references from contractors with whom the architect works.

• Does the architect carry liability insurance?

• Ask to see examples of the architect's work – finished homes, job sites, and architectural plans. Does the work look and feel like what you want?

• Find out how many projects the architect has in progress. Will you get the attention you deserve?

• Decide if you like the architect. For successful collaboration, there must be a good personal connection. As you both suggest, reject, and refine ideas, a shared sense of humor and good communication will be what makes the process workable and enjoyable. Ask yourself, "Do I trust this person to deliver our dream and take care of business in the process?" If the answer is anything less than a strong and sure, "yes!," keep looking.

UNDERSTANDING ARCHITECTS' FEES AND CONTRACTS

Fees and fee structures vary greatly among architects, and comparing them can be confusing, even for the experienced client. Architects, like licensed professionals in other fields, are prohibited from setting fees as a group and agreeing on rates. They arrive at their fees based on:

(A) an hourly rate
(B) lump sum total
(C) percentage of construction cost
(D) dollars per square foot
(E) size of the job
(F) a combination of the above

Sample Budgets, Costs & Fees

CONTRACTOR:

Demolition & Protection: $2,500
Wood flooring:...$2,500
Countertops:..$7,000
Tile backsplash: $2,000
Lighting/Electrical: $6,000
Plumbing: $6,000

Subtotal: $26,000
Contractor overhead & profit (15%):..$3,900
Contractor Total $29,900

OWNER:

Cabinetry, furnished & installed: $40,000
High end appliances:..$15,000
Painting:..$2,500
Owner Total $57,500

Contractor + Owner $87,400
Architect or Designer Fee (15%)...............$13,110
Total Project Cost......................................$100,510

Assumes very good quality materials, contractors, and subcontractors. Construction cost estimated does not include structural work, windows, drywall or general carpentry. Range of fees is approximate.

A HIGH-QUALITY NEW HOME CONSTRUCTION SAMPLE

Size: ....**4,500 square feet**
Construction cost: ....**$200 per square foot**
(does not include the site cost or major landscaping)
Project structure: ....**Upscale Chicagoland location;**
moderately high to high level of detail and complexity

Includes:
  Four or five bedrooms
  Four bathrooms
  Great room
  Home office
  Large American-style kitchen
  Dining room
  Three or four car garage
  Finished basement

Architect's fee: ....Survey results ranged from a low of $30,000 to a high range of $90,000-$120,000, based upon the type and quality of services offered.
Note: Architect's fee is approximately 15% of the cost of a project.

WHY YOU SHOULD WORK WITH A TOP ARCHITECT

1. They are expert problem solvers. A talented architect can create solutions to your design problems, and solve the problems that stand in the way of achieving your dream.

2. They have creative ideas. You may see a two-story addition strictly in terms of its function – a great room with a master suite upstairs. An architect immediately applies a creative eye to the possibilities.

3. They provide a priceless product and service. A popular misconception about architects is that their fees make their services an extravagance. In reality, an architect's fee represents a small percentage of the overall building cost.

The final quoted fee will include a set of services that may vary greatly from architect to architect. From a "no frills" to a "full service" bid, services are vastly different. For example, a no frills agreement budgets the architect's fee at two to seven percent of the construction cost; a full service contract budgets the architect's fee at 12 to 18 percent. Some firms include contractor's selection, bid procurement, field inspections, interior cabinetry, plumbing and lighting design, and punch list. Others don't.

One concrete basis for comparison is the architectural drawings. There can be a vast difference in the number of pages of drawings, the layers of drawings and the detail level of the specifications. Some include extra sketchbooks with drawings of all the construction details and in-depth written specs which call out every doorknob and fixture. Some offer impressive three-dimensional scale models to help you better visualize the end result, and computerized virtual walk throughs.

The benefit of a more detailed set of drawings is a more accurate, cost-effective construction bid. The more details noted in the drawings and text, the fewer contingencies a contractor will have to speculate on. The drawings are the sum total of what your contract with a builder is based upon. If a detail isn't included in the drawings, then it's not part of the project and you'll be billed extra for it.

Services should be clearly outlined in your contract. Many local architects use a standard American Institute of Architects (AIA) contract, in a long or short form. Some use a letter of agreement.

Have your attorney read the contract. Be clear that the level of service you desire is what the architect is prepared to deliver.

THE DESIGN PHASE

The architect will be in communication with you as your project progresses through the phases of schematic design, design development, preparation of construction documents, bidding and negotiating with a contractor, and contract administration (monitoring the construction). If any of these services will not be supplied, you should find out at your initial meeting.

The creativity belongs in the first phases. This is when you move walls, add windows, change your mind about the two-person whirlpool tub in favor of a shower surround, and see how far your budget will take you.

The time involved in the design process varies depending on the size of the project, your individual availability, and coordinating schedules.

A good architect will encourage you to take as much time as you want in the first phases. It's not always easy to temper the euphoria that comes with starting to build a dream home but the longer you live with the drawings, the happier you'll be. Spread the plans on a table and take an extra week or month to look at them whenever you walk by.

Think practically. Consider what you don't like about your current home. If noise from the dishwasher bothers you at night, tell your architect you want a quiet bedroom, and a quiet dishwasher. Think about the nature of your future needs. Architects note that their clients are beginning to ask for "barrier-free" and ergonomic design for more comfortable living as they age, or as their parents move in with them, and first floor master bedroom suites.

BUILDING BEGINS: BIDDING AND NEGOTIATION

If your contract includes it, your architect will bid your project to contractors he or she considers appropriate for your project, and any contractor you wish to consider. You may want to include a contractor to provide a "control" bid. If you wish to hire a specific contractor, you needn't go through the bidding process, unless you're simply curious about the range of responses you may receive. After the architect has analyzed the bids and the field is narrowed, you will want to meet the contractors to see if you're compatible, if you're able to communicate clearly, and if you sense a genuine interest in your project. These meetings can take place as a contractor walks through a home to be remodeled, or on a tour of a previously built project if you're building a new home.

If your plans come in over budget, the architect is responsible for bringing the costs down, except, of course, if the excess is caused by some item the architect had previously cautioned you would be prohibitive.

Not all people select an architect first. It's not uncommon for the builder to help in the selection of an architect, or for a builder to offer "design/build" services with architects on staff, just as an architectural firm may have interior designers on staff. ■

AMERICAN INSTITUTE OF ARCHITECTS

AIA/Chicago
222 Merchandise Mart, Suite 1049
Chicago, IL 60654
(312) 670-7770
www.aiachicago. org

AIA/Northeast Illinois
421 Green Valley Drive, Naperville, IL 60540
(630) 527-8550
aia@earthlink.net

AIA is a professional association of licensed architects, with a strong commitment to educating and serving the general public. They frequently sponsor free seminars called, "Working With an Architect" which features local architects speaking on home design and building. They have produced an educational package including a video entitled, "Investing in a Dream," and a brochure, "You and Your Architect." It's available at many local libraries throughout the area.

AIROOM ARCHITECTS & BUILDERS ....**(847) 679-3650**
6825 N. Lincoln Ave., Lincolnwood   Fax: (847) 677-3308
See Add on Page: 274   800 Extension: 6003
Principal/Owner: Michael Klein
Website: www.airoom.com   e-mail: info@airoom.com

ANTUNOVICH ASSOCIATES...**(312) 266-1126**
224 W. Huron Street, Chicago   Fax: (312) 266-7123
See Add on Page: 166   800 Extension: 1048
Principal/Owner: Joseph Antunovich
Website: www.antunovich.com
Description: Antunovich Associates are an architectural, interior design, planning firm committed to providing creative design solutions that respond to our client's needs.

BALSAMO, OLSON & LEWIS LTD. ....**(630) 629-9800**
1 S. 376 Summit Avenue, Oakbrook Terrace   Fax: (630) 629-9809
See Add on Page: 178, 179   800 Extension: 6022
Principal/Owner: Brad Lewis, Salvatore Balsamo
Website: www.balsamoolsonlewis.com   e-mail: bolarch@aol.com

BALTIS ARCHITECTS, INC. ....**(312) 587-1100**
748 W. Buena Ave. #2, Chicago   Fax: (773) 529-5782
See Add on Page: 154   800 Extension: 1088
Principal/Owner: Joanne Mascaro-Baltis / Bo Baltis
e-mail: baltisarch@21stcentury.net

BAUHS DRING MAIN ....**(312) 649-9484**
1 E. Delaware Street, Suite 500, Chicago   Fax: (312) 649-9508
See Add on Page: 119   800 Extension: 6027
Principal/Owner: Todd Main

BECKER ARCHITECTS, LTD. ....**(847) 433-6600**
595 Elm Place, Suite 225, Highland Park   Fax: (847) 433-6787
See Add on Page: 168, 169   800 Extension: 6029
Principal/Owner: Richard Becker, AIA
Website: www.beckerarchitects.com   e-mail: rb@beckerarchitects.com

PAUL BERGER & ASSOCIATES...**(312) 664-0640**
712 N. Wells Street, Ste. 3, Chicago   Fax: (312) 664-0698
See Add on Page: 196, 197   800 Extension: 1248
Principal/Owner: Paul Berger
e-mail: paulb@pbadesign.com

MANDY BROWN ARCHITECTS ....**(708) 524-0220**
125 N. Marion Street, Suite #302, Oak Park   Fax: (708) 524-1501
See Add on Page: 142, 143   800 Extension: 1099
Principal/Owner: Mandy Brown
e-mail: mandy_brown@yahoo.com
Description: Award winning full service architectural firm with emphasis on quality and excellence in design and service.

JEROME CERNY ARCHITECTS, INC. ....**(847) 382-4899**
234 West Northwest Highway, Barrington   Fax: (847) 381-5479
See Add on Page: 194, 195   800 Extension: 6051
Principal/Owner: Jon Welker
Website: www.jeromecerny.com   e-mail: jon@jeromecerny.com

STUART COHEN & JULIE HACKER ARCHITECTS.................**(847) 328-2500**
1322 Sherman, Evanston   Fax: (847) 328-2922
See Add on Page: 127 - 131   800 Extension: 6065
Principal/Owner: Stuart Cohen/Julie Hacker

CORDOGAN CLARK..**(312) 943-7300**
716 North Wells, Chicago   Fax: (312) 943-4771
See Add on Page: 187   800 Extension: 6069
Principal/Owner: John Cordogan/John Clark
Website: www.cordoganclark.com   e-mail: chicago@cordoganclark.com

continued on page **132**

BAUHS DRING MAIN

Music we see ... a song we enter

The architect's vision reveals harmonies and rhythms uniquely your own.

Together, you compose the grace notes of color, form and

scale, creating a home to enclose your dreams; expand your spirit.

Live the music of your life.

Architects and
Planners

One East Delaware
Suite 500
Chicago, Illinois 60611

T 312.649.9484
F 312.649.9508

. TRADITIONAL

GREGORY . ARCHITECT LTD
ARCHITECTURE AND DESIGN

2643 POPLAR AVENUE
EVANSTON, ILLINOIS 60201

TELEPHONE   847 492 1776
FACSIMILE   847 492 1736

WWW.MAIRE.COM

CONTEMPORARY

GREGORY MAIRE COMBINES EXCITING
IDEAS AND LUXURIOUS MATERIALS
TO CREATE A PERSONAL SETTING OF
GREAT STYLE.

Jeffery Pathmann + Associates
Unique Residential Design

18 Middletree Lane
Hawthorn Woods, Illinois 60047
847.438.5040 • 847.438.3223 fax

Fine Architecture

Construction Management

KQA

Kathryn Quinn

Architects

363 West Erie
Chicago, Illinois 60610
t 312.337.4977
f 312.337.6792

VISBEEN ASSOCIATES INC ■ ARCHITECTS ■ INTERIOR DESIGN

4139 EMBASSY DRIVE SOUTHEAST ■ GRAND RAPIDS, MICHIGAN 49546
616 ■ 285 ■ 9901 ■ FAX 616 ■ 285 ■ 9963

STUART COHEN & JULIE HACKER ARCHITECTS
Custom Residential Architecture 847 328 2500

Kitchen & Cabinetry Design: Cohen & Hacker.
Furnishings: Sandra Saltzman Interiors. Contractor: John P. Teschky Inc.
Cabinetry: Paoli Woodworking. Photos: Jon Miller, Hedrich Blessing.

STUART COHEN & JULIE HACKER ARCHITECTS

Custom Residential Architecture 847 328 2500

Architecture: Cohen & Hacker.
Contractor: Michael Von Behren Builder.
Photos: Jon Miller, Hedrich Blessing.

STUART COHEN & JULIE HACKER ARCHITECTS
Custom Residential Architecture 847 328 2500

Architecture: Cohen & Hacker.
Contractor: Michael Von Behren Builder.
Photos: Jon Miller, Hedrich Blessing.

STUART COHEN & JULIE HACKER ARCHITECTS
Custom Residential Architecture 847 328 2500

Architecture: Cohen & Hacker. Contractor: John P. Teschky Inc.
Furnishings: Sandra Saltzman Interiors.
Landscape: Peter Lindsay Schaudt. Photos: Jon Miller, Hedrich Blessing.

Architects

continued from page **118**

CRIEZIS ARCHITECTS, INC....**(847) 784-9400**
1775 Winnetka Road, Suite 100, Northfield Fax: (847) 784-9100
See Add on Page: 191 800 Extension: 1080
Principal/Owner: Demetrios A. Criezis/ Susan Schneider-Criezis
e-mail: crarchinc@aol.com

DONAHUE DESIGN, INC. ....**(847) 615-8055**
37 Sherwood Terrace, Suite 122, Lake Bluff Fax: (847) 615-8851
See Add on Page: 147 800 Extension: 1122
Principal/Owner: Thomas Donahue, AIA
e-mail: donahuedesign@aol.com
Description: Donahue Design, Inc. is a design/build architectural firm specializing in custom luxury and addiitons on the far North Shore.

FLORIAN ARCHITECTS...**(312) 670-2220**
432 North Clark Street, Suite 200, Chicago Fax: (312) 670-2221
See Add on Page: 150 800 Extension: 1079
Principal/Owner: Paul Florian
Website: florianarchitects.com e-mail: chris@florianarchitects.com

FRAERMAN ASSOCIATES ARCHITECTURE ....**(847) 266-0648**
1342 Linden Avenue, Highland Park Fax: (847) 266-0649
See Add on Page: 138 800 Extension: 6108
Principal/Owner: James Fraerman
e-mail: fraermanarch@speakeasy.com

GEUDTNER & MELICHAR ARCHITECTS ....**(847) 295-2440**
711 N. McKinley Road, Lake Forest Fax: (847) 295-2451
See Add on Page: 133 800 Extension: 6118
Principal/Owner: Diana Melichar
e-mail: diana@gm-arch.com

GRUNSFELD & ASSOCIATES ....**(312) 202-1800**
2110 E. Ontario Street, Sute 1390, Chicago Fax: (312) 202-1810
See Add on Page: 182 - 185 800 Extension: 1164
Principal/Owner: Ernest Grunsfeld

SCOTT HIMMEL, ARCHITECT..**(312) 332-3323**
360 North Michigan Avenue, Suite 1100, Chicago Fax: (312) 332-3345
See Add on Page: 200, 201 800 Extension: 1237
Principal/Owner: Scott Himmel

R. SCOTT JAVORE & ASSOCIATES..**(847) 835-4442**
375 Park Avenue, Glencoe Fax: (847) 835-4044
See Add on Page: 176 800 Extension: 1089
Principal/Owner: R. Scott Javore
e-mail: javore@worldnet.att.net
Description: R. Scott Javore & Associates, Ltd. is an architectural firm that specializes in Architecture, Interior Design and Historical preservation. A brochure describing our architectural services and project experience is available upon request.

ERIK JOHNSON & ASSOCIATES ....**(312) 644-2202**
154 West Hubbard, Suite 306, Chicago Fax: (312) 527-4166
See Add on Page: 152, 337 800 Extension: 1168
Principal/Owner: Erik Johnson

KAISER GUTHEIM PARTNERSHIP INC. ....**(773) 342-4695**
1734 W. Cortland, Chicago Fax: (773) 342-7007
See Add on Page: 177 800 Extension: 1170
Principal/Owner: Jay & Jean Kaiser
e-mail: kgp1836@aol.com
Description: Design/Build specialists- personal service rehab and new construction.

continued on page **144**

Geudtner
&
Melichar
Architects

Photo Credit: HNK Photography

Architecture ☐ Interior Design

711 N. McKinley Road, Lake Forest, IL 60045 • (847) 295-2440

ARCHITECTS

20 West Hubbard St.   Chicago,   Illinois   60610   312.464.0222

Lake Michigan View Addition

Residential Recording Studio

Barrington Estate

Master Bathroom Canopy

L̷A DESIGN

1088 W. Everett Road
Lake Forest, IL
847.615.0707

North Shore Mansion Renovation

1342 Linden Avenue

Highland Park, IL 60035

847-266-0648

fax 847-266-0649

FRAERMAN
ASSOCIATES
ARCHITECTURE

STUART D.
SHAYMAN
ASSOCIATES

ARCHITECTS

1780 Ash Street
Northfield, IL 60093
847.441.7555
FAX 847.441.7588

Charles L. Page Architect
100 Evergreen Lane Winnetka, IL 60093
8 4 7 . 4 4 1 . 7 8 6 0

Charles Page, North Shore Architect and Builder, is responsible for building some of the Chicago area's most impressive homes

Custom Residential Architecture
Interior Design
Historic Preservation

Mandy Brown, Architects
125 N. Marion Street, Suite 302
Oak Park, IL 60301
PH (708) 524-0220
Fax (708) 524-1501

continued from page **132**

KEMPER CAZZETTA, LTD....**(847) 382-8322**
209 E. Franklin Street, Barrington   Fax: (847) 382-4852
See Add on Page: 164, 165   800 Extension: 6180
Principal/Owner: John C. Cazzetta, Cheryl Ferguson & Jack Kemper
Description: We have a second location at: 412 Greenbay Road Kenilworth,
Illinois

FRANK J. KLEPITSCH, AIA ....**(312) 922-7126**
53 West Jackson Blvd., Suite 530, Chicago   Fax: (312) 922-3799
See Add on Page: 203   800 Extension: 1214
Principal/Owner: Frank Klepitsch
Description: Specializing in Architecture, Interior Design, Design/Build, and
Historic Renovation.

KONSTANT . ARCHITECTURE . PLANNING ....**(847) 967-6115**
5300 Golf Road, Skokie   Fax: (847) 967-0111
See Add on Page: 167   800 Extension: 1171
Principal/Owner: Paul Konstant
Website: www.konstantarchitecture.com

LA DESIGN..**(847) 615-0707**
1088 W. Everett, Lake Forest
See Add on Page: 136, 137   800 Extension: 1165
Principal/Owner: Randolph Liebelt

LARSON ASSOCIATES ....**(312) 786-2255**
542 South Dearborn, Suite 610, Chicago   Fax: (312) 789-2290
See Add on Page: 175, 292, 293, 336   800 Extension: 1119
Principal/Owner: George A. Larson
Description: Established in 1978, Larson Associates provides personalized and
creative architectural and interior design services as well as custom furniture,
design accessories, purchasing and art consulting.

GREGORY MAIRE ARCHITECTS, LTD. ....**(847) 492-1776**
2643 Poplar Avenue, Evanston   Fax: (847) 492-1736
See Add on Page: 120, 121   800 Extension: 1142
Principal/Owner: Gregory Maire
Website: www.maire.com e-mail: gregory@maire.com

MASTRO DESIGN, INC...**(630) 582-1534**
160 Greenfield Drive, Bloomingdale   Fax: (630) 582-1635
See Add on Page: 146   800 Extension: 1023
Principal/Owner: Pat Mastrodomenico
Website: mastrodesign.com

MORGANTE WILSON ARCHITECTS...**(773) 528-1001**
3813 N. Ravenswood Avenue, Chicago   Fax: (773) 528-6946
See Add on Page: 108, 109, 145   800 Extension: 1101
Principal/Owner: Elissa Morgante & Fredrick Wilson
Website: www.morgantewilson.com e-mail: mwa@mcs.net

CHARLES L. PAGE ARCHITECT ....**(847) 441-7860**
100 Evergreen Lane, Winnetka   Fax: (847) 441-7862
See Add on Page: 140, 141, 224, 225   800 Extension: 1034
Principal/Owner: Charles Page
Description: Design/ Build firm. (for 40 years)

JAMES PAPOUTSIS ACHITECT..**(312) 786-2000**
53 W. Jackson, Suite 657, Chicago   Fax: (312) 786-9242
See Add on Page: 151   800 Extension: 1090
Principal/Owner: James Papoutsis
Website: www.onearchitect.com e-mail: james@onearchitect.com
Description: We emphasize and specialize in architectural design integrating
interiors, lighting and furniture design striving to achieve a complete work of art.

continued on page **174**

MASTRO DESIGN, INC.
ARCHITECTS & BUILDERS
160 GREENFIELD DR. BLOOMINGDALE, IL 60108
630-582-1534

DONAHUE DESIGN, INC.

Architect

Developer

Builder

37 Sherwood Terrace Suite 122 • Lake Bluff, IL 60044 • 847.615.8055

SHAFER ARCHITECTS PC

417 SOUTH DEARBORN STREET SUITE 910
CHICAGO ILLINOIS 60605

312 360 9969

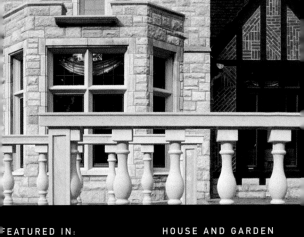

Photography: Rich Sistos

Photography: Rich Sistos

ERIK JOHNSON & ASSOCIATES

Architecture / Interior Design

154 West Hubbard Suite 306 Chicago, IL 60610

312.644.2202 Fax 312.527.4166

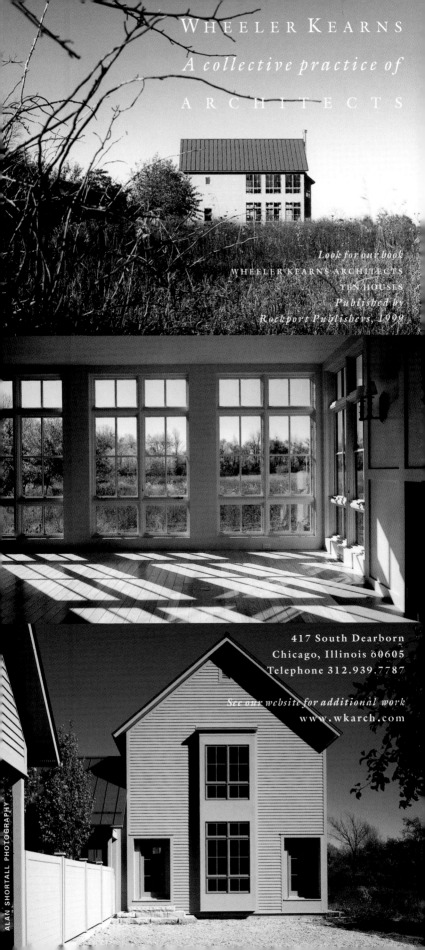

Baltis Architects

ARCHITECTURE • PLANNING • INTERIOR DESIGN

748 West Buena Avenue, #2
Chicago, Illinois 60613
312.587.1100   fax 773.529.5782

Stephen Synakowski Architects and Planners

Lake Forest, Illinois   **Telephone (847) 295-6926**

ARCHITECTURE   LANDSCAPE DESIGN   HISTORIC BUILDINGS   INTERIOR DESIGN

Archi

Old Forms
Find New Function

The Chicago area, with its deep-rooted history, combines a mix of many architectural forms into its residential realm. Although new, many home exteriors reflect a taste of nostalgia. Many times, this longing for the past is combined with modern materials, cutting-edge forms and modern technology. Whether Colonial, Victorian or Art Nouveau, any home's beauty is in the eye of its beholder. Outwardly, homes may reflect different periods of architectural history while inside the homes' floor plans are consistently characterized by an open design wherein the kitchen, living and dining areas form an unbroken whole.

An architect can borrow from a traditional form to create a home that feels like an "old soul" with 21st Century flair. Photo courtesy of Stuart Cohen & Julie Hacker Architects. Photo by John Miller/Hedrich Blessing

tects

Cheryl Ferguson of Kemper Cazzetta, Barrington, Ill., sees more clients asking for the historic European looks of English Manor, English Tudor and "Chateauesque" homes, "Our clients are affluent and educated with an appreciation for that which is stately and unpretentious," she says. Exterior materials, such as stone, impart a high-quality look with a more casual feel. "We like being able to combine a vintage look with state-of-the-art products and materials," she says.

Julie Hacker, Stuart Cohen & Julie Hacker Architects, Evanston, Ill., likens this desire for the old to the idea for something permanent in this ever-changing world. "Something that's old, that's always been there, is more comfortable to people," she says, "more buyers can relate to the traditional." However, she says, the architect can transform the traditional form to suit

The building industry is experiencing a revival of interest in quality and craftsmanship, with people becoming increasing aware of the integrity of materials and construction.

Photo courtesy of Stuart Cohen & Julie Hacker Architects. Photo by John Miller/Hedrich Blessing

Vaulted ceilings add height and spaciousness to a living space, and the treatment of several windows in a single configuration brings light and openness to the room.

Photo courtesy of Cordogan, Clark & Associates

Archi

Combining the modern, sheet-metal look of the siding with the home's Victorian lines not only keeps the home consistent with the rest of the neighborhood, it creates an abstraction that makes a bold statement.

Photo courtesy of
Cordogan, Clark & Associates

the contemporary lifestyle—borrowing from those forms and detailing—but re-crafting them into something livable for today's family. One reflection of this is the almost omnipresent movement of "open" floor plans.

Borrowing from Wright's Prairie design, open floor plans, combining living areas into one "whole" room, reflect the changing needs of today's homebuyers. Gone are the days where a kitchen is closed off from the rest of the

home. Rather, it has become a gathering area, a place to mingle and socialize, while also allowing open flow to the living and family rooms. Space is also added in volume ceilings that add height and grandeur to living areas. Rooms can be divided by other means, such as ceiling height changes, says John Clark, Cordogan, Clark & Associates, Chicago, Ill. One plan Clark designed involved

Photo courtesy of
Cordogan, Clark & Associates

The unique treatment of this entryway exemplifies the trend towards a blending of styles, which incorporate different points from different architectural styles, but aren't emblematic of one overarching style.

Photo courtesy of
Cordogan, Clark & Associates

"Uniting living areas into one "whole" room reflects the changing needs of today's homebuyers. Rooms can be divided by other means, such as ceiling height changes, rather than walls", says John Clark, Cordogan, Clark & Associates, Chicago, Ill. One plan Clark designed involved a "Wrightian pinwheel" where all of the living areas "rotate" around a central square.

a "Wrightian pinwheel" where all of the living areas "rotate" around a central square, such as the kitchen.

Where past meets the present is in the details. Hacker sees a new trend in "unfitted" kitchens, wherein kitchens, instead of being outfitted entirely with built-in cabinetry, are furnished with unfixed, moveable cupboards, tables and hutches. Here and throughout the home, many homeowners are mixing styles, combining antiques with more contemporary furniture to blend past and present, as well as a partner's contrasting tastes. Ferguson agrees, "cabinetry is looking more like free-standing furniture that has a common

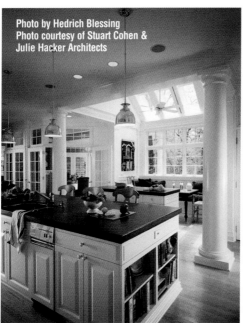

Photo by Hedrich Blessing
Photo courtesy of Stuart Cohen &
Julie Hacker Architects

The use of unfixed, moveable cupboards, tables and hutches reflects the newest trend in "unfitted" kitchens, with cabinetry looking increasingly like freestanding furniture that shares a common countertop.

Archi

countertop—but it doesn't necessarily match." One of her clients, an antiques collector, incorporated an antique seed bin as part of his counter island.

Mixing the old and new—even outside—can work, too. Clark says one client wanted low-maintenance aluminum siding during a remodel project. Clark suggested using agricultural-building metal siding. Combining the modern, sheet-metal look of the siding with the home's Victorian lines not only kept the home consistent with the rest of the neighborhood, it created an abstraction that made a bold statement.

Made better than ever to reduce glare and conserve energy, windows are offered in a wide array of stock sizes and styles to accommodate myriad architectural designs. Using several windows in a single configuration was once thought to fit only contemporary designs. Windows that look authentic can add to a traditional home's appeal as well as offer light and openness.

Photo by Hedrich Blessing
Photo courtesy of Stuart Cohen &
Julie Hacker Architects

tects

Christopher Rudolph, Rudolph Architects, Chicago, Ill., agrees with this blending of styles. "Today, a home may be built to embody points of other architectural styles, but not necessarily copy one particular style," he says. Rudolph's designs are strongly influenced by Prairie School. Arranging door openings so the space has a sense of scene and suggestion, using several lighting sources, and incorporating walls that are not full height can give the space a special, open appeal. Windows are another way to heighten the sense of open space.

Windows have evolved in several ways during the last decade. Made better than ever to reduce glare and conserve energy, windows are offered in a wide array of stock sizes and styles to accommodate myriad architectural designs. Using several windows in a single configuration was once thought to fit only contemporary designs. Windows that look authentic can add to a traditional home's appeal as well as offer light and openness, says Hacker. Sunrooms and conservatories offer another means to allow more natural light into a home. "Conservatories create a wonderful, elegant space for day or night," adds Ferguson.

Instead of any distinctive home style, Clark sees a renewed interest in quality and craftsmanship. People are more concerned with the integrity of materials and construction. For instance, granite has become a preferred countertop material for many of his buyers, as opposed to solid surfacing material. Also, many homes are incorporating radiant flooring (where heating pipes or coils are laid under the flooring) as an ancillary heating source.

Clark also sees a trend in leaving natural finishes as they are. "Materials aren't so manipulated," he says, "they're left to speak for themselves." Many times, homebuyers prefer a comfortable, less formal setting where wood is left unpainted and furnishings look weathered and old. Rudolph concurs, saying, "natural wood and fireplaces add distinctive, warming elements to the home by very simple means." Although most buyers prefer the grand oak staircases, Ferguson says that wrought iron for staircases and

Open floor plans create large living spaces encompassing the kitchen. Homeowners today see the kitchen as a place to gather and socialize, while also providing flow to the living room.

Photo by Hedrich Blessing
Photo courtesy of Stuart Cohen & Julie Hacker Architects

Today, a home may be built to embody points of other architectural styles, but not necessarily copy one particular style. Arranging door openings so the space has a sense of scene and suggestion, using several lighting sources, and incorporating walls that are not full height can give the space a special, open appeal.

Photo courtesy of Randolph Architects
Photo by HNK Architectural Photography

balconies is making a comeback—some even with a rust patina to elicit an "old" look.

One trend that Clark would like to see is clients approaching home design with no preconceptions. "People tend to copy something they've seen before or build in spaces for resale value," he says, "people end up living in the house for a long time, so they should get what they want." A house has to last, it has to function, it has to be a place you enjoy coming back to, says Clark. ■

—*Barb McHatton*

163

Many new home exteriors reflect a nostalgia for the past, combined with a sense of the present through the use of modern materials and innovative designs.

Photo courtesy of Randolph Architects

KEMPER CAZZETTA

ARCHITECTURE • LANDSCAPE ARCHITECTURE
PLANNING • INTERIOR DESIGN

209 E. Franklin Street • Barrington, IL 60010 • (847) 382-8322
412 Green Bay Road • Kenilworth, IL 60043 • (847) 256-2584

"Dedicated to creating personal spaces which display tradition, detail and creativity."

KEMPER CAZZETTA

ARCHITECTURE • LANDSCAPE ARCHITECTURE
PLANNING • INTERIOR DESIGN

209 E. Franklin Street • Barrington, IL 60010 • (847) 256-2584
412 Green Bay Road • Kenilworth, IL 60043 • (847) 256-2584

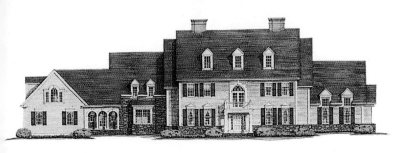

"A full-service design firm specializing in residential architecture from gentleman's estates to country cottages."

ANTUNOVICH ASSOCIATES

ARCHITECTS
PLANNERS

224 WEST HURON ST. • SUITE 7 EAST • CHICAGO, IL 60610
TEL: 312.266.1126 • FAX 312.266.7123

*Antunovich Associates is
Dedicated to a Creative and
Collaborative Approach to
Solving its Clients Design and
Construction Needs.*

Konstant
Architecture
Planning

5300 Golf Road
847•967•6115
Skokie • Il 60077

595 Elm Place, Suite 225	Tel 847.433.6600
Highland Park, Illinois 60035	Fax 847.433.6787
www.beckerarchitects.com	

Becker Architects Limited

595 Elm Place, Suite 225	Tel 847.433.6600
Highland Park, Illinois 60035	Fax 847.433.6787
www.beckerarchitects.com	

You are about to embark on a journey unlike anything you have known before. This relatively short trip will lead you through page after page of exquisite home building. R.M. Swanson & Associates is renowned as a premier design/build firm uncontested in quality and innovation. Founded by Richard M. Swanson in 1983, the company has cultivated a rich reputation. In 1985, the company entered its first Gold Key competition and won. Every year since has found R.M. Swanson & Associates receiving the award, a testament to the quality and sheer brilliance of their homes.

The beauty of each home is immediately evident, but closer inspection provides a better appreciation for the work put into each home. R.M. Swanson & Associates puts their name in the details, relentless in their pursuit to make each element of a home a stand alone work of art. Custom home building requires a precise dedication and critical nature. Unwilling to settle for less than perfect, R.M. Swanson & Associates puts every ounce of energy into ensuring the reality is somehow better than the dream.

Each home speaks for itself. Richard Swanson grew up in the construction industry and his years of training show in the homes he designs and builds. Inspired by the dreams of his clients, Richard Swanson has proven that he does what so many builders claim to do: he listens. When building custom homes, it is imperative that the needs and wants of the client are clearly understood. Richard Swanson is proud to have consistently built the most challenging of designs successfully. Listening and understanding have played vital roles in the success of R.M. Swanson & Associates.

R.M.
SWANSON
& ASSOCIATES

Architecture • Land Planning • Construction

810 S. Waukegan Road, Suite 210 • Lake Forest, IL 60045
(847) 234-6655 • Fax (847) 234-6635

R.M.
SWANSON
& ASSOCIATES

Architecture • Land Planning • Construction

810 S. Waukegan Road, Suite 210 • Lake Forest, IL 60045
(847) 234-6655 • Fax (847) 234-6635

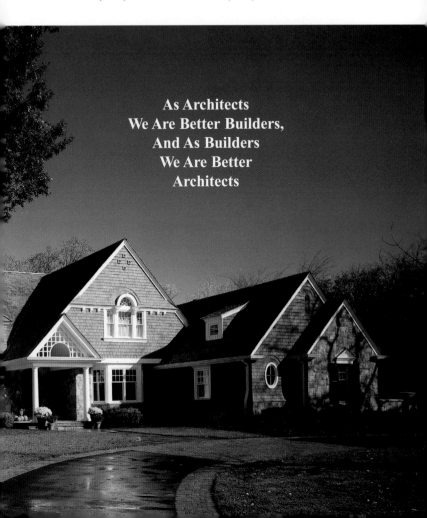

**As Architects
We Are Better Builders,
And As Builders
We Are Better
Architects**

continued from page **144**

PAPPAGEORGE HAYMES, LTD. ....**(312) 337-3344**
814 N. Franklin, Chicago   Fax: (312) 337-8009
See Add on Page: 198, 199   800 Extension: 1240
Principal/Owner: David Haymes

JEFFERY PATHMANN AND ASSOCIATES ....**(847) 438-5040**
18 Middletree Lane, Hawthorn Woods   Fax: (847) 438-3223
See Add on Page: 122, 123   800 Extension: 1097
Principal/Owner: Jeffery Pathmann
e-mail: patharchs@aol.com
Description: Pathmann architects provides complete construction management
services to its' clients.

PERIHELION LIMITED ....**(847) 695-7092**
100 E. Chicago Street, Suite 803, Elgin   Fax: (847) 695-7765
See Add on Page: 188   800 Extension: 1126
Principal/Owner: Eric Pepa
Website: www.perihelionarch.com   e-mail: epepa@perihelionarch.com

THE POULTON GROUP, LTD. ....**(847) 615-1178**
268 Market Square, Lake Forest   Fax: (847) 615-1177
See Add on Page: 190, 253   800 Extension: 6259
Principal/Owner: David J. Poulton, AIA
Description: We are a small exclusive high-end residential Design/Build firm provid-
ing both new construction, renovation, preservation and interior design services.

KATHRYN QUINN ARCHITECTS, LTD. ....**(312) 337-4977**
363 W. Erie, Chicago   Fax: (312) 337-6792
See Add on Page: 124, 125   800 Extension: 1133
Principal/Owner: Kathryn Quinn
e-mail: kquinnarch@aol.com

RUDOLPH ARCHITECTS ....**(773) 784-0804**
1807 W. Sunnyside Avenue, 2D, Chicago   Fax: (773) 704-1259
See Add on Page: 189   800 Extension: 1209
Principal/Owner: Christopher Rudolph, AIA
e-mail: rudolpharc@aol.com
Description: Our commitment to constructional order stems from the Modern
movement and an IIT education, while our sensibilities regarding materials and
formal relationships are guided by the Prairie School.

RUGO-RAFF ....**(312) 464-0222**
20 West Hubbard, Chicago   Fax: (312) 464-0225
See Add on Page: 134, 135   800 Extension: 1210
Principal/Owner: Steven Rugo

SEARL & ASSOCIATES, ARCHITECTS ....**(312) 251-9200**
500 N. Dearborn 9th Floor, Chicago   Fax: (312) 251-9201
See Add on Page: 192, 193   800 Extension: 1016
Principal/Owner: Linda Searl
Website: www.searlarch.com   e-mail: lsearl@searlarch.com

SHAFER ARCHITECTS ....**(312) 360-9969**
417 S. Dearborn #910, Chicago   Fax: (312) 360-9930
See Add on Page: 148, 149   800 Extension: 1265
Principal/Owner: Thomas L. Shafer
Website: www.shaferarchitects.com   e-mail: shaferarchitects@worldnet.att.net

EDWARD J. SHANNON, AIA ....**(847) 842-9398**
114 Applebee Street, Barrington   Fax: (847) 304-1898
See Add on Page: 202   800 Extension: 1104
Principal/Owner: Edward Shannon
e-mail: ejs@e-architect.com
Description: I offer personalized, full architectural services for residential clients.
Project types include: custom homes, additions, renovations and vacation
homes.

continued on page **186**

LARSON ASSOCIATES

Architecture • Interior Design

542 SOUTH DEARBORN   CHICAGO, IL 60605

312-786-2255   FAX: 312-786-2290

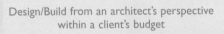

Kaiser Gutheim Partnership INC.

Architecture   and   Construction

Design/Build from an architect's perspective
within a client's budget

1734 W. Cortland St.

Chicago, IL 60622

773.342.4695

www.kgp-inc.com

BALSAMO, OLSON & LEWIS LTD.
One South 378 Summit Ave., Suite 1F
Oakbrook Terrace, Illinois 60181
630.629.9800
www.balsamoolsonlewis.com

STYCZYNSKI WALKER & ASSOCIATES
architects

Photography by: Paul Schusmann

Photography by: Paul Schusmann

STYCZYNSKI WALKER & ASSOCIATES
architects

Photography by: Paul Schusmann

Photography by: Paul Schusmann

642 Executive Drive • Willowbrook, Illinois 60521 • 630 789-2513
www.swa-architects.com

GRUNSFELD & ASSOCIATES ARCHITECTS

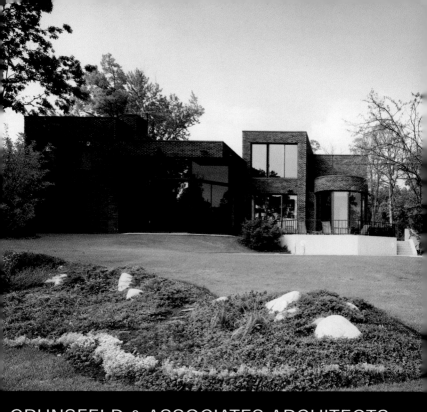

GRUNSFELD & ASSOCIATES ARCHITECTS

211 EAST ONTARIO STREET CHICAGO, ILLINOIS 60611 312-202-1800

continued from page **174**

JONATHAN SPLIT, LTD. ....**(773) 769-1017**
4764 North Ashland Avenue, Chicago   Fax: (773) 769-1703
See Add on Page: 202   800 Extension: 1181
Principal/Owner: Jonathan Split

STUART D. SHAYMAN & ASSOCIATES ....**(847) 441-7555**
1780 Ash Street, Northfield   Fax: (847) 441-7588
See Add on Page: 139   800 Extension: 1179
Principal/Owner: Stuart Shayman
e-mail: sdsarch@aol.com

STYCZYNSKI WALKER & ASSOCIATES ....**(630) 789-2513**
642 Executive Drive, Willowbrook   Fax: (630) 789-2515
See Add on Page: 180, 181   800 Extension: 1105
Principal/Owner: A. William Styczynski
Website: swa-architects.com e-mail: swa_architects@msn.com

R.M. SWANSON & ASSOCIATES, INC. ....**(847) 234-6655**
810 Waukegan Road, Lake Forest   Fax: (847) 234-6635
See Add on Page: 170, 171, 172, 173   800 Extension: 6313
Principal/Owner: Rick Swanson
e-mail: rmswanson@mindspring.com

STEPHEN SYNAKOWSKI ARCHITECTS AND PLANNERS ..**(847) 295-6926**
155 South Wooded Lane, Lake Forest   Fax: (847) 295-6926
See Add on Page: 155   800 Extension: 6315
Principal/Owner: Stephen Synakowski
Description: Tasteful Traditional & Contemporary Architectural & Landscape
Design.

VISBEEN ASSOCIATES INC. ....**(616) 285-9901**
4139 Embassy SE, Grand Rapids   Fax: (616) 285-9963
See Add on Page: 126   800 Extension: 1109
Principal/Owner: Wayne E. Visbeen, AIA, IIDA
e-mail: visbeenaia@aol.com
Description: In 1992 Wayne Evan Visbeen AIA, IIDA began Visbeen Associates
Inc. to provide architectural and interior design services for high end residential
homes specializing in lakefront and estates.

WHEELER KEARNS ARCHITECTS ....**(312) 939-7787**
417 S. Dearborn, Suite 500, Chicago   Fax: (312) 939-5108
See Add on Page: 153   800 Extension: 1167
Website: www.wkarch.com

"All great architecture is the design of
space that contains, cuddles,
exalts or stimulates."

Philip Johnson

CORDOGAN, CLARK & ASSOCIATES INC.
ARCHITECTURE ▪ INTERIORS

312.943.7300 CHICAGO ▪ AURORA 630.896.4678

PERIHELION, Ltd.
Architecture and Design

100 East Chicago Street
Suite 803
Elgin, Illinois 60120
Ph. 847.695.7092   Fax 847.695.7765
www.perihelionarch.com

RUDOLPH ARCHITECTS

□ □

1807 WEST SUNNYSIDE VENUE, CHICAGO, ILLINOIS 60640-5804

7 7 3 . 7 8 4 . 0 8 0 4

POULTON GROUP

David J. Poulton, AIA
268 Market Square
Lake Forest, IL 60045

1 ▪ 847 ▪ 615 ▪ 1178
1 ▪ Fax ▪ 615 ▪ 1177

Architecture ▪ Construction ▪ Historic Preservation ▪ Renovation ▪ Interior Design

CRIEZIS
A R C H I T E C T S

Criezis Architects, Inc.
1775 Winnetka Road. Suite 100 Northfield, IL 60093
Phone (847) 784-9400   Fax (847) 784-9100
E-Mail: crarchinc@aol.com

Jerome Cerny Architects, Inc. is dedicated to the creation of original architectural designs that respond to the desires of each individual client. I purchased this significant architectural firm in 1981, and proudly continue to build on its long-standing reputation for creative architectural solutions, attention to detail, and commitment to high quality materials. Jerome Cerny, a master of the understated, deftly created a casual elegance in homes by focusing more on the homeowner and less on the

presentation of the house itself. His concept of the home as a cocoon, a safe haven from the noise and stress of daily life, is still alive today at the firm that bears his name.

Our company offers architecture that is essentially established and traditional in character, with a definite transitional feel that's appealing to families of all ages.

*W*e listen to our clients, putting our knowledge and
talents at their disposal. They are among the most involved
of all luxury custom home clients because we establish an
attentive relationship that fosters communication and trust.

Jerome Cerny Architects, Inc.

Designer of Luxury Custom Homes Nationwide

 Paul Berger & Associates

712 N. Wells Street #3, Chicago, IL 60610
312.664.0640   Fax 312.664.0698

Home
your spirit, your dreams, your vision
our expertise
your Home.

PAPPAGEORGE/HAYMES LTD.

814 NORTH FRANKLIN SUITE 400

CHICAGO, ILLINOIS 60610

312 337 3344

SCOTT HIMMEL
architect

360 North Michigan Avenue
Suite 1100 Chicago Illinois 60601
telephone 312 332 3323
facsimile 312 332 3345
interior architecture and decoration

© Doug Snower Photography

EDWARD J. SHANNON **ARCHITECT/A.I.A.**

114 Applebee St. • Barrington, Il 60010 • T.847.842.9398 F.304.1898

Custom Single Family • Vaction Homes • Additons/Remodelings

jonathan **SPLITT** architects, ltd.

773 769 1017

FRANK J. KLEPITSCH, AIA
A R C H I T E C T

ARCHITECTURE
DESIGN BUILD
INTERIOR DESIGN
HISTORIC RENOVATION

53 West Jackson, Suite 530
Chicago, Illinois 60604
3 1 2 . 9 2 2 . 7 1 2 6
8 4 7 . 2 9 5 . 0 7 2 6
FAX 312.922.3799

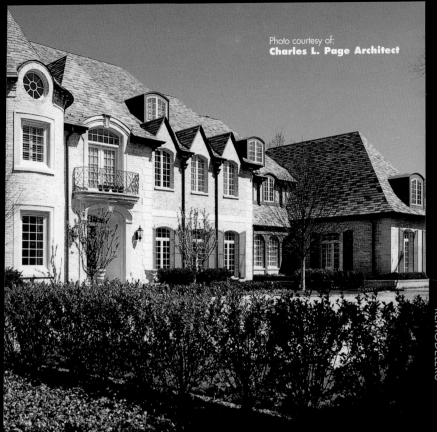

Photo courtesy of:
Charles L. Page Architect

CUSTOM HOME BUILDERS

&

REMODELERS

JMD

BUILDERS, INC.

444 Lake Cook Rd. Suite 10
Deerfield Illinois 60015
847.945.9670

"*The*
beautiful
rests on the
FOUNDATION
of the
necessary. "

Ralph Waldo Emerson

photo courtesy of:
Orren Pickell Designers & Builders

From the Ground Up

One of the key players in every home building and remodeling success story is the contractor. Architects envision possibilities, but contractors create new realities. While design/build teams of architects and contractors are becoming increasingly popular, the home in which you will be living will be the direct result of your contractor's efforts and expertise.

So much of your satisfaction in the final outcome depends upon the selection of the right contractor. It is essential to choose a company or individual with whom you have a good rapport, who has excellent references as well as experience with your type of project.

While the planning phase of a new home or remodeling project may be exciting, creating the finished product is hard work. Seek out a contractor whose attention to quality detail, willingness to listen to your concerns, and in-depth knowledge of the trades assures you a smoother road on the way to your new home.

THE TEAR-DOWN TREND

Land for new residential construction is getting harder to find, and "tear-down" renovations are becoming more common. There are often mixed emotions in an existing neighborhood as old structures come down. If you are considering a "tear-down" property, be sure you work with a builder and architect who are sensitive to the character of the neighborhood, and will help you build a home that fits in.

HOME BUILDER SOURCES

The Home Builders Association of Greater Chicago 1919 Highland Ave., Bldg. A Suite 225 Lombard, IL 60148 (630) 627-7575 www.hbagc.com

Northern Illinois Home Builders Association 29 w 140 Butterfield Rd., suite 101 Warrenville, IL 60555 (630) 393-4490 www.nihba.com

National Association of the Remodeling Industry (NARI) (847) 948-7595 www.narigc.org

SETTING THE STANDARD FOR QUALITY

A strong commitment to providing top quality materials and craftsmanship is the most important contribution a builder can make to your professional team. Working in concert with your architect, interior designer, kitchen and bath designer and landscape architect/designer, a custom home builder will take the designs, and your dreams, and make them happen. Selecting a builder who shares your dedication to building only the best is one of the best ways you can build quality into your new home. This kind of quality is as tangible as it is intangible. You can see it in the materials used – not necessarily the most expensive, but always the best for the situation. More interestingly, you can feel it. There's an unmistakable sense of integrity in a well-built home, of a dream fulfilled.

MAKE "QUALITY-DRIVEN" DECISIONS

Instead of instructing a builder to "build me a big house," or a "big kitchen" today's custom home buyer is more likely to say, "Build me the best house or kitchen my budget will allow." The emphasis has shifted from quantity ("I want it all") to quality ("I want the best"), and from taking the lowest bid to fairly compensating the builder who submits the best package of products and services. Smart, value-oriented customers realize that dollars spent today will soon be forgotten, whereas the level of quality those dollars bought will be appreciated for years.

As a custom home client, you must determine what's most important to you and what investment you'll make to achieve it. Good builders will help you set priorities and meet your goals. They've been through the process and know to be exacting, setting their expectations as high as their high-end clients do.

IS IT A(ARCHITECT) BEFORE B(BUILDER) OR B BEFORE A?

Answering this question can seem like the "chicken or the egg" riddle: Do you hire the builder first, the architect first, or choose a design/build firm, where both functions are under the same roof?

If you work first with an architect, his or her firm will recommend builders they know have a track record in building homes of the same caliber as yours. Most likely, your architect contract includes bidding and negotiation services with these builders, and you may expect help in analyzing bids and making your selection. Your architect contract also may include construction administration, where the architect makes site visits to observe construction, review the builder's applications for payment, and help make sure the home is built according to the plans.

Perhaps you've seen previous work or know satisfied clients of a custom home builder, and wish to work with him. In this scenario, the builder will recommend architects who are experienced in successfully designing homes and/or additions similar to what you want. The builder will support you and the architect will cost control information through realistic cost figures, before products are integrated into the house.

If you like the idea of working with one firm for both the architectural design and building, consider a design/build firm. Design/build firms offer an arrangement that can improve time management and efficient communication, simply by virtue of having both professional functions under the same roof. There is also added flexibility as the project develops. If you decide you want to add a feature, the design/build firm handles the design process and communicates the changes internally to the builder. When you interview a design/builder firm, it's important to ascertain that the firm has a strong architectural background, with experienced custom home architects on staff.

All scenarios work and no one way is always better than the other. Make your choice by finding professionals you trust and with whom you feel comfortable. Look for vision and integrity and let the creative process begin.

FINDING THE RIGHT BUILDER

The selection of a builder or remodeler is a major decision, and should be approached in a thoughtful, unhurried manner. Allow plenty of time to interview and research at least two candidates before making your choice. Hours invested at this point can save months of time later on.

At the initial interview, the most important information you'll get is not from brochures, portfolios, or a sales pitch, but from your own intuition. Ask yourself: Can we trust this person to execute plans for our dream home, likely the biggest expenditure of our lifetime? Is there a natural two-way communication, mutual respect, and creative energy? Does he have the vision to make our home unique and important? Is his sense of the project similar to ours? Will we have any fun together? Can we work together for at least a year?

If you answer "Yes!", you've found the most valuable asset – the right chemistry.

TEN GOOD QUESTIONS TO ASK A BUILDER'S PAST CLIENTS

1. Are you happy with your home?
2. Was the house built on schedule?
3. Did the builder respect the budget and give an honest appraisal of costs early on?
4. Did the builder bring creativity to your project?
5. Were you well informed so you properly understood each phase of the project?
6. Was the builder accessible and on-site?
7. Does the builder provide good service now that the project is complete?
8. How much help did you get from the builder in choosing the products in your home?
9. Is the house well built?
10. Would you hire the builder again?

IT TAKES HOW LONG?

Some typical construction time frames:

Total Kitchen Remodel: From total demolition to installation of new cabinets, flooring, appliances, electrical, etc. SIX – EIGHT WEEKS

A 1,400 Sq. Ft. Addition: New first floor Great Room & powder room, extension of the existing kitchen; master suite upstairs. FOUR – SIX MONTHS

Total Home Remodel: An 1,800 sq. ft. Colonial expanded to 4,000 sq. ft. All spaces redefined, added third floor, three new baths, new high-end kitchen, deck. SIX – NINE MONTHS

These estimates depend on factors such as the size of the crew working on your project, the timeliness of decisions and delivery of materials.

TAKE TIME TO CHECK REFERENCES

The most distinguished builders in the area expect, even want, you to check their references. More luxury home clients are taking the time to do this research as the move toward quality workmanship continues to grow.

Talk to clients. Get a list of clients spanning the last three to five years, some of whom are owners of projects similar to yours. Call them and go visit their homes or building sites. Satisfied customers are only too happy to show you around and praise the builder who did the work. If you can, speak with a past client not on the builder's referral list. Finding one unhappy customer is not cause for concern, but if you unearth a number of them, cross that builder off your list.

Visit a construction site. Clients who get the best results appreciate the importance of the sub-contractors. Their commitment to quality is at the heart of the job. Do the sub-contractors appear to be professional? Are they taking their time in doing their work? Is the site clean and neat?

Contact subcontractors with whom the builder has worked. If they vouch for the builder's integrity and ability you'll know the firm has earned a good professional reputation. Meeting subcontractors also provides a good measure for the quality of workmanship you'll receive.

Visit the contractor's office. Is it well-staffed and organized? Do they offer the technology for virtual walk-throughs? Do you feel welcome there?

Find out how long the builder has been in business. Experienced custom builders have strong relationships with top quality sub-contractors and architects, a comprehensive knowledge of products and materials, and know how to provide the best service before, during and after construction.

Ask how many homes are currently being built and how your project will be serviced. Some builders work on several homes at once; some limit their total to ten or twelve a year.

LAYING A FOUNDATION FOR SUCCESS

Two documents, the contract and the timeline, define your building experience. The contract lays down the requirements of the relationship and the timeline delineates the order in which the work is done. While the contract is negotiated once at the beginning of the relationship, the timeline continues to be updated and revised as the project develops.

THE CONTRACT

The American Institute of Architects (AIA) provides a standard neutral contract which is widely used in the area, but some firms write their own contracts. As with any contract, get legal advice, read carefully, and assume nothing. If landscaping is not mentioned, then landscaping will not be provided. Pay careful attention to:

• Payment schedules. When and how does the builder get paid? How much is the deposit (depends on the total cost of the project but $10,000 to $25,000 is not uncommon) and will it be applied against the first phase of the work? Do you have the right to withhold any payment until your punch list is completed? Will you write checks to the builder (if so, insist on sworn waivers) or only to the title company? Remodeling contracts typically use a payment schedule broken into thirds – one-third up front, one-third half-way through the project, and one-third at completion. You may withhold a negotiated percentage of the contract price until you're satisfied that the terms of the contract have been met and the work has been inspected. This should be stipulated in the contract. Ten percent is the average amount to be held back, but is negotiable based on the overall size of the project.

Builders and remodeling specialists who attract a quality-minded, high end custom home client, are contacted by institutions offering attractive construction or bridge and end loan packages. Ask your contractor for referrals if you want to do some comparative shopping.

• The total cost - breakdown of labor and materials expenses.

• Change order procedures. Change orders on the average add seven to ten percent to the cost of a custom home. Be clear on how these orders are charged and the impact they eventually will have on the timetable.

• The basic work description. This should be extremely detailed, including everything from installing phone jacks to the final cleaning of your home. A comprehensive list of specified materials should be given, if it hasn't already been provided by your architect.

• Allowances. Are they realistic? This is one place where discrepancies will be evident. Is Contractor A providing $75,000 for cabinets while Contractor B is providing $150,000?

• Warranty. A one-year warranty, effective the date you move in, is standard in this area.

TRUTH ABOUT CHANGE ORDERS

The building process demands an environment that allows for changes as plans move from paper to reality. Although you can control changes through careful planning in the preliminary stages of design and bidding, budget an extra seven to ten percent of the cost of the home to cover change orders. Changes are made by talking to the contractor, not someone working at the site. You will be issued a change order form, which you will sign and return to the contractor. Keep your copies of the forms together in one folder. Avoid last minute sticker shock by being diligent in keeping a current tab on your change order expenses.

213

SOURCES FOR HISTORIC PROPERTIES

Landmarks Preservation Council of Illinois 53 West Jackson Chicago, IL 60604 (312) 922-1742 Contact them for information about your home, and the state's tax freeze program to promote historic renovation or restoration.

The National Trust for Historic Preservation 1785 Massachusetts Avenue, N.W. Washington, D.C. 20036 (202) 588-6000 Having a home listed on the National Register doesn't restrict homeowners from demolishing or making changes, (local restrictions do that) but offers possible financial assistance and tax credits for renovations, and limited protection against federal 'takings.' The organization sponsors programs, publishes newsletters and books, and advocates preservation.

Local foundations and historical societies are established in most of the Chicago area communities that have older homes.

THE TIMELINE

This changeable document will give you a good indication if and when things will go wrong. Go to the site often enough to keep track of the progress according to the timeline. Do what you need to do to keep the project on schedule. One of the main causes of delays and problems is late decision-making by the homeowner. If you wait until three weeks prior to cabinet installation to order your cabinets, you can count on holding up the entire process by at least a month. (You'll also limit your options to cabinets that can be delivered quickly.)

THE SECOND TIME'S A CHARM

Today's lifestyles demand a home that's flexible. As homeowners become increasingly sophisticated in their knowledge and awareness of the exciting possibilities that can be built into a home, they're designing custom additions and renovations that match their individual style. People who entertain formally, who like to have caterers and chefs come into their kitchens to prepare a special meal, build fabulous multi-zone kitchens with elegant dining areas. Those who operate a business build dedicated offices, with separate entrances and conference areas. Empty nesters add on or re-configure existing space for a luxury first floor master suite, and use the upper level as storage and guest rooms for visiting children and grandchildren.

Renovating a home offers the unique excitement of reinventing an old space to serve a new, enhanced purpose. It's an evolutionary process, charged with creative thinking and bold ideas. If you enjoy a stimulating environment of problem solving and decision making, and you're prepared to dedicate the needed time and resources, remodeling will result in a home which lives up to all of your expectations. You'll be living in the neighborhood you love, in a home that fits your needs.

Top caliber remodeling projects are achieved by remodeling specialists who create excellent plans which meet the needs of their client, the best quality workmanship and materials, and considerable client involvement.

They work on jobs as contained as updating a bathroom or adding storage, and as complex as renovating or enlarging a classic or historic home.

A successful addition or renovation is so elegantly seamed into the original structure, both inside and out, that the work is all but unnoticeable. An achievement of this magnitude requires an extensive amount of care in planning and execution.

THE LUXURY OF SUPERIOR SERVICE

Clients of top quality remodeling specialists expect a high level of individualized service, and when they fulfill their client responsibilities in the project, they aren't disappointed. Involved clients are granted a high degree of personal attention from the very beginning of the process.

As the planning and eventually the building project unfolds, a top remodeler will keep you up to date and on track with your decision-making.

This service and accessibility will save you time and money and add to your enjoyment of the project. You may speak to each other every day during the most intensive period of decision making.

UPDATING THE CLASSICS

Many homeowners at the beginning of the new century are attracted to the historic architecture in these older neighborhoods. Their maturity and classicism are factors that persuade homeowners to make an investment in an old home and restore, renovate or preserve it, depending on what level of involvement interests them and the significance of the house. Renovations include additions and updating or replacing systems in the house. Restorations involve restoring the building to the specifications original to the house. Preservation efforts preserve what's there.

Like any remodeling project, it's an emotional and personal experience, only more so. Staying within the confines of a certain period or style is difficult and time consuming. That's why it's crucial to find an experienced architect and builder who share a reverence for tradition and craftsmanship to bring about a successful result. At your interview, determine if his or her portfolio shows competence in this specialty. It's vital to find a professional who understands historic projects and knows experienced and qualified contractors and/or subcontractors who will do the work for you. Ask if he or she knows experienced contractors who work in historic districts and have relationships with knowledgeable, experienced craftsmen. If you want exterior features, like period gardens or terraces, ask if it will be included in the overall plan. Make sure he or she has sources for you to find period furnishings, sconce shades or chimney pots.

There are many construction and design issues particular to old homes. The historic renovation and preservation experts featured in the following pages bring experience, creativity and responsibility to each project.

A LUXURY ADDITION ON AN HISTORIC HOME

Suburban Arts and Crafts-Prairie Home, circa 1915.
• All windows, trim, casings, and other details to match the original brick.
• Full, finished basement, with bar and workout area.
• First level family room, dining room and new kitchen.
• Upper level master suite and office. Stone terrace and garden.

Total Project Cost: $500,000, including architectural fees.

CLEAN UP TIME: Now or Later?

Your remodeling contract should be specific about clean-up. Will the site be cleaned up every day, or at the end of the project? Everyday clean-up may add to the price, but is well worth the extra expenditure.

CREATE A RECORD

You have a team of highly qualified professionals building your home, but the ultimate responsibility is on your shoulders. So keep track of the project. Organize a binder to keep all of your samples, chips, change orders, and documents together. Make copies for yourself of all communication with your suppliers and contractor. Take notes from conversations and send them to the contractor. This can help eliminate confusion before a problem occurs.

SETTING PRIORITIES

Choosing the "must-have" features and learning to live without others can be a highly-charged issue for the custom home client. Your builder will help you make these decisions, by giving you accurate quotes and emphasizing the features you need to build a quality home.

RESPECT YOUR ELDERS

Before you fall in love with an old house, get a professional opinion. Find out how much is salvageable before you make the investment. Can the wood be restored? Have the casings been painted too many times? Is the plaster wavy and buckled? Can the house support ductwork for central air conditioning or additional light sources?

Are you really compatible? The biggest mistake prospective historic home owners make is planning to change the nature of the house. If the house can't be made livable to your standards, while staying true to the architecture and style of the home and neighborhood, look for another property. People who live in historic neighborhoods expect new owners will do their part to keep the distinctive character of the area intact. Be sensitive to and aware of that expectation.

Notable remodelers are often contacted for their expert advice prior to a real estate purchase and realtors maintain relationships with qualified remodelers for this purpose. They also keep remodelers informed of special properties suitable for custom renovations as they become available.

PRIVACY? WHAT'S THAT?

Remodelers overwhelmingly agree their clients are happier if they move to a temporary residence during all, or the most intensive part, of the renovation. The sight of the roof and walls being torn out, the constant banging and buzzing of tools, and the invasion of privacy quickly take their toll on children and adults who are trying to carry on family life in a house full of dust. Homeowners who are well-rested from living in clean, well-lighted temporary quarters enjoy better relationships with each other, their remodeler and sub-contractors.

Not only will you save your sanity by vacating your home, you may also save a significant amount of money while shortening the time it takes to complete the job. A plumber, for instance, won't have to make two trips to your house – once to make it temporarily livable and again to do the majority of the required plumbing work. Contractors always protect the inside of a home from the elements during construction, but if you will be in the house, additional protection must be provided. By staying home, you may add as much as two percentage points to the cost of the remodeling project and weeks or months to the timeline.

Common hideaways are rental homes, suite-type hotels, the unoccupied home of a relative, or a long vacation trip.

CONTEXTUALISM

Popular styles and trends take a back seat to establishing harmony with the neighborhood and within a house itself.

Property owners want their newly built home to fit in with the other houses in their neighborhood – to respect and complement any established architecture. Homeowners who remodel or add on, who forego moving because they love their homes and neighborhoods, are ardent supporters of contextual design, which works within the aesthetic of the original home. They insist on an addition that blends in with the existing structure, stays in context with other rooms and doesn't intrude on the look or feel of the neighborhood. The result: a home of perfect proportion that is appealing to the eye, fits the land, and doesn't overpower the neighborhood.

A WORD ABOUT FINANCING OF REMODELING PROJECTS

Payment schedules in remodeling contracts typically require a deposit or a first payment at the start of the project with subsequent payments due monthly or in conjunction with the progress of the work.

It is within your rights to withhold a negotiated percentage of the contract price until you're satisfied that the terms of the contract have been met and the work has been inspected. This should be stipulated in the written contract. Ten percent is the average amount to be held back, but is negotiated based on the overall size of the project.

Remodeling specialists who attract a quality-minded clientele are kept abreast of the most attractive remodeling loans on the market by lenders who specialize in these products. Ask your remodeler for referrals to these financial institutions. ■

THAT'S ENTERTAINING

The need for more efficient, flexible and expanded space for entertaining is one of the main reasons Chicago area homeowners decide to remodel their homes. As home becomes more central to our lifestyle, comfortable entertaining becomes a priority, especially in the new, multi-functional kitchen.

Custom
Home Builders

AIROOM ARCHITECTS & BUILDERS ....**(847) 679-3650**
6825 N. Lincoln Ave., Lincolnwood   Fax: (847) 677-3308
See Add on Page: 274   800 Extension: 6003
Principal/Owner: Michael Klein
Website: www.airoom.com   e-mail: info@airoom.com

BGD & C ....**(312) 255-8300**
875 N. Michigan Avenue, Chicago   Fax: (312) 255-8393
See Add on Page: 276, 277   800 Extension: 1035
Principal/Owner: Rodge Owen & Charles Grode
e-mail: bgdc@hotmail.com

BURACK & COMPANY ....**(847) 266-3500**
1741 Green Bay Road, Highland Park   Fax: (847) 266-3707
See Add on Page: 236   800 Extension: 6040
Principal/Owner: Robert Burack

CRONIN CUSTOM HOMES ....**(630) 513-5800**
2550 Fox Field Drive, St. Charles   Fax: (630) 513-5813
See Add on Page: 241   800 Extension: 1070
Principal/Owner: Joe Cronin & Kevin Cronin

DIOR BUILDERS, INC. ....**(847) 934-1500**
116 W. Northwest Highway, Palatine   Fax: (847) 934-1508
See Add on Page: 238, 239   800 Extension: 6086
Principal/Owner: Peter Di Lorio
Website: www.diorhomes.com   e-mail: info@diorhomes.com

DISTINCTIVE CUSTOM HOMES ....**(847) 295-4500**
PO Box 142, Lake Forest   Fax: (847) 295-1914
See Add on Page: 259   800 Extension: 1259
Principal/Owner: Robert D. Salm/ Jamie P. Childs
e-mail: robtsalm@aol.com

FERRIS HOMES ....**(847) 509-9600**
624 Anthony Trail, Northbrook   Fax: (847) 509-9601
See Add on Page: 254   800 Extension: 1003
Principal/Owner: Andrew Ferris
Website: www.ferrishomes.com   e-mail: info@ferrishomes.com

FIELDCREST BUILDERS ....**(847) 234-1300**
1300 Gavin Court, Lake Forest   Fax: (847) 234-1389
See Add on Page: 255   800 Extension: 1155
Principal/Owner: Joe Dakis

continued on page **226**

JOSEPH LICHTENBERGER
Custom Homes

27 West 031 North Avenue • West Chicago, Illinois 60185

Tel: 630.293.9660 • Fax: 630.293.9683

www.ldchomes.com

JMD

BUILDERS, INC

444 Lake Cook Rd. Suite 10
Deerfield Illinois 60015

847.945.9670

Page Builders, Inc.
100 Evergreen Lane Winnetka, IL 60093
8 4 7 . 4 4 1 . 7 8 6 0

The Page Company provides complete services from site acquisition through concept, design, planning, construction, finishing and landscaping for over 35 years on the North Shore.

Page Builders, Inc.
100 Evergreen Lane Winnetka, IL 60093
847 . 441 . 7860

Page Builders is known for their authentic interpretation of French and English traditional architecture

Custom Home Builders & Remodelers

continued from page 218

GIRMSCHEID BUILDERS ....**(847) 367-5258**
1511 Sunnyview Drive, Libertyville — Fax: (847) 367-5282
See Add on Page: 242, 243 — 800 Extension: 1159
Principal/Owner: Terry Girmscheid

GLEN ELLYN HOMES ....**(630) 469-1070**
489 Taft Avenue, Glen Ellyn — Fax: (630) 469-1356
See Add on Page: 268, 269 — 800 Extension: 6121
Principal/Owner: Doug Walksler / Tom Gale
e-mail: gehomes@aol.com
Description: Custom homes and premium properties in Chicago's Western
Suburbs.

GREAT HAVEN BUILDERS ....**(847) 382-8360**
51 Oak Ridge Lane, Barrington — Fax: (847) 304-1404
See Add on Page: 252 — 800 Extension: 1128
Principal/Owner: Greg Crowther
Website: www.greathaven.com e-mail: greathaven.com

ARTHUR J. GREENE CONSTRUCTION CO. ....**(847) 367-4044**
702 Deerpath Drive, Vernon Hills — Fax: (847) 367-4002
See Add on Page: 272, 273 — 800 Extension: 1222
Principal/Owner: Stephen C. Rice

JERRY GUTNAYER ....**(847) 498-8444**
2918 Cherry Lane, Northbrook — Fax: (847) 498-8445
See Add on Page: 264, 265 — 800 Extension: 1233
Principal/Owner: Jerry Gutnayer
Description: Custom Home Builder: Design- Build

HOMES BY JAMES, INC. ....**(847) 228-6181**
235 S. Leonard Lane, Arlington Heights — Fax: (847) 228-6867
See Add on Page: 275 — 800 Extension: 1166
Principal/Owner: James W. Malapanes, Jr.

JDS BUILDER OF CUSTOM HOME ....**(630) 789-6202**
6212 Elm Street, Burr Ridge — Fax: (630) 789-6255
See Add on Page: 278, 279 — 800 Extension: 1083
Principal/Owner: Donna Slesser/ James D. Slesser
Website: www.jdshomes.com e-mail: JSle879254

JMD BUILDERS, INC. ....**(847) 945-9670**
444 Lake Cook Road, Suite 10, Deerfield — Fax: (847) 945-9671
See Add on Page: 206, 207, 222, 223 — 800 Extension: 6171
Principal/Owner: Jerry Dardick
e-mail: jerry@jmdbuilders.com

LICHTENBERGER HOMES ....**(630) 293-9660**
27W031 North Avenue, West Chicago — Fax: (630) 293-9683
See Add on Page: 220, 221 — 800 Extension: 1140
Principal/Owner: Joseph Lichtenberger

JOHN MARSHALL CONSTRUCTION, INC. ....**(847) 279-7840**
1583 Barclay Blvd., Buffalo Grove — Fax: (847) 279-7841
See Add on Page: 267 — 800 Extension: 1107
Principal/Owner: John Marshall
Website: www.jmarshallconstruction.com e-mail: JMCINC1976@aol.com
Description: Since 1976, John Marshall Construction, Inc. has demonstrated
commitment to quality and decision to customer service as a design-build com-
pany.

CHIC MARTIN SIGNATURE HOMES ....**(847) 837-0660**
262 Hawthorne Village Commons, Vernon Hills — Fax: (847) 837-8495
See Add on Page: 270, 271 — 800 Extension: 1086
Principal/Owner: Chic Martin

continued on page 226

SPEND THE REST OF YOUR LIFE IN THE HOME OF YOUR DREAMS

CRYSTAL KEY AWARD WINNER, 1999

CUSTOM HOMES MAGAZINE HAS HONORED ORREN PICKELL DESIGNERS & BUILDERS AS AMERICA'S CUSTOM HOME BUILDER OF THE YEAR, 2001

1996-1998

web:

llbuild

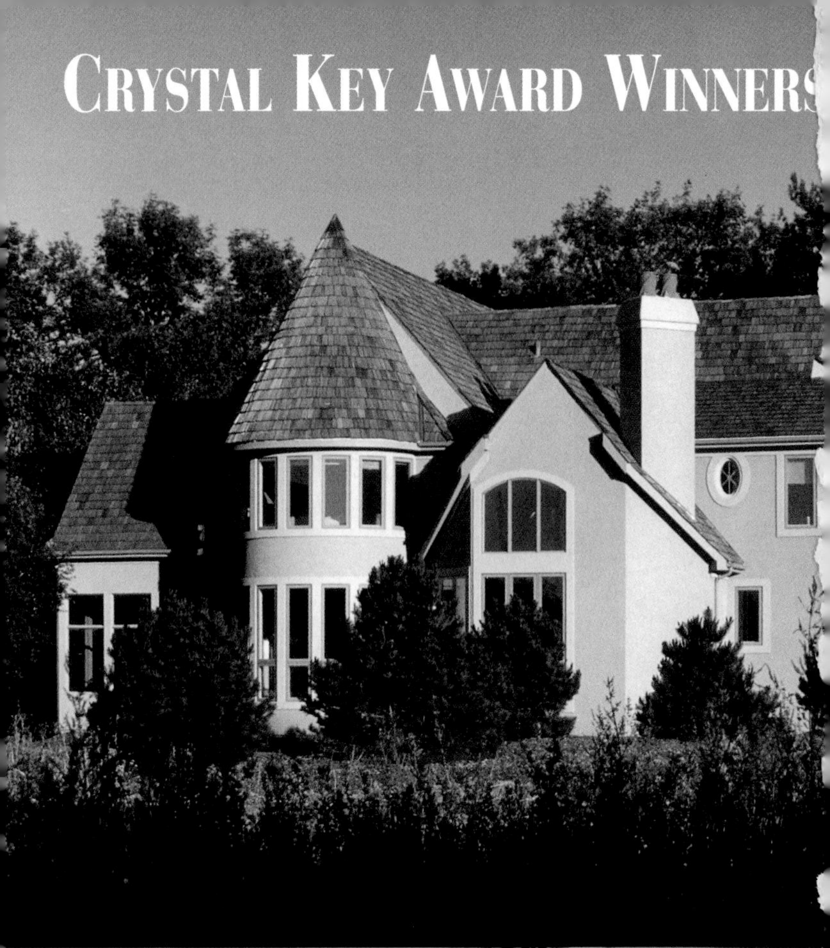

Research us on the

Pickel

YOU'VE WAITED FOR THIS YOUR WHOLE LIFE

It may have begun in your childhood, somewhere in your imagination. Your home, just as you want it. Life without compromise, every single day.

Your Orren Pickell professionals give form to your custom homebuilding or remodeling fantasies and bring your dreams into sharp focus. We guide you through every detail. We never skimp, using only master craftsmen and the finest materials every step of the way. Just look at the results.

GOLD KEY AWARD WINNER, 2000

At Orren Pickell Designers & Builders, we have the resources and expertise to take you through every phase of the custom homebuilding process.

The time has come to live your dream. So relish the complete experience, from start to finish, with the Orren Pickell team.

Site Selection

We will help you find your ideal site. If you already have a site, our designs will reflect the terrain and surrounding neighborhood.

Architectural Design

Our award-winning professional architects use computer-aided design and virtual reality technology. Watch your dreams materialize.

Landscaping

Experts will guide you through every consideration, from the driveway approach to the type of grass, from the vistas to the positioning of trees, shrubs, and flowers.

Kitchen and Cabinetry

Award-winning interior designers and master carpenters are on the staff of CabinetWerks, an Orren Pickell company. Their only job is to help you.

Construction Group

You'll experience the dedication of our talented and experienced craftsmen. You'll find that their commitments to highest quality work, on time and within budget, are renewed every day.

Maintenance Division

Your one-year service guarantee begins the day you move into your new home. Many homeowners are so happy with this program that they extend it, assuring that everything is kept fine-tuned for years to come.

Remodeling and Renovation

You'll appreciate the cleanliness, reliability, and painstaking attention to detail of our master craftsmen. Their pride and professionalism extend to highest quality remodeling, renovation, and/or restoration projects.

Behind-the-Scenes

Yours will be the ultimate designing/building experience. Our estimators will keep you on budget while the team guides you through this exciting creative process. We're all there to ensure that your home meets your, and our, highest standards.

Do this for yourself.
Call Orren Pickell Designers & Builders today.
Spend the rest of your life in the home of your dreams.

ORREN PICKELL
DESIGNERS & BUILDERS

2201 Waukegan Road • Suite W-285 • Bannockburn, IL 60015
Ph: 847.914.9629 Fax: 847.914.9781
www.pickellbuilders.com

Creating your Luxury Dream Home

It's What's Inside that Counts

What does it mean to build a custom, luxury home? Luxury is something that is not a necessity but provides added comfort or pleasure. You must determine what luxury means to you.

Initially, your architect will play an important role in defining this process by helping to interpret your vision. Together, you will bring your dream closer to reality with sketches, material selections, revisions, layouts, more revisions and final blueprints.

While you may already know you want a dramatic curved staircase in the entry, a two-story stone fireplace in the great room, or hardwood floors in your gourmet kitchen, it's the details behind these features and the quality of the workmanship that will create the feeling of turning this one-of-a-kind house into a home.

It is the custom home builder's job to fulfill your vision with integrity and quality. All luxury homes demand a four-step process, unique to any other kind of home building — education, communication, information and service:

Education: A builder should help each client understand everything there is to know about the strengths and weaknesses of various materials selections, the impact of a specific design or structural decisions, and what to expect during each phase of the building process.

Communication: Hundreds of decisions will be made by your design/build team. To ensure clear communication, hold regular status meetings.

Information: Your builder should be open with all information about your home—good or bad, large or small, so informed choices can be made.

Service: The importance of providing superior customer service, on-time and on-budget cannot be stressed enough. A custom home contractor should work diligently to ensure that the entire process runs smoothly.

Ultimately, it's a combination of these ingredients—design, craftsmanship, materials, relationships, processes and services—that translate into the unmistakable look and feeling of a luxury home.

Jerry Dardick

Jerry Dardick, *JMD Builders Inc.*

BURACK & COMPANY

WINDSOR BUILDERS, INC.

320 Melvin Dr., Suite 9   Northbrook IL 60062   847.562.9545   Fax 847.562.9546

CRONIN
CUSTOM HOMES
2560 Foxfield Dr. • St. Charles, IL 60174 630-513-5800

Creating
Custom
Spaces

Each person's vision of a dream home is very different. Some may opt for extra square footage, while others may indulge in high-tech bells and whistles, elaborate interior spaces, or all of the above. Making each home as unique as the people who live there is the challenge posed to Chicago-area luxury homebuilders. Lifestyles are dictating that each home be fitted with unique rooms that complement the families living there. Luxury homebuyers are treating themselves to larger, more magnificent homes. Chicago-area builders are rising to the challenge and, in doing so, are changing the meaning of the words "custom home" forever.

Imposing on the outside, inside this luxury home is an insulated, safe haven with both multi-purpose and specialty rooms that reflect the owner's personality and are designed to be enjoyed and lived in 100 percent of the time.
Photo courtesy of Orren Pickell Designers & Builders

Photo by Linda Oyama Bryan

Specialty rooms are built for one purpose—for its owner to spend some leisure time enjoying his or her hobbies. Orren Pickell, Orren Pickell Designers & Builders, Bannockburn, Ill., designs many of these specialty rooms—each with the owner's unique interests in mind. One billiard room displays the owner's autographed baseballs and photos of sports figures. A wine cellar incorporates the owner's love of the sea with a fish tank spanning the entire wall opposite the wine racks. An indoor basketball court provides a perfect play space for visiting grandchildren.

Another specialty room, the media room, is designed to house elaborate home theaters and entertainment systems. One home theater designed by Charles Page, Charles Page Architects/Builders, Winnetka, Ill., contained an elaborate theater setup including curtains that opened, seats that vibrated and an "unbelievable" sound system, he says. Yet another specialty room Page designed features a dojo to integrate one woman's interest in kick-boxing and karate.

Many rooms are planned to have several uses—this is an evolving trend

HomeB

that both luxury homebuyers and builders are embracing more and more. Page says empty nesters are building new homes that are as big or bigger than the homes they raised their children. "They're pampering themselves," he says. Now, they have the knowledge to design spaces that reflect their individual tastes, personalities and needs.

In fitting with the larger trend toward multi-use rooms, many buyers are opting for the flexible spaces that are always in use. Pickell agrees with this trend, as do more savvy homebuyers, "We design spaces that can be lived in 100 percent of the time." Luxury homebuyers know what rooms they use and capitalize on that knowledge. The Transition House, a concept house built by Pickell, features rooms designed to accommodate the changing needs of today's family. "Empty nesters are still anxious about building only two or three bedrooms, so we add a fourth bedroom." This way, the extra square footage and expense is justified because grandchildren, boomerang kids or elderly parents have a place to stay within the home, and the rooms serve a dual purpose.

Specialty rooms are built for one purpose in mind—simply for its owner to spend some leisure time enjoying his or her hobbies. These rooms are designed with the owner's unique interests in mind. An indoor basketball court provides a perfect play space for visiting grandchildren. Another specialty room, the media room, is designed to house elaborate home theaters and entertainment systems.
Photo courtesy of Orren Pickell Designers & Builders
Photo by Linda Oyama Bryan

248

HomeB

Photo courtesy of Charles L. Page Architect

yoga spaces and excercise rooms, once tucked away in the basement where good views are scarce, now afford breathtaking views from the upper levels of the home. Pickell says many of his clients simply change bedrooms when the seasons change. This way, owners do not have to change out their closets with winter and summer clothing.

As carefully planned as every room in the home, storage is also a big issue with today's luxury homebuyers. "Many people design their storage space even before they design their kitchen," says Pickell. Furthermore, families accumulate many "things"—from figurine collections to trophies to family heirlooms—and they want to show them off. Many cabinet systems are designed specifically for this purpose. Glass-front, glass-shelf cabinets are used to display collections and add to an open feel within the home. Niches and specialized cabinetry find a place for everything. Another design incorporates French doors that open into a library. When open, the doors enclose curio cabinets within the room; when the doors are closed, they function as entry doors.

Another new concept, called the Family Workshop, combines all of the family's activities and hobbies into an organized, family-centered area. In another concept home, the Organization House, Pickell incorporated lockers and mail slots

uilders

In homes such as this one, "extra" rooms can be converted to flexible space, such as a reading/reflection room or a craft area. Yoga spaces and exercise rooms, once tucked away in the basement where good views are scarce, now afford breathtaking views from the upper levels of the home.

HomeB

As carefully planned as every room in the home, storage is also a big issue with today's luxury homebuyers. Glass-front, glass-shelf cabinets are used to display collections and add to an open feel within the home. Niches and specialized cabinetry find a place for everything.

for each member of the family. This area also includes a complete computer workstation. A craft station includes pull-out art areas, retractable work tables and a gift-wrapping area complete with storage for ribbons, bows, tape, scissors, etc. A laundry area has sweater racks, individual racks for white and colored laundry, a laundry chute, ironing area and retractable dry-cleaning hooks. "It's harder not to put things away," says Pickell.

In many homes, laundry rooms are moving to the second floor where most of the laundry originates. Page says some homes even incorporate multiple laundry rooms on the first and second floors of the home. "One woman requested a stacked washer/dryer in her dressing room," he says.

"It's an exciting time to be designing homes," says Page. He feels trends have evolved more rapidly during the last five years than ever before. Luxury homebuyers know what is special and unique to their lives—it's up to the builder to execute them in rooms and spaces that reflect their individual personalities and needs. ■

—*Barb McHatton*

uilders

GREAT·HAVEN
BUILDERS

- Custom Home Building & Remodeling
- General Contracting & Construction Management
- Quality Assurance Guarantee
- C.P.M. Computer Driven Scheduling
- Visit us at www.greathaven.com

Every home should be a
GREAT·HAVEN

Great Haven, Inc., 51 Oak Ridge Lane, Barrington, IL 60010
Phone: 847-382-8360 Fax: 847-304-1404

POULTON GROUP

David J. Poulton, AIA
268 Market Square
Lake Forest, IL 60045

1 ▪ 847 ▪ 615 ▪ 1178
1 ▪ Fax ▪ 615 ▪ 1177

Architecture ▪ Construction ▪ Historic Preservation ▪ Renovation ▪ Interior Design

FIELDCREST
BUILDERS, INC.

1300 GAVIN CT.

LAKE FOREST

ILLINOIS 60045

847.234.1300

Stonegate Builders, Inc.

"BUILDING FOR YOUR FUTURE"

1510 Old Deerfield Road, Suite 228, Highland Park, IL 60035
847.579.1525   847.579.1252 Fax

"Handcrafted with pride."

As Seen in the Chicago/Midwest Design Index

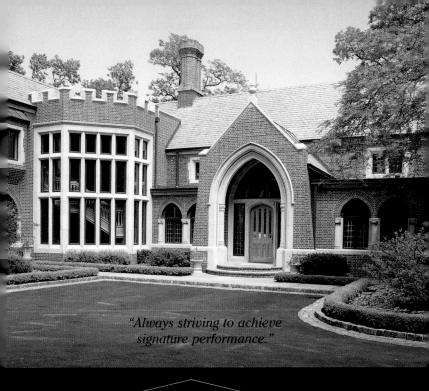

*"Always striving to achieve
signature performance."*

Stonegate Builders, Inc.

"BUILDING FOR YOUR FUTURE"

1510 Old Deerfield Road, Suite 228, Highland Park, IL 60035
847.579.1525   847.579.1252 Fax

Custom Home Builders & Remodelers

continued from page **218**

THE MEYNE COMPANY..**(773) 207-2100**
1755 W. Armitage, Chicago   Fax: (773) 207-0488
See Add on Page: 260, 261   800 Extension: 1071
Principal/Owner: Mark Evans

MIHOVLOVICH BUILDERS, INC. ....**(847) 395-4795**
24977 Nicholas Way, Antioch   Fax: (847) 395-4935
See Add on Page: 219   800 Extension: 1147

CHARLES L. PAGE ARCHITECT ....**(847) 441-7860**
100 Evergreen Lane, Winnetka   Fax: (847) 441-7862
See Add on Page: 140, 141, 224, 225   800 Extension: 1113
Principal/Owner: Charles Page
Description: Design/ Build firm. (for 40 years)

ORREN PICKELL DESIGNERS & BUILDERS ....**(847) 914-9629**
2201 Waukegan Road, Suite W-285, Bannockburn   Fax: (847) 914-9781
See Add on Page: 227 - 234   800 Extension: 1131
Principal/Owner: Orren Pickell
Website: www.pickellbuilders.com   e-mail: esucherman@pickellbuilders.com
Description: Includes: Orren Pickell Designers & Builders; Orren Pickell Design
Group; Orren Pickel Remodeling Group; Orren Pickell Maintenance Division; and
CabinetWerks

THE POULTON GROUP, LTD. ....**(847) 615-1178**
268 Market Square, Lake Forest   Fax: (847) 615-1177
See Add on Page: 190, 253   800 Extension: 6259
Principal/Owner: David J. Poulton, AIA
Description: We are a small, exclusive high-end residential Design/build firm
providing both new construction, renovation, preservation and interior design
services.

258

SEBERN HOMES..**(630) 377-7767**
P.O. Box 1306, St. Charles   Fax: (847) 464-4527
See Add on Page: 240   800 Extension: 1127
Principal/Owner: Ken Bernhard
Website: www.sebernhomes.com

SEVVONCO, INC. ....**(847) 359-3591**
201 E. Dundee Road, Suite A, Palatine   Fax: (847) 359-5123
See Add on Page: 280, 281   800 Extension: 1178
Principal/Owner: Scot Sevon

STONEGATE BUILDERS, INC...**(847) 579-1525**
1510 Old Deerfield Road, Highland Park   Fax: (847) 579-1526
See Add on Page: 256, 257   800 Extension: 1182
Principal/Owner: John Stalowey

STONERIDGE CUSTOM HOMES, INC. ....**(630) 852-1515**
6908 Galway Court, Darien   Fax: (630) 852-9051
See Add on Page: 262   800 Extension: 1183
Principal/Owner: Sue Boparai
Website: www.stoneridgebuilders.com   e-mail: homes@stoneridgebuilders.com
Description: Stoneridge Custom Homes combines proven commitment to build-
ing homes of the highest quality at a fair cost with an interactive style to help
clients create the home of their dreams.

TRIODYNE-WANGLER CONSTRUCTION CO., INC..................**(847) 647-8866**
5950 W. Touhy Avenue, Niles   Fax: (847) 647-0785
See Add on Page: 263   800 Extension: 6323
Principal/Owner: William Wangler / Joseph Wangler

continued on page **266**

George Lambros Photography

Quality Residential Construction Since 1906

George Lambros Photography

William Kildow Photography

The Meyne Company
A division of Bulley & Andrew, LLC

1775 W. Armitage Avenue
Chicago, Illinois 60622
(312) 207-2100
www.meyne.com

**NEW CONSTRUCTION   RENOVATION
HISTORICAL RESTORATION**

TRIODYNE-WANGLER
CONSTRUCTION COMPANY INC.

5950 West Touhy Avenue, Niles, IL 60714-4610

(847) 647-8866 FAX: (847) 647-0785

The Art

of

Living

Idea Homes^{SM}

Jerry Gutnayer

Custom Home Builder

2918 Cherry Lane • Northbrook, IL 60062

(847) 498–8444 • Fax (847) 498–8445

continued from page **258**

WINDSOR BUILDERS, INC...**(847) 562-9545**
320 Melvin Drive, Suite 9, Northbrook   Fax: (847) 562-9546
See Add on Page: 237   800 Extension: 6333
<u>Principal/Owner:</u> Matthew Kurtyka
<u>e-mail:</u> windsorbld@aol.com

"When you're talking about
building a house,
you're talking
about dreams."

Robert A.M. Stern

All Photography by: Jenn Marshall

JOHN MARSHALL
Construction, Inc.

John Marshall Construction, Inc

General Contractors - Design/Build
1583 Barclay Boulevard
Buffalo Grove, IL 60089
Tel: 847.279.7840
Fax: 847.279.7841

GLEN ELLYN HOMES

489 Taft Avenue Glen Ellyn, Illinois 60137   630.469.1070

Chic Martin
SIGNATURE HOMES

262 Hawthorne Village Commons
Vernon Hills, IL 60061-1526
847-837-0660 Fax 847-837-8495

Chic Martin

SIGNATURE
CM HOMES

262 Hawthorne Village Commons
Vernon Hills, IL 60061-1526
847-837-0660 Fax 847-837-8495

Adler's Glen

Evergreen

Conway Farms

- **Home Additions**

  Kitchens

  Custom Homes

Our unique approach combines top design talent with over 43 years of building experience to provide our clients with seamless integration from start to finish.

Visit our 30,000 sq. ft. Design and Build Showroom filled with ideas for your home.

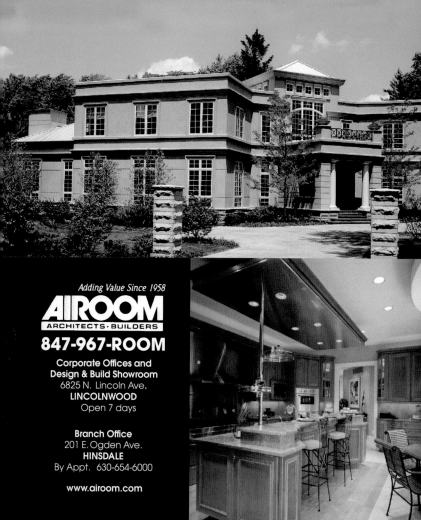

H·O·M·E·S
by
JAMES INC.
CUSTOM HOME BUILDER

235 South Leonard Lane
Arlington Heights, IL 60005

847-228-6181 • 847-228-6867

Design & Construction

BGD&C

Bowen Group Design/Build & Construction

875 North Michigan Avenue • Suite 1414 • Chicago, Illinois 60611 • 312.255.8300

JDS

BUILDER OF CUSTOM HOMES

6212 ELM STREET • BURR RIDGE, IL 60521
(630) 789-6202 • www.jdshomes.com

JDS

BUILDER OF CUSTOM HOMES

6212 ELM STREET • BURR RIDGE, IL 60521

(630) 789-6202 • www.jdshomes.com

SEVVONCO

Custom Builders and Remodelers of the Millennium Series Homes

Sevvonco builds for living in the 21st century. In 1998, we introduced the **Millennium I** and are now debuting the **Millennium II**.
The Millennium II is the first **Health House®** in Illinois recognized by the American Lung Association. This showcase residence also meets the EPA's Energy Star® criteria and is built utilizing sound green construction practices.
For a personal tour or additional information, please contact our office.

Sevvonco meets the distinctive needs of discerning homeowners for quality craftsmanship and comfort. Whether building a new home, remodeling or renovating... Sevvonco takes pride in a personal yet educated approach to homebuilding.

SEVVONCO

The Extra Step Builder
201 E. Dundee Road
Palatine, IL 60074
Tel. 847.359.3591 • Fax. 847.359.5123
www.sevvonco.com
email: sevvonco@mindspring.com

Raising the Standard for Home Environments.

Millennium II
Showcase for the 21st Century

Remodeling
Specialists

CONCEPT DESIGN CONSTRUCTION ....**(773) 549-3211**
2671 N. Lincoln Ave., Chicago   Fax: (773) 549-1765
See Add on Page: 283   800 Extension: 1001
<u>Principal/Owner:</u> Ted Cohn

KEYSTONE BUILDERS, INC. ....**(847) 432-4392**
3585 Old Mill Road, Highland Park   Fax: (847) 432-4395
See Add on Page: 284, 285   800 Extension: 1219
<u>Principal/Owner:</u> Joanna E. Szymel
<u>Website:</u> www.keystone-builders.com   <u>e-mail:</u> sales@keystone-builders.com
<u>Description:</u> Specializing in Design/Build custom homes, additions, kitchens, baths and renovations. For design consultation, please call.

LICHTENBERGER HOMES ....**(630) 293-9660**
27W031 North Avenue, West Chicago   Fax: (630) 293-9683
See Add on Page: 220, 221   800 Extension: 1145
<u>Principal/Owner:</u> Joseph Lichtenberger

CONCEPT DESIGN CONSTRUCTION

2671 NORTH LINCOLN ■ CHICAGO, ILLINOIS ■ 60614

PHONE: 773-549-3211 ■ FAX: 773-549-1765

The Sign of Excellence is in

DESIGN/BUILD, CONSTRUCTION MANAGEMENT, AND RENOVATIONS.

You may have noticed our sign popping up around the neighborhood as we begin building new homes or creative renovation projects for your neighbors. If you're thinking about improving your home or building a new home, please give us a call to talk about your ideas. From a gallery of styles for your kitchens and baths, to elegant home expansions, we can help you develop ideas that will give you the best value for each dollar you invest.

Your Neighborhood.

KEYSTONE
BUILDERS, INC.

*Call us today for more information
on our professional services.*

(847) 432-4392

ARCHITECT, DESIGN/BUILD, STRUCTURAL ENGINEERING
AND INTERIOR DESIGNERS.

3585 Old Mill Road, Highland Park, IL 60035

Please Visit our Website: www.keystone-builders.com

Roofing
Specialists

CEDAR ROOFING CO. INC. ....**(847) 247-4400**
27820 N. Irma Lee Circle, Lake Forest   Fax: (847) 247-4405
See Ad on Page: 287   800 Extension: 1242
<u>Principal/Owner:</u> Matt Wilkinson
<u>Website:</u> www.cedarinc.com

"From raw materials of the earth,
sleek floors, elegant arches, sweeping staircases."

Orren Pickell

Proudly Serving the North Shore for Over 20 years

Cedar Roofing Company has long been considered the North Shore's resident expert on cedar shakes and shingles.

Our expertise also includes slate and tile, cedar shingle siding, modified bitumen flat roofing, asphalt shingles, custom sheet metal, and gutters & downspouts.

Historic
Renovation

THE POULTON GROUP, LTD. ....**(847) 615-1178**
268 Market Square, Lake Forest   Fax: (847) 615-1177
See Add on Page: 190, 253   800 Extension: 1201
Principal/Owner: David J. Poulton, AIA
Description: We are a small, exclusive high-end residential Design/Build firm providing both new construction, renovation, preservation and interior design services.

SAWMAN & COMPANY ....**(847) 573-1361**
125 Marimac Lane, Vernon Hills   Fax: (847) 573-1362
See Add on Page: 289   800 Extension: 1213
Principal/Owner: Steve Smola

"All great architecture
is the design of space
that contains, *cuddles,*
exalts or stimulates."
Philip Johnson

SAWMAN & CO. Inc

125 Marimac Lane · Vernon Hills, IL 60061
Tel: (847) 573-1361 · Fax: (847) 573-1362

Finally... Chicago's Own Home & Design Sourcebook

The CHICAGO HOME BOOK, a comprehensive hands-on design sourcebook to building, remodeling, decorating, furnishing and landscaping a luxury home in Chicago and its suburbs, is a "must-have" reference for the Chicagoland homeowner. At over 700 pages, this beautiful, full-color hard cover volume is quite simply the most complete, well-organized reference to the Chicagoland home industry. It covers all aspects of the process, with hundreds of listings of local home industry professionals, accompanied by hundreds of inspiring photographs. You will also find articles to assist in planning and completing a project. The CHICAGO HOME BOOK tells you how to find what you need when you need it.

Order your copy today!

CHICAGO HOME BOOK

Published by
The Ashley Group
1350 E. Touhy Avenue • Des Plaines, IL 60018
888-458-1750
E-mail: ashleybooksales@cahners.com

Photo courtesy of:
Richard Menna Interior Design

INTERIOR
DESIGNERS

LARSON ASSOCIATES
Interior Design • Architecture

542 South Dearborn   Chicago, IL 60605
312-786-2255   fax: 312-786-2290

"**Art** imitates **Nature** in this:

Not to *dare*
is to
dwindle. "

John Updike

Inner Beauty

photo courtesy of:
Jayson Home & Garden
photo by:
Judy A. Slagle

It may be as simple as a fresh look at the familiar. Or it may be an involved process requiring major renovation. In either case, interior designers can bring your ideas to life by demystifying the daunting task of designing a home.

With their years of professional experience and the tools that they have at their fingertips, designers can orchestrate, layer by layer, design elements that together compose an inviting and harmonious décor. For this collaboration to be a success however, requires communication and trust. By listening to your dreams and by understanding your needs, designers can fashion workable rooms that are a visual delight, reflect your personality and speak to your spirit. The end result of a productive partnership should be a happy homeowner who can exclaim, "I've always known that this was a great house, but now it's home!"

FIVE THINGS YOU SHOULD KNOW

1. Know what level of guidance you want: A person to handle every detail, someone to collaborate with you, or simply an occasional consultation?

2. Know what you're trying to achieve. Start an Idea Notebook, filling it with pictures of rooms you like and don't like. This will help you define your style and stay true to your goal.

3. Know your budget. Prices of high end furnishings know no upper limit. Adopt a "master plan," to phase in design elements if your tastes are outpacing your pocketbook.

4. Know what's going on. Always ask; don't assume. Design is not a mystical process. Good designers can explain your project (and they'll want to).

5. Know yourself. Don't get blinded by beauty. Stay focused on what makes you feel "at home," and you'll be successful.

WHERE STRUCTURE MEETS INSPIRATION

A great interior designer, like a great architect or builder, sees space creatively, applying years of education and experience to deliver a distinguished residence at the highest level of quality in an organized, professional manner. Intensely visual, these talented individuals imprint a home with the spirit and personality of the family living there.

Creativity, that special talent to see the possibilities in a living room, library, or little reading nook, is the most important asset an interior designer will bring to a project. Particularly in upper-end interiors, where the expense of the antique accessories, sumptuous fabrics and imported furnishings is often a secondary concern, the creative vision driving the design choices and placement decisions is what makes a room extraordinary.

Just as an inventive spirit allows talented designers to apply their flair for putting things together in creative and welcoming ways, education and business experience are what get the wonderful concept off the computer or drawing paper and into reality.

A top quality interior designer who is licensed by the state is well educated in the field of interior design, usually holding a bachelor's or master's degree in the subject. This educational background coupled with practical experience is vital. You need not know where to get the best down-filled pillows, or when French fabric mills close each summer. You need not learn the difference between French Country and English Country, how to match patterns, or correctly balance a floor plan. Rely on a knowledgeable designer for that information.

A great interior designer also handles the "nuts and bolts" business end of the project. With skill and experience in placing and tracking orders, scheduling shipping, delivery, and installation, the designer can bring your project to its perfect conclusion.

AN INTERIOR DESIGNER IS A TEAM MEMBER

Choose an interior designer when you select your architect, builder, and landscape architect. A skilled designer can collaborate with the architect on matters such as window and door location, appropriate room size, and practical and accent lighting plans. In new construction and remodeling, try to make your floor plan and furniture choices simultaneously, to avoid common design problems, like traffic corridors running through a formal space, or awkward locations of electrical outlets.

CREATE THE BEST CLIENT-DESIGNER RELATIONSHIP

Talk to the best interior designers in the area and they'll tell you how exciting and gratifying it is for them when a client is involved in the process. This is happening more and more as homeowners turn their attention to hearth and home, and dedicate the time and resources to achieve a style they love.

To establish the most successful and pleasant relationship with an interior designer, make a personal commitment to be involved.

Start by defining your needs, in terms of service and the end result. Have an interior designer involved during the architectural drawing phase of a new or renovation project, and get the process started early. Be clear about how much help you want from a designer. Some homeowners have a strong sense of what they want and simply need a consultant-type relationship. Others want significant guidance from a professional who will oversee the entire process.

Set up a relationship that encourages an open exchange of ideas. In pursuit of personal style, you must be comfortable trusting a professional designer to interpret your thoughts and needs. You must be comfortable saying, "No, I don't like that," and receptive to hearing, "I don't think that's a good idea."

Be forthcoming about your budget. Not all interiors are guided by a budget, but the majority are. Your designer must know and respect your financial parameters and priorities. If a gorgeous dining room table is a top priority, objets d' art can be added later as you find them. Prices of exquisite furniture, custom carved cabinets, and other high end furnishings know no upper limit. Be realistic about what you will spend and what you expect to achieve. Do some research in furniture stores and specialty shops, starting with those showcased in this section. If your expectations temporarily exceed your budget, phase in the decor over a period of time.

Lastly, be inquisitive as the design unfolds. This is a creative effort on your behalf, so let yourself enjoy it, understand it and be stimulated by it.

START THINKING VISUALLY: STOP, LOOK AND CLIP

Before you start scheduling initial interviews with interior designers, start compiling an Idea Notebook – it's the best tool for developing an awareness of your personal style. Spend a weekend or two with a pair of scissors, a new Idea Notebook, and a stack of magazines, (or add a section to the Idea Notebook you made to inspire your architecture and building plans).

UNDERSTANDING "ECLECTIC"

Eclectic means "not following any one system, but selecting and using what seems best from all systems."

Its popularity in interior design stems from the unique look it creates. Mixing the best from different styles creates a dynamic that's totally different from an application of one chosen style. The overall effect is casual and comfortable, "dressed up" in a less formal way.

Eclectic can mean a mixing of styles within one room, like a rich Oriental rug paired with a denim sofa, or between rooms, like an 18th Century dining room leading into an Early American kitchen. The possibilities for accents and appointments are unlimited because there are no restrictions.

297

IMMERSE YOURSELF

The more exposure you have to good design, the easier it becomes to develop your own style.

• **Haunt the bookstores that have large selections of shelter magazines, and stacks of books on decorating, design and architecture. Some good book stores are:**

Chicago Architecture Foundation Bookstore 224 South Michigan Avenue (773) 922-3431

Prairie Avenue Book Shop 418 South Wabash Street (312) 922-5184 www.pabook.com

• **Attend show houses, especially the Designer Showcase homes presented twice annually by ASID, and visit model homes, apartments or lofts**
• **Visit the Merchandise Mart's 13th Floor, which is open to the public, and take advantage of their special educational seminars.**

Make this a record of your personal style. Include pictures of your favorite rooms, noting colors, fabrics, tile, carpet, fixtures, the way light filters through a curtain, anything that strikes your fancy. Circle the design elements in a room that you'd like to incorporate into your own home décor and make comments regarding those elements you don't care for. Think hard about what you love and loathe in your current residence. Start to look at the entire environment as a rich source of design ideas. Movies, billboards, architecture, clothing – all are fascinating sources for visual stimulation.

Then, when you hold that initial meeting, you too will have a book of ideas to share. Although a smart designer will be able to coax this information from you, it's tremendously more reliable to have visual representations than to depend on a verbal description. It also saves a tremendous amount of time.

THE INTERIOR DESIGN PROCESS: GETTING TO KNOW YOU

Give yourself time to interview at least two interior designers. Invite him or her to your home for a tour of your current residence and a look at items you wish to use in the new environment. If you're building or remodeling, an interior designer can be helpful with your overall plans when they're given the opportunity to get involved early in the building process.

During the initial meeting, count on your intuition to guide you toward the best designer for you. Decorating a home is an intimate and very personal experience, so a comfortable relationship with a high degree of trust is absolutely necessary for a good result. You may adore what a designer did for a friend, but if you can't easily express your ideas, or if you feel he or she isn't interested in your point of view, don't pursue the relationship. Unless you can imagine yourself working with a designer two or three homes from now, keep interviewing.

You may wish to hire a designer for one room before making a commitment to do the whole house. Some designers maintain a high degree of confidentiality regarding their clients, but if possible, get references and contact them, especially clients with whom they've worked on more than one home. Be sure to ask about the quality of follow-up service.

Be prepared to talk in specific terms about your project, and to honestly assess your lifestyle. For a home or a room to work well, function must be considered along with the evolving style. Designers ask many questions; some of them may be:

• What function should each room serve? Will a living room double as a study? Will a guest room also be an exercise area?

• Who uses the rooms? Growing children, adults, business associates? Which are shared and which are private?

• What safety and maintenance issues must be addressed? A growing family or a family pet may dictate the degree of elegance of a home.

• What kind of relationship do you want to establish between the interior and the landscape?

• Style: Formal, casual or a bit of both?
Are you comfortable with color?
Are you sentimental, practical?
Are you naturally organized or disorganized?

• What kind of art do you like? Do you own art that needs to be highlighted or displayed in a certain way? Do you need space for a growing collection?

• Do you feel at home in a dog-eared, low maintenance family room or do you soothe your soul in an opulent leather chair, surrounded by rich cabinetry and Oriental rugs?

• What kind of furniture do you like? Queen Anne, contemporary, American Arts and Crafts, casual wicker, or eclectic mixing of styles?

• What words describe the feeling you want to achieve? Cheerful, cozy, tranquil, elegant, classic?

COMPUTING THE INTERIOR DESIGN FEE

Designers use individual contracts, standard contracts drawn up by the American Society of Interior Designers (ASID), or letters of agreements as legal documents. The ASID contract outlines seven project phases – programming, schematic, design development, contract documents, contract administration, project representation beyond basic services, and additional services. It outlines the designer's special responsibilities, the owner's responsibilities, fees, and payments to the designer, including reimbursement of expenses.

Payments may be due at the completion of each project phase, monthly or quarterly, or as orders are made. You can usually expect to pay a retainer, or a

PROFESSIONAL DESIGNATIONS

ASID (American Society of Interior Designers)/ Chicago 1647 Merchandise Mart (312) 467-5080 Offers referrals to homeowners. ASID sponsors two local Designer Showcase homes annually, one in Evanston, one in Oak Park.

IIDA (International Interior Design Association) 341 Merchandise Mart (312) 467-1950 www.iida.org email: IIDAhq@iida.org Offers referrals to Chicagoland homeowners.

Designers who add ASID or IIDA after their names are certified members of the organization.

EMBRACE THE MASTER PLAN

Gone are the days when Chicago area homeowners felt the need to move into a "finished" interior. They take their time now, letting the flow of their evolving lifestyle and needs guide them along the way.

299

MAKE LIGHTING A PRIORITY

The trend toward a comprehensive lighting programs as part of good interior design is catching on in Chicago area luxury homes. Appropriate light and well designed accent lighting are very important to the overall comfort and functionality of a home. Neither the stunning volume ceiling nor the cozy breakfast nook can reach their potential if the lighting is wrong. Ask your interior designer for his or her lighting ideas. These choices need to be made in coordination with the building timeline, so plan and place orders early.

CAN YOU WEAR WHITE AFTER LABOR DAY?

There are colors and emotions for every season. Let your designer know if you want to be able to change the look and feel of your home to reflect the seasons.

50 percent deposit on goods as they are ordered, 40 percent upon the start of installation, and the balance when the job is completed.

Design fees, which may be based on "current market rate," are computed as a percentage of a job, on a flat fee or hourly basis, or may be tied to retail costs. Expect hourly fees of approximately $100 an hour, varying by experience, reputation and workload. If an hourly rate is being used, ask if there is a cap per day, and if different rates are charged for an assistant's or drafter's time. Percentages may be figured as a certain amount above the retail or trade price, and can range from 15 to 100 percent. Separate design fees may be charged by the hour, room, or entire project. It is imperative to trust your designer and rely on his or her reputation of delivering a top quality project in an honest, reliable fashion. You must feel you're being given a valuable service for a fair price.

If you work with a designer of staff at a retail store, a design service fee ranging from $100 to $500 may be charged and applied against purchases.

FROM THE MIND'S EYE TO REALITY

Once you've found a designer whom you like and trust, and have signed a clear, specific agreement, you're ready to embark on the adventure.

A designer who knows his or her way around the masses of products and possibilities will guide you through upscale retail outlets, and to craftsmen and women known only to a fortunate few in the trade. You can be a "kid in a candy store."

Just as you've allowed time to carefully consider and reconsider architectural blueprints, temper your enthusiasm to rush into decisions regarding your interiors. Leave fabric swatches where you see them day after day. Look at paint samples in daylight, evening light and artificial light. If possible, have everyone in the family "test sit" a kitchen chair for a week before ordering the whole set, and play with furniture placement. This small investment of time will pay handsomely in an end result that suits you perfectly.

Be prepared to wait for your interiors to be installed. It's realistic to allow eight months to complete a room, and eight to 12 months to decorate an entire home.

Decide if you want your interiors to be installed piecemeal or all at once. Many designers recommend waiting for one installation, if you have the patience. Homeowners tend to worry and try to outthink their original decisions when pieces are brought in as they arrive. By waiting for one installation, they treat themselves to a stunning visual and emotional thrill. ■

DALE CAROL ANDERSON, LTD. ....**(773) 348-5200**
2030 N. Magnolia, Chicago
See Add on Page: 342, 343
Principal/Owner: Dale Carol Anderson
Fax: (773) 348-5271
800 Extension: 1258

ANI INCORPORATED ....**(630) 323-1800**
111 S. Garfield Avenue, Hinsdale
See Add on Page: 314, 315
Principal/Owner: Ann Neumann
e-mail: aniinc@aol.com
Description: Interior Design, Architecture, Construction form this unique combination of DESIGN, BUILD, FURNISH for remodeling and restoration of homes and businesses.
Fax: (630) 323-1875
800 Extension: 6004

ARKULES & ASSOCIATES ....**(847) 433-0788**
340 N. Deere Park W., Highland Park
See Add on Page: 363
Principal/Owner: Linda Arkules Cohn
Fax: (847) 433-4248
800 Extension: 1121

ASI INTERIORS ....**(312) 932-9400**
980 N. Michigan Avenue, Suite 1085, Chicago
See Add on Page: 312, 313
Principal/Owner: Denise Antonucci/ Jerry Sanfilippo
e-mail: asi980@aol.com
Fax: (312) 654-9426
800 Extension: 1012

LAURA BARNETT DESIGNS ....**(312) 654-1706**
213 W. Institute Place, Suite 706, Chicago
See Add on Page: 304
Principal/Owner: Laura Barnett, IIDA
Description: Firm was founded in 1980 and can handle every aspect of each project: interior architecture, furnishings, window and wall treatments, etc.
Fax: (312) 654-8706
800 Extension: 6023

CANNON/ BULLOCK ....**(323) 221-9286**
4975 Valley Blvd., Los Angeles
See Add on Page: 646, 647
Principal/Owner: Richard Bullock & Richard Cannon
Website: www.cannonbullock.com e-mail: mail@cannonbullock.com
Fax: (323) 221-9287
800 Extension: 1082

CHAMPAGNE FURNITURE GALLERY, INC. ....**(312) 923-9800**
65 W. Illinois Street, Chicgao
See Add on Page: 367, 670
Principal/Owner: Patricia Champagne, IIDA
Website: champagnefurniture.com e-mail: sales@champagnefurniture.com
Description: Retail store exhibiting six elegantly furnished, fully accessorized rooms; offering full service interior design.
Fax: (312) 923-9802
800 Extension: 1026

DARLEEN'S INTERIORS ....**(630) 357-3719**
2852 W. Ogden Avenue, Naperville
See Add on Page: 364, 660
Principal/Owner: Darleen McFarlan
Fax: (630) 357-9724
800 Extension: 1255

LAUREN SEAMAN ENSLIN DESIGN, ASID ....**(312) 944-1999**
200 E. Delaware Place #33E, Chicago
See Add on Page: 373
Principal/Owner: Lauren Seaman Enslin, ASID
800 Extension: 1254

SUSAN FREDMAN & ASSOCIATES ....**(847) 509-4121**
425 Huehl Road, #6B, Northbrook
See Add on Page: 344, 345
Principal/Owner: Susan Fredman
Website: www.susanfredman.com e-mail: info@susanfredman.com
Description: For over 25 years, this award-winning firms with a staff of 20 including 13 top ASID designers consistently displays design ingenuity, creativity and sound business practice.
Fax: (847) 509-4111
800 Extension: 6113

continued on page **310**

TOM·STRINGER·INC
INTERIOR DESIGN

CHICAGO | LOS ANGELES

·

62 WEST HURON
CHICAGO, IL 60610
312.664.0644
·

101 SOUTH ROBERTSON BLVD
LOS ANGELES, CA 90048
310.385.9399
·

EMPHASIZING
THE CREATION
OF A TOTAL
ENVIRONMENT

COMMITTED
TO
SERVICE

CELEBRATING
OUR 20TH
ANNIVERSARY
1980-2000

LAURA BARNETT DESIGNS
213 WEST INSTITUE PLACE   SUITE 706
CHICAGO, IL   60610

312.654-1706

SANDRA SALTZMAN INTERIORS

1430 NORTH ASTOR STREET
CHICAGO, ILLINOIS 60610
312.642.8381 Fax 312.642.8402
SAVGA10@AOL.COM

Gregga Jordan Smieszny

Bruce Gregga
Alex Jordan
Dan Smieszny

1203 N. State Pkwy
Chicago, IL 60610
Phone 312 787 0017
Fax 312 787 5108
Email info@GJSInc.com

continued from page **301**

GELIS & ASSOCIATES ....**(312) 943-7464**
222 East Pearson #204, Chicago   Fax: (312) 943-0373
See Add on Page: 332   800 Extension: 1008
Principal/Owner: Madeline Gelis
Description: Over 20 years of experience in interior design and architectural renovations throughout the country, featured in national design publications.

GRAY & WALTER, LTD. ....**(847) 853-1940**
1018 11th Street, Wilmette   Fax: (847) 853-9751
See Add on Page: 370, 371   800 Extension: 1162
Principal/Owner: Kenneth Walter
e-mail: kennethwalter@msn.com

GREGGA, JORDAN, SMIESZNY INC. ....**(312) 787-0017**
1203 N. State Parkway, Chicago   Fax: (312) 787-5108
See Add on Page: 308, 309   800 Extension: 1120
Principal/Owner: Bruce Gregga, Alex Jordan & Dan Smieszny

LOIS GRIES INTERIOR DESIGN ....**(312) 222-9202**
400 N. Wells Street, Chicago   Fax: (312) 222-9207
See Add on Page: 358   800 Extension: 1067
Principal/Owner: Lois Gries
Website: www.loisgries.com   e-mail: loisbgries@aol.com
Description: Full service interior design, including all interior finishes and furnishings.

ERIK JOHNSON & ASSOCIATES ....**(312) 644-2202**
154 West Hubbard, Suite 306, Chicago   Fax: (312) 527-4166
See Add on Page: 152, 337   800 Extension: 1169
Principal/Owner: Erik Johnson

KAUFMAN SEGAL DESIGN ....**(312) 649-0680**
900 N. Franklin #700, Chicago   Fax: (312) 649-0689
See Add on Page: 372   800 Extension: 1049
Principal/Owner: David Kaufman & Thomas Segal

LARSON ASSOCIATES ....**(312) 786-2255**
542 South Dearborn, Suite 610, Chicago   Fax: (312) 789-2290
See Add on Page: 175, 292, 293, 336   800 Extension: 1223
Principal/Owner: George A. Larson
Description: Established in 1978, Larson Associates provides personalized and creative architectural and interior design services as well as custom furniture design,accessories, and art consulting.

LORI LENNON & ASSOCIATES ....**(847) 482-0165**
350 South Ashland Lane, Lake Forest   Fax: (847) 482-0166
See Add on Page: 368, 369   800 Extension: 1264
Principal/Owner: Lori Lennon
e-mail: llintdesn@aol.com

RICHARD MENNA DESIGNS ....**(312) 644-8153**
220 W. Kinzie Street, Chicago   Fax: (312) 644-9732
See Add on Page: 360, 361   800 Extension: 1144
Principal/Owner: Richard Menna

ERIC MULLENDORE ARCHITECT/INTERIOR DESIGNER ....**(773) 275-2798**
920 W. Castlewood Terrace, Chicago   Fax: (773) 275-2799
See Add on Page: 374   800 Extension: 1060
Principal/Owner: Eric Mullendore
e-mail: emullendore@aol.com
Description: As licensed architects and interior designers, we have the ability to meet all of your design needs.

OLAFSEN DESIGN GROUP, LTD. ....**(312) 644-4738**
233 East Erie Street, Suite 305, Chicago   Fax: (312) 664-7396
See Add on Page: 338   800 Extension: 1075
Principal/Owner: Bill Olafsen

continued on page **340**

POWELL/KLEINSCHMIDT

Interior Architecture

Suite 810
645 North Michigan Avenue
Chicago, Illinois 60611
312 642 6450 Fax 312 642 5135
www.PowellKleinschmidt.com

Photography by Barry Rustin

A·S·I
interiors INC

980 N. Michigan Ave. – Suite 1085
Chicago, Illinois 60611
312.932.9400

Denise Antonucci – ASID
Jerry Sanfilippo – ASID

CUSTOM
FURNITURE

QUALITY, KNOWLEDGE, EXPERIENCE & SERVICE SINCE 1967

A N I INCORPORATED

DESIGN • BUILD • FURNISH

INTERIOR DESIGN / EXTERIOR DESIGN

111 S. GARFIELD AVENUE • HINSDALE, ILLINOIS 60521-4229
PHONE: 630-323-1800 • FAX 630-323-1875

INTERIOR
DESIGN

REMODELING

CUSTOM INTERIOR AND EXTERIOR DESIGN

A N I INCORPORATED

DESIGN · BUILD · FURNISH

INTERIOR DESIGN / EXTERIOR DESIGN

111 S. GARFIELD AVENUE • HINSDALE, ILLINOIS 60521-4229
PHONE: 630-323-1800 • FAX 630-323-1875

ARCHITECTURAL DETAILS

JAMES E. RUUD, INC.
INTERIORS

ASID ALLIED   IIDA ASSOCIATE

312 • 573 • 1951

WWW.JERUUDINC.COM

d e s i g n

s t y l e

v e r s a t i l i t y

s e r v i c e

Classic, contemporary or eclectic,
Richar has been offering his distinctive
flair for creating interior environments
to an international clientele with high-profile
status—and even higher expectations—
since 1983.

Exploring a full spectrum of styles,
periods and innovative approaches,
it's the unique mood created that has
become his trademark.

Service is his top priority—
Richar believes the best design work
results from a client relationship based
upon mutual trust, respect and
exchange of ideas.

Richar always delivers.

1 2 4 4   n o r t h   w e l l s   s t r e e t
c h i c a g o   i l   6 0 6 1 0
t e l e p h o n e   3 1 2 . 9 5 1 . 0 9 2 4
f a x   3 1 2 . 9 5 1 . 8 5 3 5

Photos by Kip Jacobs

PAGE ONE INTERIORS,

Adele Lampert:

"When designing this luxurious bath, we specified all plumbing mechanics, lighting designs, and finished materials such as the Piel Serpentine marble to the architect. Our company provided all the cabinetry. The curve form was repeated gracefully in the tub and deck, and stained windows and soffit. We even specified radiant heat and towel warmers for a bath fit for a king and queen!"

LAURA BARNETT DESIGNS, INC.,

Laura Barnett:

"When this home was purchased, furniture from two existing houses needed to be used. The four chairs were originally upholstered in two-tone pink and arranged around the silver-leaf table. The sofa was uphol-stered in brightly striped canvas. For the new house, we needed a pair of sofas, so a matching sofa was ordered. When it arrived in a black and white pattern, we had the striped sofa re-upholstered in the same fabric, with details to match. The silver table now serves as the base for a large glass top. The furnishings look brand new in their new home!"

321

Photo by Judy A. Slagle

ners

MARY RUBINO INTERIORS,

Mary Rubino:

"My client desired clearly defined areas for dining and relaxing within the openness of a long, narrow space. We solved this with furniture selection and placement. Placing a long, low sofa perpendicular to the long wall divided the room; the low bench behind the sofa offered an anchor for the dining area. Finally, the square dining table fit perfectly in the center. Everything went exactly according to (floor) plan…but when the table arrived, my client's eyes widened in horror. 'I'm sorry, I hate it…' He said it looked too wide. I explained that no other proportion would fit as well in that space, so he agreed to live with it while he thought it over. Within a week, he called, saying he loved it. He simply was unaccustomed to a square shape as a dining table. Today it is his favorite piece. And it makes a great story."

Photo by Douglas Fogelson

Desi

Photo by Buschauer

ANI INCORPORATED,

Ann Neumann:

"Our client had a traditional home and like many older homes, a small parlor-sitting room off the foyer. To create the illusion of greater space, we utilized mirrors and created a raised, panel wall made out of glass. In order to maintain the traditional look, four-inch bevels on top of the mirrors were added and a beveled, etched and a leaded glass transom was fashioned to echo the wall covering in the foyer. Artwork was functional as well as decorative, as seen in the bronze figures that form the base of the coffee table. The result was a traditional living area that looks larger than it actually is and holds eight people comfortably!"

iners

VISBEEN ASSOCIATES, INC.,

Wayne E. Visbeen:

"European Cottage reflects a casual sophistication in this living and dining space. The rooms share the vaulted ceiling and the two-sided, tapered stone fireplace, which sets the tone for this provincial style. Casual elegance describes the earthy palette and use of faux finishes, including the distressed oak floors. A mix of old and new makes for a comfortable space with the custom metal mantel scrolls and fire screen, and the old-world furniture."

324

Photo by Erhard Pfeiffer

Desi

CHAMPAGNE
FURNITURE GALLERY, INC.,

Patricia A. Champagne:

"This is an average-sized room in a condo building with a lofted ceiling. We kept the furnishings to a minimum to create the illusion of greater space. The painting and tall tree play up the height, which adds to the feeling of more space. The small sectional keeps the design clean rather than cluttering the room with numerous pieces, such as a sofa and several chairs. The neutral color pallet is the final touch in visually expanding the size of the space."

DARLEEN'S INTERIORS,

Bill Marler:

"The custom designed window coverings were styled to architecturally beautify the windows and enhance the golf course view. To bring the spacious room together, the ceiling was darkened, and the king size bed was placed on an angle for visual appeal, adding depth and dimension to the room. Soft fabrics were draped over the bed pulling the flow of colors from the walls and floor together with the dark sheer drapery to accentuate the furniture."

Desi

OLAFSEN DESIGN GROUP, LTD.,

William D.B. Olafsen:

"The generous scale of the room, handsome coffered ceiling and elegant French doors set the stage for dramatic furnishings and bold colors. Luxurious fabrics, generously proportioned furniture and carefully detailed lampshades enhance the client's collection of Chinese antiques and nineteenth century paintings to create an elevated, warm and welcoming interior."

327

Photo by Tony Bernardi/Photofields

iners

SUSAN FREDMAN & ASSOCIATES,

Susan Fredman:

"This room was designed like a painting with a great deal of attention initially given to the broad strokes, including the floor plan and overall balance of the room. Next, we addressed the smaller, finer brushstrokes, such as the combination of textures, mix of shapes and focused on the use of a singular color. Even finer details are found in the custom iron drapery valance bracket, the crackle finish on the sofas and the playful shape of the chairs. The client wanted a beautiful space that would encourage an intimate feeling for conversation, cocktails or reading. The end result was the creation of an atmosphere that provides nourishment for both the heart and eyes."

328

Photo by Janet Mesic Mackie

Desi

Photo by Bruce Van Inwigen

KAUFMAN SEGAL DESIGN,

David Kaufman:

"This vintage gray stone was renovated in the 1970's and stripped of all the original charm and character. Our approach was to return the splendor and detail the space deserved. During the construction phase, we added crown molding, custom millwork and an antique fireplace mantel. Furniture pieces were upholstered in lavish skills, velvets and damasks, and mixed in with antique Biedermier and Empire pieces to give the room a formal flair while still being warm and inviting."

Interior Design Spotlight continued on page 348.

ners

The

Group

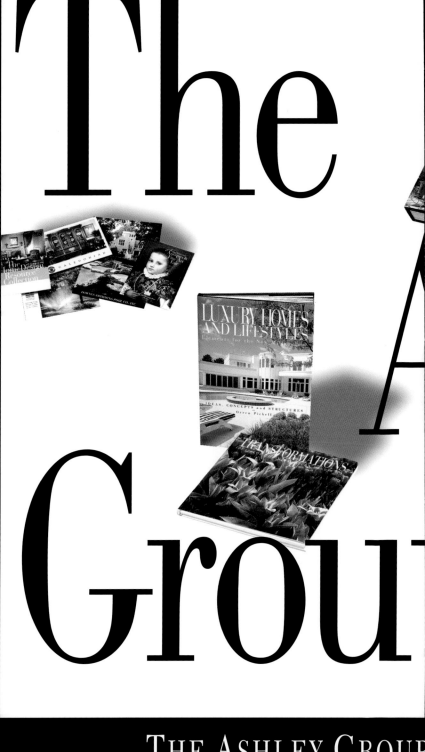

ashley
o

RESOURCE COLLECTION

...visual resource images, and strives to provide the highest
...resources available, to upscale consumers and professionals.
Group, visit our website at www.ashleygroup@cahners.com.
...a member of the Reed Elsevier plc group, is a leading
...vertical markets, including entertainment,
...encompasses more than 140 Web sites as well as *Variety*,
...market-leading business-to-business magazines

G E L I S
& ASSOCIATES INC

ARCHITECTURE • INTERIOR DESIGN
222 EAST PEARSON #204
CHICAGO, ILLINOIS 60611
312.943.7464

A. SPRINGER INTERIORS, LTD.

633 NORTH LOMBARD AVENUE
OAK PARK, ILLINOIS 60302
708.848.6240 Fax: 708.848.6266
ASpringerint@AOL.com

847.550.6363

LARSON ASSOCIATES

Interior Design • Architecture

542 SOUTH DEARBORN   CHICAGO, IL 60605
312-786-2255   FAX: 312-786-2290

ERIK JOHNSON & ASSOCIATES

Architecture / Interior Design
154 West Hubbard Suite 306 Chicago, IL 60610
312.644.2202 Fax 312.527.4166

Olafsen Design Group

William D.B. Olafsen, ASID
233 East Erie, Suite 305
Chicago, Illinois 60611
312.664.4738

Our strategic focus integrates the architecture
and the client's lifestyle into the details
of every project. The result. . .designs of quality,
comfort, and uniqueness.

FRANK S. PERRY · IIDA
RESIDENTIAL INTERIORS, INC.

STUDIO 312·280·0850
FAX 312·280·8978

continued from page **310**

PAGE ONE INTERIORS ....**(847) 382-1001**
320 E. Main Street, Barrington   Fax: (847) 382-0484
See Add on Page: 316   800 Extension: 6246
Principal/Owner: Adele Lampert, ASID

FRANK S. PERRY RESIDENTIAL INTERIORS, INC. ....**(312) 280-0850**
Chicago
See Add on Page: 339   800 Extension: 1197
Principal/Owner: Frank Perry

POWELL / KLEINSCHMIDT ....**(312) 642-6450**
645 N. Michigan Avenue, Suite 810, Chicago   Fax: (312) 642-5135
See Add on Page: 311   800 Extension: 1025
Principal/Owner: Robert Kleinschmidt
Website: www.PowellKleinschmidt.com   e-mail: info@powellkleinschmidt.com

GAIL PRAUSS INTERIOR DESIGN, LTD ....**(708) 524-1233**
421 N. Marion Street, Oak Park   Fax: (708) 524-1237
See Add on Page: 341   800 Extension: 1230
Principal/Owner: Gail Prauss
Website: www.praussinteriors.com   e-mail: gpid@flash.net

EVA QUATEMAN INTERIORS, LTD. ....**(773) 472-0522**
399 W. Fullerton Parkway, Chicago   Fax: (773) 665-8615
See Add on Page: 359   800 Extension: 1215
Principal/Owner: Eva Quateman

RICHAR INTERIORS INC. ....**(312) 951-0924**
1244 N. Wells, Chicago   Fax: (312) 951-8535
See Add on Page: 318, 319   800 Extension: 1042
Principal/Owner: Richar
e-mail: Richar@net56.net

MARY RUBINO INTERIORS, INC. ....**(847) 424-0432**
620 Judson Avenue, Suite 3, Evanston   Fax: (847) 424-0432
See Add on Page: 362   800 Extension: 6276
Principal/Owner: Mary Rubino
Website: http://st9.yahoo.com/maryrubinointeriors
e-mail: marubino@earthlink.net

JAMES E. RUUD, INC. ....**(312) 573-1951**
1410 N. State Parkway, Suite 228, Chicago   Fax: (312) 573-1971
See Add on Page: 317   800 Extension: 1129
Principal/Owner: James Ruud
Website: www.jeruudinc.com   e-mail: jeruudinc@aol.com

S & B INTERIORS, INC. ....**(877) 666-2616**
11270 SW 59th Ave., Pinecrest   Fax: (305) 661-2722
See Add on Page: 305   800 Extension: 1017
Principal/Owner: Sandi Samole
Website: www.sandbinteriors.com   e-mail: sandi@sandbinteriors.com
Description: Complete Interior Design Services for Residential and Commercial
clients nationwide. From conception to completion, we design and build your
dreams.

SANDRA SALTZMAN INTERIORS ....**(312) 612-8381**
1430 N. Astor Street, Chicago   Fax: (312) 642-8402
See Add on Page: 306, 307   800 Extension: 1027
Principal/Owner: Sandra Saltzman
e-mail: sam2productions@aol.com

PETRINA SCLAFANI ....**(312) 961-4320**
850 N. State Street, Unit F, Chicago
See Add on Page: 346, 347   800 Extension: 1228
Principal/Owner: Petrina Sclafani

continued on page **366**

GAIL PRAUSS INTERIOR DESIGN, LTD.

Photography by Charles Mayer

Photography by James Yochum

Gail Prauss Interior Design is a full service design firm, committed to excellence, utilizing high quality products, furnishings, and fabrications. Attention to architectural detailing, along with custom lighting design and wall finishes, add to the ambience of our interiors. Our work is influenced by our clients functional and aesthetic preferences, reflecting styles from traditional to contemporary.

421 N. Marion Street Oak Park, IL 60302 708/524.1233
www.praussinteriors.com

DALE CAROL ANDERSON LTD.

INTERIOR DESIGN

ANTIQUES

CUSTOM DESIGN FURNITURE

ALSO REPRESENTS
BERNARD AND BENJAMIN STEINITZ

PARIS

NEW YORK

PALM BEACH

CHICAGO

2030 N. MAGNOLIA
CHICAGO, ILLINOIS 60614
TEL 773. 348. 5200

SUSAN FREDMAN
AND ASSOCIATES

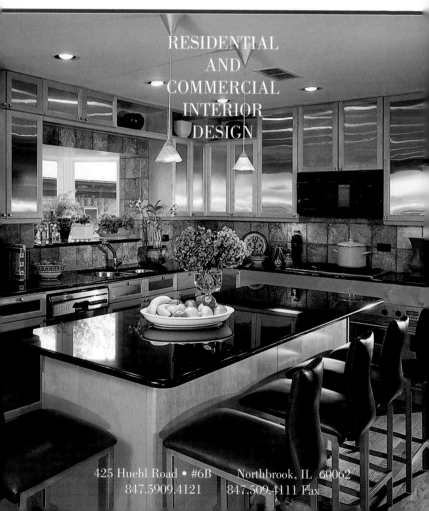

RESIDENTIAL
AND
COMMERCIAL
INTERIOR
DESIGN

425 Huehl Road • #6B   Northbrook, IL 60062
847.5909.4121   847.509.4111 Fax

DESIGNS BY
Petrina

tel: 312-274-1461 • email: petrinas@dotplanet.com

DESIGNS BY

Petrina

tel: 312-274-1461 • email: petrinas@dotplanet.com

CANNON/BULLOCK,

Richard Bullock:

"This grand and dark old Tudor-style home from the 1920's needed some cleaning and lightening to work for its young new owners. A pale moss wash over the once dark walls, soft horizontal stripes in satin for window side panels, and a repeating series of white, crackle finished plates brought light and a tranquil order to the room and left space for guests to be the focus. A select few first-rate antiques from Europe and Asia provide a subtle dramatic backdrop."

Desi

Photos by Robert Stein

S & B INTERIORS, INC.,

Sandi Samole:

"The challenge for this home was to create defined yet open spaces with natural materials in a living sculpture. I began by placing a two-sided glass sculpture over a dual-purpose floating console/buffet. The use of 'functional art' in furnishings and accessories is an important factor in our design schemes as seen in the functional and artistic area achieved by creating a second column opposite the structural one and adding a light soffit. Reflecting the concept of a 'living sculpture' that utilizes all natural materials, the countertop in the dining room is durable Black Galaxy granite, while the foyer side is elegant Portoro Gold marble. Continuing this theme in the great room is a fireplace/media wall made of stone, marble, wood and glass. Even the wall sculpture mixes these mediums."

iners

A. SPRINGER INTERIORS, LTD.,

Annette Springer:

"The clients wanted a home which would blend into their early 1900's community. This house is a combination of Prairie and Contemporary styles. All of the doors, moldings, trims, staircase and fireplaces were custom designed to reflect the linear aspects of the Prairie school.

The center stairwell unites the home making the basement and loft feel like an integral part of the living space. The open layout creates a perfect environ-ment for entertaining either an intimate group or large party. The use of mahogany creates a warm counterpart to the brushed stainless and natural stone repeated throughout."

Photo by Rich Sistos

Desi

Photo by Barry Rustin

LAUREN SEAMAN ENSLIN DESIGN, ASID,

Lauren Seaman Enslin:

"The client desired an intimate setting for the study and enjoyment of musical pursuits. Featured are the owner's collection of fine antique furnishings that were restored for the space, their heirloom piano (not shown) and occasion seating. A highlight of the room is a large-scale charcoal drawing depicting cabaret life at the turn of the century. The period setee was accented with gold leaf and hand rubbed to an aged patina. Its cushions were refurbished with goose down and newly upholstered in a tapestry chenille, trimmed with custom wetting. Loop fringe surrounds the pillows. A heavily carved gold leaf mirror reflects the adjacent sheer amber window coverings. An area rug of wool and silk with hand-dyed yarns from Tibet ground the space and echo the warm tone quality the room emanates."

ners

SANDRA SALTZMAN INTERIORS,

Sandra Saltzman:

"As an Interior Designer my responsibility to the client is in fact my process of respecting the architecture while bringing the essence of ornamentation of design to the forefront in the specific areas of contrast, series and symmetry of elements."

352

Photo by Photofields

Desi

Photo by B. Rustin

ASI INTERIORS,

Denise Antonucci:

"The constraints within this space made for a challenging task. By designing a casual private chamber, we created a special ambiance. A variety of materials were used to enhance this room. With three entryways and no windows, a wash of color helped to infuse the room with an elegant softness of its own. A custom textured rug combined with soft fabrics and antique custom pillows provided a subtle elegance. The simplicity of accessorizing works to envelop the space and create a sense of drama."

ners

POWELL/KLEINSCHMIDT,

William Arnold,

"Interior design should create, through the careful use of light and materials, a unique sense of place. In this instance, we enhanced and revealed the character of the existing space by creating 'place' where none existed before. This was done through attention to quality details and integrity of form in both furniture and architecture. The result of close collaboration, this room reflects my clients' interests and exhibits their unique point of view."

354

Photo by Hedrich Blessing

ERIC MULLENDORE, ARCHITECT/INTERIOR DESIGNER,

Eric Mullendore:

"This dressing room adjoins a master bath area. The two spaces are unified by having one floor finish, a beige Italian mosaic marble tile with custom borders and center medallions. It defines the geometry of the rooms and gives the appearance of a series of Oriental carpets. The closet cabinetry, though finely detailed, is constructed of cherry-laminated plywood, a relatively inexpensive material. Glass transoms atop the closets allow light to pass between the areas."

ners

DALE CAROL ANDERSON,

Dale Carol Anderson:

"The design goal in this wintergarden was to evoke the look and feel of the 'orangerie' of a French chateau. To maximize the amount of glass, the framework of the new structure was metal. Without walls, the floor was the only expanse available to set the mood and sense of age. Through painstaking research, color selection, sourcing and editing, a floor was designed that duplicated the style and craftsmanship found in basilicas of the 1400's. Furniture and accessories were carefully selected from a broad mix of periods and styles; all had the common elements of age, organic themes and whimsy. Through the weaving of the disparate elements of severe structure and lush layered design details, the wintergarden took on the luxurious warmth and mood evoked by its ancestors."

Photo by Tony Soluri

Desi

GAIL PRAUSS INTERIOR DESIGN, LTD.,

Gail Prauss:

"The coolness of the white cabinetry and black granite counter-tops are juxtaposed against the warmth of color and wood. Simplicity and geometry create a strong, yet quiet architectural influence are a perfect backdrop to art and accessories in the Asian style. The richness of a ribbon mahogany soffit enhances the warmth of saffron walls and ceiling. The lighting design adds a soft ambiance to the setting."

ners

Dedicated to excellence in Interior Design.

Designers Building
400 N. Wells Suite 416
Chicago, Il 60610

Lois Gries, ASID
v 312.222.9202
f 312.222.9207
www.loisgries.com
email: loisbgries@aol.com

Lois Gries interior design

EVA QUATEMAN

Richard Menna Interior Design

IIDA

220 W. Kinzie
Chicago, IL
60610

312.644.8153
F

AX 312.644.9732

MARY RUBINO INTERIORS, INC.
design and purchasing

Photographed by Douglas Fog

Translating personalities into homes...

classic modern style

international influences

mixing periods and regions

innovative approach, thoughtful service

A.B. Brown University

L'Universita Degli Studi di Bologna

M.A. University of Chicago

620 JUDSON AVENUE SUITE 3 EVANSTON, ILLINOIS 60202 847.424.0432

ARKULES +
ASSOCIATES

LINDA ARKULES COHN   BARBARA ARKULES
           INTERIOR DESIGN

Architect: Gibbons, Fortman & Weber

CHICAGO

340 N. DEERE PARK W.	TEL	847.433.0788
HIGHLAND PARK, IL 60035	FAX	847.433.4248

SCOTTSDALE

5224 E. ARROYD RD.	TEL	602.840.7332
PARADISE VALLEY, AZ 85253	FAX	602.840.6459

BARBARA YOUNG INTERIORS · LTD

211 W. Burlington Avenue, Clarendon Hills, IL 60514
PH (630) 654-0015 FAX (630) 654-0092

- DESIGN AND
  SPACE PLANNING
- COLOR
  COORDINATION
- ART SELECTION
- CABINETRY
- LIGHTING
- CARPET AND
  AREA RUGS
- FURNISHINGS
- ACCESSORIES
- WINDOW
  TREATMENTS

Design Connection

Cabinetry Design

continued from page **340**

LOREN REID SEAMAN & ASSOCIATES ....**(847) 550-6363**
22742 N. Lakewood Lane, Lake Zurich
See Add on Page: 334, 335
Principal/Owner: Loren Seaman

Fax: (847) 550-6464
800 Extension: 1053

A. SPRINGER INTERIORS, LTD. ....**(708) 848-6240**
633 N. Lombard, Oak Park
See Add on Page: 333
Principal/Owner: Annette Springer
e-mail: aspringerint@aol.com

Fax: (708) 848-6266
800 Extension: 1227

Description: Business begun in 1987. Dominique Thomas is an associate of the
firm. We address all aspects of interior design.

TOM STRINGER, INC. ....**(312) 664-0644**
62 West Huron, Chicago
See Add on Page: 302, 303
Principal/Owner: Thomas D. Stringer

Fax: (312) 664-2611
800 Extension: 1148

BARBARA YOUNG INTERIORS LTD. ....**(630) 654-0015**
211 W. Burlingtlon, Clarendon Hills
See Add on Page: 365
Principal/Owner: Barbara Young

Fax: (630) 654-0092
800 Extension: 1236

Finally...
Chicago's Own
Home & Design
Sourcebook

The CHICAGO HOME BOOK, a comprehensive hands-on
design sourcebook to building, remodeling, decorating, furnishing
and landscaping a luxury home in Chicago and its suburbs,
is a "must-have" reference for the Chicagoland homeowner.
At over 700 pages, this beautiful, full-color hard cover
volume is quite simply the most complete, well-organized
reference to the Chicagoland home industry. It covers all aspects
of the process, with hundreds of listings of local home industry
professionals, accompanied by hundreds of inspiring photographs.
You will also find articles to assist in planning and completing a
project. The CHICAGO HOME BOOK tells you how to
find what you need when you need it.

Order your copy today!

CHICAGO
HOME
BOOK

Published by
The Ashley Group
1350 E. Touhy Avenue • Des Plaines, IL 60018
Toll Free 888-458-1750   Fax 847.390.2902
E-mail: ashleybooksales@cahners.com

*Concentrating on meeting the client's complete needs
from interior architectural planning and furnishings to
accessories, for lasting design excellence.*

LORI LENNON AND ASSOCIATES

847-482-0165

Lake Forest, Illinois

LoriLennonDesign@aol.com

GRAY &
WALTER
ASS^oC

1018 11th Street • Wilmete, IL 60091 • 847/853-1940 • Fax 847/853-9751

159 West Kinzie St. • Chicago, IL 60610 • 312/329-1007 • Fax 312/527-4445

KAUFMAN
DESIGN
SEGAL

900 NORTH FRANKLIN • CHICAGO, IL 60610
TEL: 312.649.0680 • FAX: 312.649.0689

LAUREN
SEAMAN
ENSLIN
DESIGN

200 EAST DELAWARE PLACE   CHICAGO   312.944.1999

LANDSCAPING

Photography by Linda Oyama Bryan

ILT VIGNOCCHI

LANDSCAPE ARCHITECTS & CONTRACTORS

Wauconda   Oak Brook   Lincolnshire

tel: 847 487 5200
website: www.iltvignocchi.com

Photography by Linda Oyama Bryan

ILT VIGNOCCHI
LANDSCAPE ARCHITECTS & CONTRACTORS
Wauconda   Oak Brook   Lincolnshire

tel: 847 487 5200
website: www.iltvignocchi.com

> " I trust in *nature* *for the* stable laws of *beauty.* "
>
> Robert Browning

photo courtesy of:
**Downes Swimming
Pool Co.**

379

Natural Selection

Landscaping is the only design area that is by nature intended to evolve over time. The philosophy behind landscape design has evolved as well. From traditional European formality to the naturalism of Prairie Style, to the simplicity and order of Far Eastern influences, your landscape should be as unique a design statement as your home itself.

More and more people are blurring the divisions between inside and outside environments, with expanses of windows, patios designed to act as "outdoor rooms," and various types of glass and screened enclosures to enjoy the outdoors whatever the weather. Landscape becomes almost an architectural element at times, creating an interplay and synthesis of indoors and outdoors.

Water gardens are growing in popularity as people learn that they are ecosystems in their own right, requiring little additional time or attention once they are established. Think of it: the soothing splash of a waterfall or babbling brook right in your own backyard!

VIEWS AND VISTAS

First you choose your views, then you build your home. To create a harmonious balance between your home and its surroundings, your architect should be invited to visit the site of your new home, and to meet with your landscape architect. The site can often serve as a catalyst, inspiring a design that responds to the uniqueness of the site. When all the team members are included, important details (like the location of your air conditioning units) can be discussed and settled, making for the best results for you and your family.

THE LANDSCAPE BUDGET

**Basic:
10% of the cost of your home & property
In-depth:
The 10 to 25% rule of thumb applies to your landscapes too. Starting at $90,000:
• Finish grading
• Sodded lawns
• Foundation plantings (all around the house) including some smaller trees
• Walkways of pavers or stone
City Dwellers!**

GETTING BACK TO THE GARDEN

Think of the land as a canvas for a work of environmental art. Think of the landscape professional as an artist who uses nature to translate your needs and desires into a living, breathing reality. A formal English garden or seemingly artless arrangements of native plantings, a winding cobblestone walkway leading from a hand-laid brick driveway or dramatically lit oak trees above a steaming spa – these are the kinds of possibilities you can explore. When you work with a professional who is personally committed to superior work and service, designing a landscape is full of creativity, new ideas and satisfying results.

GETTING A LANDSCAPE STARTED

Selecting a landscape professional to create and maintain a distinctive landscape is one of the most important decisions you'll make as a homeowner. In making your decision, consider these questions:

• Are you landscaping a new construction home? There are critical decisions to be made early in the home building planning process that concern the landscape. Interview and work with professionals who have considerable experience in doing excellent work with new construction projects. Make them part of your team and have them meet with your architect, interior designer and builder early in the project.

• Do you want to hire a landscape architect or a landscape designer? Landscape architects have met the criteria to be registered by the state. Many hold university degrees in landscape architecture. A landscape designer generally has had training and/or experience in horticulture and landscaping and may also have a background in art.

• Do you want full service? If you want to work with one source, from design through installation to maintenance, only consider those who offer comprehensive service.

Allow time to interview at least two professionals before making a decision. Start early, especially if you plan to install a swimming pool, which should be dug the same time as the foundation of a new home.

Invite the professional to your home to acquaint him or her with your tastes and personality through observing your choices in interior design as well as the current landscape. Have a plat of survey available. Be prepared to answer questions like:

• Do you prefer a formal or informal feel? The formality of symmetrical plantings or the informal look of a natural area?

• Is there a place or feeling you'd like to recreate? Summers spent in Arizona? Your childhood home in New England?

• What colors do you like? This will impact the flowers chosen for your gardens.

• Are you a gardener? Would you like to be? If you're fond of flower, herb or vegetable gardening, your landscape professional will build the appropriate gardens.

• How will you use the space? Will children use the backyard for recreation? Will you entertain outdoors? If so, will it be during the day or at night? Do you envision a pool, spa, gazebo or tennis court?

• Are you fond of lawn statuary, fountains, or other ornamental embellishments?

• What architectural features must be considered? A wrap-around porch, large picture windows? Brick or stone exteriors?

• To what extent will you be involved in the process? Most landscape architects and designers are happy to encourage your involvement in this labor of love. There is a great deal of pleasure to be derived from expressing your personality through the land. A lifelong hobby can take root from this experience.

Landscapers say their clients often join garden clubs after the completion of their project, and that many of their rehabbing projects are done for clients who are already avid gardeners.

Landscape professionals expect that you will want to see a portfolio, inquire about their styles, and their experience. You may wish to request permission to visit sites of their installed landscapes. If you have special concerns, such as environmental issues, ask if the landscape professional has any experience in such areas.

COMPUTING LANDSCAPE FEES

It's important to create a workable budget. It's easy to be caught off guard when you get a landscape proposal – it is a significant investment.

To make sure you give the outside of your home the appropriate priority status, plan to invest ten to 25 percent of the cost of a new home and property in the landscaping. Although landscape elements can be phased in year after year, expect that the majority of the cost will be incurred in the first year. Maintenance costs must also be considered.

Billing practices vary among professionals and depend on the extent of the services you desire. Some charge a flat design fee up front, some charge a one-time fee for a contract that includes everything, some charge a design fee which is waived if you

• Soft atmospheric lighting up to the front door and in the back yard
• Asphalt driveway
• Concrete unit pavers or stone patio, or deck
• Perimeter plantings of trees and shrubs for privacy and finished look

OUTDOOR DECOR

As Chicago area homeowners get more involved in their yards and gardens, they learn to "see" outdoor rooms and take deep pleasure in decorating them. Arbors, sculpture, tables, benches, water features, or any piece of whimsy add delightful decorating. Hedges or fences create natural partitions. The results are appealing, comfortable and richly rewarding.

A PARTY OF GARDENS

As gardening attracts more devotees in Chicago, people are re-discovering the satisfaction of creating imaginative gardens. Some ideas: One-color gardens, Fragrance gardens, Native plant gardens, Japanese gardens.

LIGHTING YOUR LOT

"Less is more" is the best philosophy when designing an outdoor lighting system. Today's beautiful, functional fixtures are themselves worthy of admiration, but their purpose is to highlight the beauty of your home while providing safe access to your property. Well established lighting companies and specialty companies offer extensive landscape lighting product lines.

382

THE FINAL EVALUATION

When the landscape is installed, conduct a final, on-site evaluation. You should evaluate the finished design, find out what elements will be installed later and learn more about how the plan will evolve over time. You, the landscape designer or architect, project manager, and maintenance manager should be involved.

select them to complete the project, and some build a design fee into the installation and/or maintenance cost.

A PROFESSIONAL DEVELOPS AN ENVIRONMENT

While you're busy imagining glorious flowers waving a welcome at you from your expertly designed tiered gardens, or snow-laden pine trees seen through your kitchen window, your landscaper will be out walking around your property, assessing practical issues like grading and drainage, the location of sewers, utility lines, and existing trees, where and when the sun hits the land, and the quality of the soil.

This important first step, the site analysis, should take place before construction has even begun, in the case of a new house. Site work helps ensure that the blueprints for your house won't make your landscape dreams impossible to achieve, and vice versa. If you've told your builder you want a breakfast nook, you'll probably get one regardless of the fact that it requires taking out a tree you value.

If you're considering installing a custom driveway or sidewalk, this early stage is the time to inform your builder. Ask your builder not to do construction outside the building envelope. You and your landscape professionals will design and build your driveway and walkways.

Expect the design process to take at least six weeks. During this time, the designer is developing a plan for the hardscape, which includes all of the man-made elements of your outdoor environment, and the many layers of softscape, which are the actual plantings. You can expect to be presented with a plan view that is workable and in harmony with your home, as well as your budget.

Hardscape elements, like irrigation systems and pavements, will be installed first, before a new house is completely finished. Softscape will go in later.

During this landscape project, you most likely have begun to appreciate the special nature of landscape and will not be surprised if your completed project does not look "complete." A landscape should be given time in the hands of nature to come to maturity: three years for perennials, five years for shrubs, and 15 years for trees.

LUXURY LIVING WITH A CUSTOM-DESIGNED POOL

The beauty and value of a custom-designed swimming pool are unmatched. A welcome design element to the landscape, a pool adds to the overall property value of the residence, and creates greater use and enjoyment of the yard. As area families spend more and more of their leisure time at home, a pool answers their dreams of living well at home.

Deciding to build a swimming pool is best done as a new home is being designed so the pool can enhance the home and landscape architecture. By integrating the pool into the overall scheme, you'll be able to establish a realistic budget. One of the biggest mistakes homeowners make when purchasing a pool is not initially getting all the features they want. It's difficult and costly to add features later.

The design process is time consuming. You may have four or more meetings with your pool professional before finalizing the design. Pool projects can be started at almost any time of year, so avoid getting caught in the busy season, spring to summer. Start getting approvals in January if you want to be enjoying your pool in the summer. The building process takes about two months, after obtaining permits. You should plan to have your pool dug at the same time as the home foundation. Pool construction is integrated with surrounding decking, so make sure your landscape architect, pool builder, or hardscape contractor is coordinating the effort.

OUTDOOR LIVING

Today's homeowners, having invested the time and resources to create a spectacular environment, are ready to "have it all" in their own backyards.

Decks, gazebos, and increasingly, screened rooms, are popular features of today's upscale homes. The extended living space perfectly suits our "cocooning" lifestyle, offering more alternatives for entertaining, relaxation, and family time at home. Many new homes tout outdoor living space as a most tantalizing feature.

Decks and terraces offer extra living space which can be utilized seven months a year and are functional enough to host almost any occasion. With thoughtful and proper design, it fulfills our dreams of an outdoor getaway spot. A multi-level deck built up and around mature trees can feel like a treehouse. A spa built into a cedar deck, hidden under a trellis, can make you believe you're in a far-off paradise.

With so many options available, building a new deck provides a unique opportunity for homeowners to give their creativity free rein.

EVERY KID'S FANTASY

In a yard with plenty of flat area: A wood construction expandable play system with: Several slides, including a spiral slide, crawl tunnels and bridges to connect fort and structures, a tic-tac-toe play panel, three swings, climbing ropes, fire pole, gymnastics equipment (trapeze, turning bar), sandbox pit, and a built in picnic table with benches. Price Tag: Around $12,000

In a smaller yard: A wood construction expandable play system with: A small fort, two swings and a single slide. Price Tag: Around $1,400

383

DREAM POOLS

Yours for $60,000: Custom-designed mid-sized pool with a deep end, spa, custom lighting, cleaning system, remote control functions, cover, deck.

Yours for $200,000: A custom-designed Roman style pool with bar stools, a small wading pool, elevated spa, and elaborate waterfall. Specialized lighting, built-in planters, automated hydraulic cover, top of the line automated cleaning system, all with remote control functions.

A TYPICAL LANDSCAPE DESIGN TIMETABLE

• One to two weeks to get the project on the boards
+
• One to two weeks to do the actual site and design work and prepare plans
+
• One week to coordinate calendars and schedule presentation meeting
+
• One to two weeks to leave the plans with client and get their feedback
+
• One week to incorporate changes, create and get approval on a final design
=
FIVE TO EIGHT WEEKS

THE TIGHT SQUEEZE. When homes get bigger, back yards get smaller. A landscape architect will be attentive to keeping all aspects of your plan in proper balance.

384

THINKING ABOUT OUTDOOR LIVING

An on-site meeting with a licensed contractor who is an expert in landscape building or a landscape architect is the first step in designing and building a deck, patio, or any outdoor structure. An experienced professional will guide you through the conceptualization by asking questions like these:

• Why are you building the structure? For business entertaining, family gatherings, child or teen parties, private time?

• Do you envision a secluded covered area, a wide open expanse, or both?

• Do you want a single level, or two or more levels (the best option for simultaneous activities)?

• Will it tie in with current or future plans?

• How do you want to landscape the perimeter?

• Do you want benches, railings, trellises, or other stylish options, like built-in counters with gas grills, or recessed lighting under benches or railings?

Don't let obstacles block your thinking. Your gas grill can be moved. Decks are often built around trees and can convert steep slopes into usable space.

Once a design has been settled upon, expect three to four weeks to pass before a deck or gazebo is completed. In the busy spring and summer months, it most likely will take longer. The time required to get a building permit (usually two to four weeks) must also be considered.

If you're landscaping during this time, be sure to coordinate the two projects well in advance. Building can wreak havoc on new plantings and your lawn will be stressed during construction.

DISTINCTIVE OUTDOOR SURFACES

Driveways, walkways, patios, decks, and wood terraces, hardscape features once relegated to "last minute" status, with a budget to match, are now being given the full and careful attention they deserve. A brick paver driveway can be made to blend beautifully with the color of the brick used on the house. Natural brick stairways and stoops laid by master crafters add distinctive detail and value. Custom-cut curved bluestone steps, hand selected by an experienced paving contractor, provide years of pride and pleasure.

Hardscape installation doesn't begin until your new home is nearly complete, but for your own budgeting purposes, have decisions made no later than home mid-construction phase.

To interview a paving or hardscape contractor, set up an on-site meeting so you can discuss the nature of the project and express your ideas. Be ready to answer questions like:

• Will the driveway be used by two or three cars, or more? Do you need it to be wide enough so cars can pass? Will you require extra parking? Would you like a circular driveway? A basketball court?

• Will the patio be used for entertaining? Will it be a family or adult area, or both? How much furniture will you use? Should it be accessible from a particular part of the house?

• Do you have existing or future landscaping that needs to be considered?

• Would you like to incorporate special touches, like a retaining wall, a small koi pond, or a stone archway?

If you're working with a full service landscape professional, and hardscape is part of the landscape design, be certain a hardscape expert will do the installation. A specialist's engineering expertise and product knowledge are vital to the top quality result you want.

GARDENER'S EDENS

Visit these artistic gardens for ideas and inspiration.
Anderson Gardens (Authentic Japanese Garden)
2214 Stoneridge Drive, Rockford (815) 877-2525
Chicago Botanic Garden
1000 Lake-Cook Rd., Glencoe (847) 835-5440
Morton Arboretum
IL. Route 53, Lisle (630) 719-2465
Cantigny
1S151 Winfield Rd., Wheaton (630) 668-5161
Montefiore
11250 S. Archer Ave., Lemont (630) 719-2465
Lincoln Park Conservatory
Lincoln Park, Chicago ■

SOURCES

Illinois Chapter, American Society of Landscape Architects
P.O. Box 4566
Oak Brook, IL 60522
(630)833-4516
www.info@il-asla.org

Illinois Chapter, Wild Ones Natural Landscapers, Ltd.
P.O. Box 4566
Oak Brook, IL 60522
(630) 833-4516
www.for-wild.org

WHY YOU NEED AN ARBORIST.

It's not just your kids, dogs, and the neighborhood squirrels trampling through your yard during construction. Excavation equipment, heavy trucks, and work crews can spell disaster for your trees. Call an arborist before any equipment is scheduled to arrive, and let him develop a plan that will protect the trees, or remove them if necessary.

385

Landscape
Architects

CHALET LANDSCAPE/ NURSERY & GARDEN SHOPS ....**(847) 256-0561**
3132 Lake Avenue, Wilmette — Fax: (847) 256-4978
See Add on Page: 389 — 800 Extension: 1118
Principal/Owner: Larry Thalmann III
Website: www.chaletnursery.com e-mail: info@chaletnursery.com
Description: Chalet Landscape Division has provided the North Shore with award winning design, construction, maintenance and Lawn Care since 1917.

ROCCO FIORE & SONS, INC...**(847) 680-1207**
28270 N. Bradley Road, Libertyville — Fax: (847) 816-1137
See Add on Page: 390, 391 — 800 Extension: 6103
Principal/Owner: Rocco Fiore / Steve Fiore

HEYNSSENS & GRASSMAN ....**(847) 360-0440**
PO Box 1152, Libertyville — Fax: (847) 360-0491
See Add on Page: 410, 411 — 800 Extension: 6147
Principal/Owner: Rene' Grassman Heynssens and Chris J. Heynssens
e-mail: heynssens@iconnect.net
Description: Registered landscape architects, specializing in the design, construction and maintenance of residential gardens.

ILT VIGNOCCHI ....**(847) 487-5200**
25865 W. Ivanhoe, Wauconda — Fax: (847) 487-5265
See Add on Page: 376, 377, 393 — 800 Extension: 6157
Principal/Owner: Donna Vignocchi
Website: www.iltvignocchi.com
Description: ILT Vignocchi has been providing and maintaining preferred residential properties with elegant outdoor environments for entertainment, relaxation, and play for over thirty years.

MILIEU DESIGN, INC. ....**(847) 465-1150**
48 E. Hintz Road, Wheeling — Fax: (847) 465-1159
See Add on Page: 387, 412 — 800 Extension: 1103
Principal/Owner: Peter Wodarz

ROSBOROUGH PARTNERS, INC...**(847) 549-1361**
15849 W. Buckley Road, Libertyville — Fax: (847) 549-1392
See Add on Page: 388 — 800 Extension: 6275
Principal/Owner: Phil Rosborough
e-mail: rosborough1@aol.com

386

Since 1947, Rocco Fiore & Sons, Inc. has been creating award-winning, personalized design, construction and maintenance services to the prestigious North Shore and Chicago metropolitan areas. All areas of expertise are fully explored. Whether working with large-scale, formal and informal settings to small-scale intimate spaces... each and every detail is considered as utmost importance. There are no shortcuts or sacrifices.

Rocco Fiore & Sons, Inc. Highland Park 847 680 1207

The Ashley Group Luxury Home Resource Collection

Call Toll Free at 888-458-1750

The Ashley Group is pleased to offer as your final destination when searching for home improvement and luxury resources the following Home Books in your local market: Chicago, Washington DC, South Florida and the Los Angeles area. These comprehensive, hands-on design source books to building, remodeling, decorating, furnishing, and landscaping luxury a home, is required reading for the serious and selective homeowners. With over 600 full-color, beautiful pages per market, these hard cover volumes are the most complete and well-organized reference to the home industry. The Home Books in each market, cover all aspects of the building and remodeling and design process, including listings of hundreds of industry professionals, accompanied by informative and valuable editorial discussing the most recent trends. Ordering your copy of any of the *Home Books* now can ensure that you have the blueprints to your dream home, in your hand, today.

Order your copies today and make your dreams come true!

O R D E R   F O R M

Landscape
Contractors

BUHRMAN DESIGN GROUP ....**(847) 680-6120**
2088 Bob-O-Link Lane, Libertyville
Fax: (847) 680-6124
See Add on Page: 398, 399
800 Extension: 1072
Principal/Owner: Lance Buhrman

CHICAGO SPECIALTY GARDENS, INC. ....**(847) 832-0406**
P.O. Box 97, Glenview
Fax: (847) 832-0435
See Add on Page: 408
800 Extension: 1110
Principal/Owner: Phil Cleland
e-mail: philgard@aol.com

CRANE LANDSCAPE & DESIGN, INC. ....**(262) 889-8802**
P.O. Box 267, Wilmot
Fax: (262) 889-4359
See Add on Page: 406
800 Extension: 1081
Principal/Owner: Robert Livingston
Website: www.cranelandscape.com e-mail: design@cranelandscape.com

HINSDALE NURSERIES, INC. ....**(630) 323-1411**
7200 S. Madison, Hinsdale
Fax: (630) 323-0918
See Add on Page: 395
800 Extension: 1073
Principal/Owner: Richard Theidel
e-mail: sales@hinsdalenurseries.com

MARIANI LANDSCAPE ....**(847) 234-2172**
300 Rockland Road, Lake Bluff
Fax: (847) 234-2754
See Add on Page: 404, 405
800 Extension: 1044
Principal/Owner: Frank Mariani

MILIEU DESIGN, INC. ....**(847) 465-1150**
48 E. Hintz Road, Wheeling
Fax: (847) 465-1159
See Add on Page: 387, 412
800 Extension: 1192
Principal/Owner: Peter Wodarz

RONALD REHLING ASSOCIATES, INC. ....**(630) 879-0577**
2 S. 311 Deerpath Road, Batavia
Fax: (630) 879-0566
See Add on Page: 403
800 Extension: 1134
Principal/Owner: Ronald Rehling

RUFFOLO, INC. ....**(847) 883-0303**
13 S. Milwaukee Avenue, Vernon Hills
Fax: (847) 883-0305
See Add on Page: 400, 401
800 Extension: 1135
Principal/Owner: John Popiolek

KLAUS SCHMECHTIG COMPANY ....**(847) 566-1233**
20860 N. Indian Creek, Mundelein
Fax: (847) 566-1488
See Add on Page: 407
800 Extension: 6191
Principal/Owner: Michael Schmechtig
Website: klausslandscapes.com

TECZA ENVIRONMENTAL GROUP ....**(847) 742-3320**
12N442 Switzer Road, Elgin
Fax: (847) 742-3171
See Add on Page: 409
800 Extension: 1031
Principal/Owner: Edward Reier

TIMBER RIDGE LANDSCAPING, INC. ....**(630) 543-5296**
PO Box 882, Addison
Fax: (630) 543-5295
See Add on Page: 402
800 Extension: 1188
Principal/Owner: Mark J. Casazza

VAN ZELST INC. ....**(847) 623-3580**
39400 N. Hwy 41, Box 250, Wadsworth
Fax: (847) 623-7546
See Add on Page: 396, 397
800 Extension: 1108
Principal/Owner: David Van Zelst
Website: www.vanzelst.com e-mail: info@vanzelst.com

Hinsdale Nurseries

Extraordinary Landscape Service

We have a feel for
Chicagoland landscapes.
After all, we've been growing
in your neighborhood for
more than 150 years.
We know what it takes
to make your landscape fit
your home, your taste
or your budget.

Call us for a
no cost consultation
and see the difference
150 years of Midwest
growing experience
will make
in your landscape.

**Landscape Design
Installation &
Maintenance
for Discerning Homeowners**

7200 S. Madison St.
Hinsdale
630-323-1411

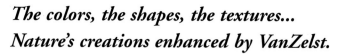

The colors, the shapes, the textures...
Nature's creations enhanced by VanZelst.

Beautifying one's surroundings always brings a sense of satisfaction and accomplishment. At VanZelst, Inc. our goals are to create and maintain beautiful landscapes which combine the art of landscape architecture with the personal preferences of each of our clients.

We take pride in the ability of our team to listen to our clients, to understand what they envision and to use all of our company's expertise and creativity to allow that vision to flourish.

Our landscape architects and team of skilled professionals are masters in their art. Please call me personally to discuss the potential for your landscape.

Sincerely,

Dave VanZelst

Van Zelst inc.
Landscape Development & Management

Photography: Linda Oyama Bryan

847.623.3580   FAX 847.623.7546

Give me solitude, give me Nature,

Give me the splendid silent sun with all his beams full-dazzling,

Give me at sunrise a garden of beautiful flowers where I can walk undisturb'd,

Give me juicy autumnal fruit ripe and red from the orchard,

Give me an arbor, give me the trellis'd grape,

Give me again O Nature

EXCERPTS FROM WALT WHITMAN

For the Landscape

B U H R M A N
design group

that Inspires Poetry

A Full Service Landscape Contractor

(847) 680-6120

2088 BOB-O-LINK LANE
LIBERTYVILLE, IL. 60048

Inspired by Nature.

Installed by Ruffolo.

We've been assisting homeowners in the North Shore area for more than 45 years - specializing in exterior design.

Ruffolo Inc
design
construction
maintenance

(847) 883-0303

The beauty of these designs is a reflection of the time and effort spent to meet your unique and specialized demands. Call us today for an estimate on your next project.

Terraced Patios

Old World Stone Work

Elegant Garden Walks

Inspired by Nature.

Installed by Ruffolo.

Finally...
Chicago's Own
Home & Design
Sourcebook

The CHICAGO HOME BOOK, a comprehensive hands-on
design sourcebook to building, remodeling, decorating, furnishing
and landscaping a luxury home in Chicago and its suburbs,
is a "must-have" reference for the Chicagoland homeowner.
At over 700 pages, this beautiful, full-color hard cover
volume is quite simply the most complete, well-organized
reference to the Chicagoland home industry. It covers all aspects
of the process, with hundreds of listings of local home industry
professionals, accompanied by hundreds of inspiring photographs.
You will also find articles to assist in planning and completing a
project. The CHICAGO HOME BOOK tells you how to
find what you need when you need it.

Order your copy today!

CHICAGO
HOME
BOOK

Published by
The Ashley Group
1350 E. Touhy Avenue • Des Plaines, IL 60018
Toll Free 888-458-1750   Fax 847.390.2902
E-mail: ashleybooksales@cahners.com

Landscape Design/Build

Maintenance

Landscape Architecture

" Contemporary and Traditional Landscapes to match your Lifestyle"

Ronald Rehling Associates, Inc.
2 S 311 Deerpath Rd.
Batavia, IL 60510
630.879.0577

MARIANI
LANDSCAPE / DESIGN·BUILD·MAINTENANCE®

300 Rockland Road
Lake Bluff, Illinois 60044
847.234.2172 Fax 847.234.2754

CRANE
Landscape & Design, Inc.

Phn: 262-889-8802
Fax: 262-889-4359
www.cranelandscape.com

SHAPE YOUR WORLDS.

KLAUS SCHMECHTIG LANDSCAPES

ESTABLISHED   IN   1960

LANDSCAPE ARCHITECTURE • CONSTRUCTION • MAINTENANCE
20860 W. INDIAN CREEK ROAD • MUNDELEIN, IL • 60069
847.566.1233
www.klauslandscapes.com

Simple Things of Beauty

Landscape Lighting • Natural Stone and Paver Installations • Micro-Irrigation
Rooftop and Deck Gardens • Ornamental Trees, Shrubs, Perennials and Annuals
Containers, Urns and Statuary • Water Features • Computer-Aided Design

CHICAGO SPECIALTY GARDENS

ILCA AWARD-WINNING DESIGN AS SEEN ON **HGTV**

CITY & SUBURBS (847) 832-0406

tecza environmental group

12 N. 442 Switzer Road • Elgin, Il 60123
847 • 742 • 3320

LANDSCAPE DESIGN
A Complete Master Plan

LANDSCAPE INSTALLATION
Ideas Come to Life

LANDSCAPE MAINTENANCE
Professional Service, Care & Attention

HEYNSSENS+
GRASSMAN

Landscape Architecture, Construction and Maintenance

TIMELE

BEAUTY

Milieu Design Inc.

GROUNDS FOR CHANGE?

48 EAST HINTZ ROAD
WHEELING, ILLINOIS 60090
PHONE: 847.465.1160
FAX: 847.465.1159
LANDSCAPE ARCHITECTURE CONSTRUCTION MAINTENANCE

Hardscape,
Masonry & Water

HIRSCH BRICK & STONE..**(847) 623-0063**
15187 Primrose Lane, Wadsworth — Fax: (847) 623-3367
See Add on Page: 417 — 800 Extension: 1263
<u>Principal/Owner:</u> Greg Hirsch

KRUGEL COBBLES..**(847) 234-7935**
3337 West Berqyn Avenue, Lake Bluff — Fax: (847) 785-9202
See Add on Page: 414, 415 — 800 Extension: 1238
<u>Principal/Owner:</u> Heath Frey

MACKEY LANDSCAPES..**(847) 740-6448**
430 N. Milwaukee Avenue, Suite 8, Lincolnshire — Fax: (847) 740-6462
See Add on Page: 418 — 800 Extension: 1058
<u>Principal/Owner:</u> Scott Mackey

RIKROCK, INC...**(847) 291-3455**
PO Box 892, Northbrook — Fax: (847) 934-7746
See Add on Page: 416 — 800 Extension: 1205
<u>Principal/Owner:</u> Rick Walsh

RUFFOLO, INC...**(847) 883-0303**
13 S. Milwaukee Avenue, Vernon Hills — Fax: (847) 883-0305
See Add on Page: 400, 401 — 800 Extension: 1014
<u>Principal/Owner:</u> John Popiolek

UNILOCK..**(630) 892-9191**
301 East Sullivan Road, Aurora — Fax: (630) 892-9215
See Add on Page: 419, 760, 761 — 800 Extension: 1149
<u>Principal/Owner:</u> Tracy Walsh, Inside Sales

413

Water Gardens Exclusively

"Artistic Integrity is the Cornerstone of Our Success."

Photos by: Linda Oyama Bryan

RIK ROCK
ARCHITECTURAL
WATER ENVIRONMENTS

P.O. Box 892•Northbrook, ILLINOIS 60065
847.291.3455

⚡ HIRSCH
BRICK & STONE

Driveways

Patios

Pool Decks

Concrete Pavers

Clay Pavers

Natural Stone

15187 PRIMROSE LANE
WADSWORTH, ILLINOIS 60083
(847) 623-0063

Every

Window

is a

Picture

Frame.

design

construction

maintenance

Mackey
Landscapes, Inc

430 N. Milwaukee Av
Lincolnshire, IL
60069
847-740-6448

Through creative use of designs, colors and textures, thousands of Chicagoland home exteriors have been beautified with the use of Unilock products.

Swimming Pools,
Spas & Sport

A COMPLETE SPA & POOL SUPPLY CENTRE ....**(608) 227-7727**
3202 W. Beltline Highway, Middleton   Fax: (608) 227-2727
See Add on Page: 421   800 Extension: 1020
Principal/Owner: Greg Griswold
Description: Once you experience the outrageous pleasure of over 110 jets of 15
HP pumps, anything less is just a hot tub!

BOILINI POOL INC. ....**(847) 615-7100**
300 Rockland Road, Lake Bluff   Fax: (847) 615-7177
See Add on Page: 424   800 Extension: 6037
Principal/Owner: Patrick M. Boilini
Website: www.boilini.com e-mail: patrick@boilini.com

DOWNES SWIMMING POOL CO. INC. ....**(800) 939-9309**
433 Denniston Court, Wheeling   Fax: (847) 465-0970
See Add on Page: 428   800 Extension: 1019
Principal/Owner: Lou Downes
Website: www.downespool.com
Description: Construction of custom granite pools, spas and water features.

POOL CRAFT, INC. ....**(847) 776-5278**
1509 W. Dundee Road, Palatine   Fax: (847) 776-5299
See Add on Page: 426, 427   800 Extension: 1033
Principal/Owner: John Mitmoen
Description: Specialists in custom pools, spas, and waterfalls.

ROSEBROOK CAREFREE POOLS, INC. ....**(847) 432-0710**
2310 Skokie Valley Road, Highland Park   Fax: (847) 432-3911
See Add on Page: 422, 423   800 Extension: 1261
Principal/Owner: John Bently
Website: www.carefreepools.com e-mail: jnbently@aol.com
Description: High-end custom design/builders of residential and commercial
pools, spas and fountains.

SPORT COURT ....**(630) 682-5500**
1547 Orchard Road, Wheaton   Fax: (630) 682-5109
See Add on Page: 429   800 Extension: 1030
Principal/Owner: Dave Vanderveen
Website: sportcourt.com
Description: World's largest builder of backyard game courts and putting
greens.

STRICTLY SPAS..**(847) 215-7727**
503 S. Milwaukee, Wheeling   Fax: (847) 215-0016
See Add on Page: 425   800 Extension: 1184

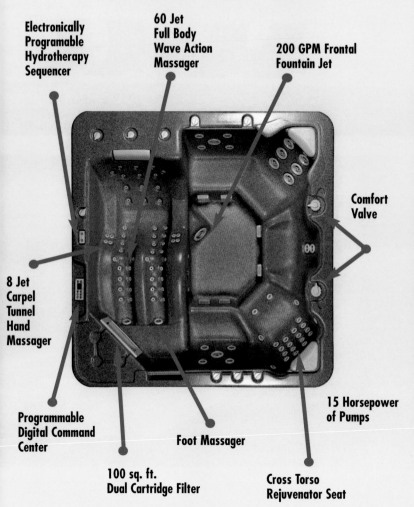

ROSEBROOK

CAREFREE *the finest* POOLS, INC.

2310 SKOKIE VALLEY ROAD
HIGHLAND PARK, ILLINOIS 60035
PHONE (847) 432-0710

www.carefreepools.com

Excellence in Pool and Spa Construction

Strictly Spas

"When Uniqueness Counts"

503 S. Milwaukee Avenue
Wheeling, IL 60090
Tel: 847.215. SPAS (7727)

Near Bob Chinn's Crabhouse

Catalina Spas

Jacuzzi WHIRLPOOL BATH

strictlyspas.com

- Spas: TVs, Stereos, Misters
- Hot tubs, Whirlpools
- Saunas – Indoor & Out
- Gazebos, Domes, Wraps
- Billiards & Game Tables

Photography by: Linda Oyama Bryan

Pool Craft, Inc.
1509 West Dundee Road
Palatine, Illinois 60074

DOWNES SWIMMING POOL CO., INC.

QUALITY POOL CONSTRUCTION AND SERVICE
"Named one of the top 100 firms in the industry"

433 Denniston Court, Wheeling, Illinois 60090
800-939-9309 • 847-465-0895 • Fax 847-465-0970
www.downespool.com

Backyard
Game Court

Decks, Conservatories &
Architectural Elements

AMDEGA CONSERVATORIES..**(847) 277-9190**
421 N. Northwest Highway, Barrington   Fax: (847) 277-9008
See Add on Page: 431   800 Extension: 1234
<u>Principal/Owner:</u> Bonnie Miske

CONCRETE SELECT ....**(847) 251-8310**
1131 Greenleaf Avenue, Wilmette   Fax: (847) 251-8353
See Add on Page: 437   800 Extension: 1095
<u>Principal/Owner:</u> Anne Williams

JLH CUSTOM DECK BUILDERS ....**(847) 550-0426**
20453 W. Main Street, Kildeer   Fax: (847) 550-9861
See Add on Page: 434, 435   800 Extension: 1123
<u>Principal/Owner:</u> John Hachmeister
<u>e-mail:</u> JLHBuild@A1ISP.net

OUT FRONT DESIGN GROUP ....**(847) 831-0287**
PO Box 501, Highland Park   Fax: (847) 831-2052
See Add on Page: 436   800 Extension: 1146
<u>Principal/Owner:</u> Martin Heller
<u>Website:</u> www.outfrontdesign.com

UNIQUE BUILDERS, INC ....**(847) 831-1388**
747 Lake Cook Rd., Deerfield   Fax: (847) 480-7311
See Add on Page: 432, 433   800 Extension: 1062
<u>Principal/Owner:</u> Joel Boyer

"A lake is the landscape's
most beautiful and expressive feature.
It is earth's eye, looking into which the
beholder measures the
depth of his own nature."

Henry David Thoreau

AMDEGA

conservatories & garden buildings

421 Northwest Highway
Suite 201
Barrington, IL 60010

◆ ◆ ◆

800.521.8990
www.amdega.com

Unique Deck Builders

Free Estimates
847/831-1388 • 1-800-427-DECK (3325)

JLH
CUSTOM DECK
BUILDERS

DECKS, ARBORS, PERGOLAS, GAZEBOS

20453 WEST MAIN STREET
KILDEER, IL 60047
847-550-0426
FAX 847-550-9861

JLH
CUSTOM DECK
BUILDERS

20453 WEST MAIN STREET
KILDEER, IL 60047
847-550-0426
FAX 847-550-9861

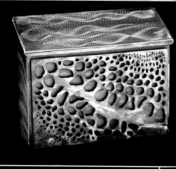
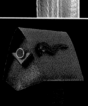

Lighting

ACTIVE ELECTRICAL SUPPLY..**(773) 282-6300**
    4240 W. Lawrence Ave., Chicago   Fax: (773) 282-5206
    See Add on Page: 440, 678, 679   800 Extension: 1064
    <u>Principal/Owner:</u> Skip Leigh

LIGHTSACPE, INC. ....**(847) 266-7551**
    3150 N. Skokie Hwy, #9, Highland Park   Fax: (847) 266-7552
    See Add on Page: 438   800 Extension: 1022
    <u>Principal/Owner:</u> Steve Achtemeier
    <u>Description:</u> Lightscape, Inc. is a service organization providing landscape lighting design, installation and maintenance to residential and commercial clientele.

LIGHTSHOW/ OUTDOOR LIGHTING PERSPECTIVES............**(708) 403-5873**
    10645 Hollow Tree Road, Orland Park   Fax: (708) 403-3857
    See Add on Page: 439   800 Extension: 1141
    <u>Principal/Owner:</u> Dick Norwood

437

Secure your home
Beautifully

Increasing your home's safety through outdoor
lighting shouldn't mean sacrificing its beauty.

Let Lightscape provide attractive, natural looking
lighting to illuminate and secure your home...beautifully.

KICHLER LANDSCAPE LIGHTING

The primary function of outdoor lighting is to provide adequate illumination for the comfort and safety of your family and guests. At *Fox Lighting Galleries*, we will enable you to create outdoor lighting that is both functional and beautiful.

Fox Lighting Galleries

Active Electrical Supply
4240 West Lawrence Avenue
Chicago, Illinois 60630
Phone 773-282-6300
Fax 773-282-5206
Hours: Mon. - Fri. 7:30AM - 5PM
Thurs. till 8pm Sat. till 2PM

"IT STARTS WITH IDEAS... BIG OR SMALL, IN WORDS OR PICTURES, IN COLORS OR SHAPES.... CRYSTAL CLEAR OR BARELY THERE. THAT'S HOW IT STARTS."

Paul A Casper & Carolyn Nichols

The
Ashley
Group

Publishers of Fine Visual Reference for the Discerning Connoisseur
1350 Touhy Ave. • Des Plaines, Illinois 60018
888.458.1750 • FAX 847.390.2902
ashleygroup@cahners.com

Photo courtesy of:
Dream Kitchens

KITCHEN
&
BATH

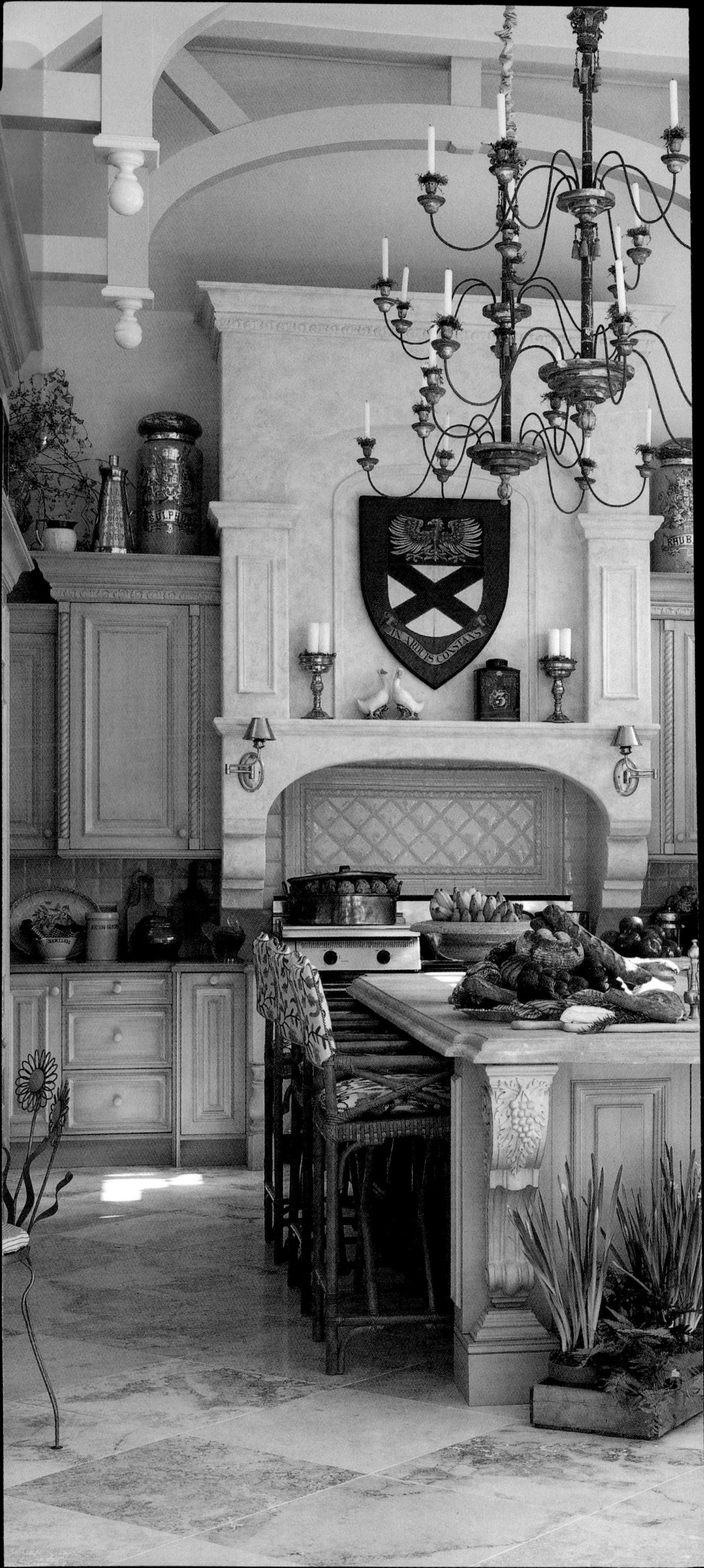
IN ARDUIS CONSTANS

" **A thing of beauty is a joy** *forever*

It's *loveliness* increases; it will never pass into *nothingness.* "

John Keats

Form, Function... Fabulous!

photo courtesy of:
**Ann Sacks
Tile & Stone**

Once designed merely for efficiency with little attention to beauty, today's kitchens and baths have become paramount to a home's comfort and style, places to nurture body and spirit.

Without a doubt, today's larger kitchen is the real family room, the heart and soul of the home. Some kitchens serve as the control center in "Smart Houses" wired with the latest technology. With the kitchen as a focal point of the home, good design means the room must be both functional and a pleasure to be in, while reflecting the "feel" of the rest of the home. From the European "unfitted" look to super-high tech, there are styles and finishes to make every taste, sophisticated to simple, feel at home in the kitchen. The bath has evolved into a truly multipurpose "cocooning" area as well. Sufficient room for exercise equipment, spacious master closets, and spa features are all in high demand, creating master suites to allow you to escape from the world. The emphasis on quality fixtures and luxury finishes remains, whatever the size of the room.

FIVE WAYS TO SPOT A TOP QUALITY KITCHEN OR BATH

1. A feeling of timelessness: Sophisticated solutions that blend appropriately with the home's overall architecture & smoothly incorporate new products and ideas.

2. A hierarchy of focal points: Visual elements designed to enhance – not compete with – each other.

3. Superior functionality: Rooms clearly serve the needs they were designed to meet, eliminate traffic problems and work well years after installation.

4. Quality craftsmanship: All elements, from cabinets, counters, and floors, to lighting, windows and furnishings, are built and installed at the highest level of quality.

5. Attention to detail: Thoughtful planning is evident – from the lighting scheme to the practical surfaces to the gorgeous cabinet detailing.

PLANNED TO PERFECTION
THE CUSTOM KITCHEN & BATH

In many ways, the kitchen and bath define how we live and dictate the comfort we enjoy in our everyday lives. Families continue to design their kitchens to be the heart of the home – in every way. It's the central gathering place. It's a work space. It's a command center for whole house electronic control systems. Bathrooms become more luxurious, more multi-functional. Having experienced the pleasures of pampering on vacations, in spas, beauty salons, and health clubs, sophisticated area homeowners are choosing to enjoy a high degree of luxury every day in their own homes.

Homeowners building a new home, or remodeling an existing one, demand flexible and efficient spaces, custom designed to fill their needs. Reaching that goal is more challenging than ever; as new products and technologies race to keep up with the creative design explosion, the need for talented, experienced kitchen and bath designers continues to grow.

The kitchen/bath designer will be a member of your home building team, which also includes the architect, contractor, interior designer and in new home construction, the landscape architect.

Professional kitchen and bath designers, many of whom are also degreed interior designers, possess the education and experience in space planning particular to kitchens and baths. They can deliver a functional design perfectly suited to your family, while respecting your budget and your wishes. Their understanding of ergonomics, the relationship between people and their working environments, and a familiarity with current products and applications, will be invaluable to you as you plan.

SEARCH OUT AND VALUE
DESIGN EXCELLENCE

Designing a kitchen or bath is an intimate undertaking, filled with many decisions based on personal habits and family lifestyle. Before you select the kitchen/bath professional who will lead you through the project, make a personal commitment to be an involved and interested client. Since the success of these rooms is so important to the daily lives of your family, it's a worthwhile investment of your time and energy.

Choose a designer whose work shows creativity and a good sense of planning. As in any relationship, trust and communication are the foundations for success. Are they open to your ideas, and do they offer information on how you can achieve your vision?

If you can't express your ideas freely, don't enter into a contractual relationship, no matter how much you admire his or her work. If these rooms aren't conceived to fulfill your wishes, your time and resources will be wasted.

What also is true, however, is that professional designers should be given a comfortable degree of latitude to execute your wishes as best as they know how. Accomplished designers earned their reputation by creating beautiful rooms that work, so give their ideas serious consideration for the best overall result.

Many homeowners contact a kitchen or bath designer a year before a project is scheduled to begin. Some come with a full set of complete drawings they simply want to have priced out. Some take full advantage of the designer's expertise and contract for plans drawn from scratch. And some want something in between. Be sure a designer offers the level of services you want – from 'soup to nuts' or strictly countertops and cabinetry.

Designers charge a design fee which often will be used as a deposit if you choose to hire them. If you expect very detailed sets of drawings, including floor plans, elevations, and pages of intricate detail, such as the support systems of kitchen islands, the toe kick and crown molding detail, be specific about your requirements. All contracts should be written, detailed, and reviewed by your attorney.

TURNING DREAMS INTO DESIGNS - GET YOUR NOTEBOOK OUT

The first step toward getting your ideas organized is to put them on paper. Jot down notes, tape photos into your Idea Notebook, mark pages of your Home Book. The second step is defining your lifestyle. Pay close attention to how you use the kitchen and bath. For example, if you have a four-burner stove, how often do you cook with all four burners? Do you need a cook surface with more burners, or could you get by with less, freeing up space for a special wok cooking module or more counter space? How often do you use your bathtub? Many upper-end homeowners are forgoing the tub in favor of the multi-head shower surround and using bathtub space for a dressing or exercise area or mini-kitchen. As you evaluate your lifestyle, try to answer questions like these:

THINKING ABOUT KITCHEN DESIGN

• What feeling do you want to create in the kitchen? Traditional feel of hearth and home? The clean, uncluttered lines of contemporary design?

THE LATEST APPLIANCES

There's a revolution in kitchen appliances, guaranteed to make your life simpler and more enjoyable: High performance stainless steel cook-top ranges with a commercial level of performance; Cook-tops with interchangeable cooking modules (like woks, griddles); Down draft ventilation on gas cook-tops; Convection ovens with oversize capacity, and electronic touchpad controls; Refrigeration products and systems you can put wherever you could put a cabinet or drawer; Flush-design appliances; Ultra-quiet dishwashers with lifelong stainless steel interiors; Refrigerators that accept decorative door panels and handles to match your cabinets; State-of-the-art warming drawers.

447

WHAT DESIGNERS OFFER YOU

1. Access to the newest products: With their considerable knowledge of products and solutions, your remodeling or budget limitations can be more easily addressed.
2. Ergonomic design for a custom fit: Designers consider all the measurements – not just floor plan space – but also how counter and cabinet height and depth measure up to the needs of the individual family members.
3. A safe environment: Safety is the highest priority. As kitchens and baths serve more functions, managing traffic for safety's sake becomes more crucial.
4. Orderly floor plans: When an open refrigerator door blocks the path from the kitchen to the breakfast room, or you're bumping elbows in the bathroom, poor space planning is the culprit.
5. Smart storage: Ample storage in close proximity to appropriate spaces is essential.

• Is meal preparation the main function of the kitchen? Gourmet cooks and gardeners want a different level of functionality than do homeowners who eat out often or want to be in and out of the kitchen quickly.

• How does the family use the kitchen? How will their needs change your requirements over the next ten years? (If you can't imagine the answer to this question, ask friends who are a few years ahead of you in terms of family life.)

• Do you want easy access to the backyard, dining room, garage?

• Is there a special view you want preserved or established?

• Do you want family and friends to be involved and close to the action in the kitchen?

• What appliances and amenities must be included? Do some research on this question. Warming drawers, refrigeration zones, wine coolers, ultra-quiet dishwashers that sense how dirty the dishes are, cooktops with interchangeable cooking modules, convection ovens with electronic touchpad controls, are all available.

• What are your storage needs? If you own a lot of kitchen items, have a relatively small kitchen, or want personally tailored storage space, ask your kitchen designer to take a detailed inventory of your possessions. Top quality cabinets can be customized to fit your needs. Kitchen designers, custom cabinet makers, or space organization experts can guide you. Consider custom options such as:

- • Slotted storage for serving trays
- • Pull-out recycling bins
- • Plate racks and wine racks
- • Cutlery dividers
- • Angled storage drawer for spices
- • Pivoting shelving systems
- • Pull-out or elevator shelves for food processors, mixers, televisions or computers

• Is the kitchen also a work area or home office? Do you need a location for a computerized home management or intercom system?

THINKING ABOUT BATH DESIGN

• What look are you trying to create? Victorian, Colonial, contemporary, whimsical?

• What functions must it fill? Exercise area, sitting room, dressing or make-up area?

• Who will use the bath? Children, teens, guests, (and how many)?

• What is the traffic pattern? How do people move in and around a bathroom? (Set up your video camera in the corner one morning to get a realistic view.)

• What amenities are desired? Luxury shower systems, whirlpool tub, ceiling heat lamps, heated towel bars, spa, heated tile floors, audio and telephone systems?

• What are your storage needs? Linen or clothes closets? Stereo and CD storage? Professionals will customize spaces for your needs.

• Do you want hooks for towels or bathrobes? Heated towel bars or rings?

THE SKY'S THE LIMIT

New high-end kitchen budgets can easily reach the $100,000 range, so it's important to identify your specific needs and wishes. The sky's the limit when designing and installing a luxury kitchen or bath in the 2000s, so don't get caught by surprise by the cost of high quality cabinetry, appliances and fixtures. Know what you're willing to spend and make sure your designer is aware of your budget. Projects have a way of growing along the way. If you've established a realistic budget, you have a solid way to keep the project moving forward and prioritizing your wishes. As you establish your budget, think in terms of this general breakdown of expenses:

Cabinets	40%
Appliances	15%
Faucets and Fixtures	8%
Flooring	7%
Windows	7%
Countertops	8%
Labor	15%

THE NEW KITCHEN – THE FLAVOR OF THE PAST – A TASTE OF THE FUTURE

Many of the fabulous new kitchens being built now don't look "new." The desire for a inviting, lived-in look that encourages friends and family to linger over coffee and conversation is leading homeowners to embrace European design ideas of furniture-quality cabinetry, and dedicated work zones. Consumers are investing in restaurant-quality appliances, gorgeous imported natural stone countertops and floors, and luxury options like dedicated wine coolers, stem glass holders, and plate racks. Tastes are turning to more classical, traditional detailing in cabinetry, with Georgian, Greek and Roman influence in its architecture.

"WHAT ABOUT RESALE?"

This is a question designers hear when homeowners individualize their kitchens and baths. It's only prudent to consider the practical ramifications of any significant investment, including investing in a new custom kitchen and bath.

Beautiful upscale kitchens and baths will only enhance the value of your home. Indeed, these two rooms are consistently credited with recouping much of their original cost. Research by professional builders' organizations and real estate companies bears this out year after year. The greatest return, however, is in the present, in the enjoyment of the space.

449

YOUR KITCHEN. COM

Technology has arrived in the kitchen. On-line grocery shopping, computers, multiple phone lines, intercom, security system & "smart house" controls. Right by the breakfast table.

A STEP UP

Custom counter height is an idea whose time has arrived in new and remodeled homes in the Chicago area. Multiple heights, appropriate to the task or the people using the particular area, are common. When one permanent height doesn't work as a solution to a problem, consider asking for a step to be built in to the toe kick panel of the cabinetry.

GET TWO DISHWASHERS

Homeowners today are installing extra dishwashers:
1. To make clean up after a party a one-night affair.
2. To serve as a storage cabinet for that extra set of dishes.
They're also installing dishwashers at a more friendly height to eliminate unnecessary bending.

That's not to say that homeowners no longer demand state-of-the-art features; quite the contrary. New, smart ideas play an ever more important role in a kitchen's daily life. Kitchens are often equipped as a central hub in a computer automated home, with everything from ovens to entertainment systems accessible by remote control. Home office or homework areas equipped with telephones, computers, printers, and fax machines are included in most every new project. With advances in refrigeration technology, homeowners now have separate integrated refrigerators and freezer drawers installed near the appropriate work zone – a refrigerated vegetable drawer near the sink, a freezer drawer by the microwave, dedicated refrigerators to keep grains or cooking oils at their perfect temperatures. Ultra-quiet dishwashers, instant hot water dispensers, roll-out warming drawers and versatile cooktops are just some of the products that meet the demands of today's luxury lifestyle.

THE "UN-FITTED" KITCHEN

As homeowners today snuggle deeper into their nests, kitchens that look generations old are more and more appealing. To achieve that look, designers are installing "unfitted" cabinetry, and countertops that look like well-coordinated, complementary furniture. Cabinets of different styles, different finishes, or from altogether different manufacturers are put together to create distinctive environments. Character-lending ledges and shelves hold ceramic canisters, bottle collections, cookbooks, or ultra-chic frosted stemware. Plate racks, European dish-drying racks and wicker basket drawers all add to the open, Old World feel.

Homeowners continue to include an island in their kitchen plan, not so often as a cooking zone but usually with a sink. Today's island helps define the work areas, directs people in the right directions and offers the perfect setting for socializing. Islands linking the kitchen to the breakfast or family room can be built with two or three levels for simultaneous use by a cook, a child busy with homework, and a friend stopping in for a chat and a snack. An extra microwave oven or small refrigerated space is often installed in the base of the island for ultimate convenience, especially when the kitchen is used for entertaining.

The classic "work triangle," with the refrigerator, sink and stove forming the points of an unobstructed traffic pattern, is no longer the automatic rule of thumb. The European concept of zones allows much more individualized, workable floor plans.

The commitment to quality extends to choosing the best appliances available. In addition to contributing top quality function, these kitchen workhorses dress up the kitchen with great style and design. Imported appliances are priced up to $20,000 for a European range, plus freight and installation.

THE NEW BATH – PRACTICALITY DRENCHED WITH PANACHE AND POLISH

Imagine it's a Thursday night at the end of a very busy week. You come home, have a great work out while listening to your favorite CDs over the loudspeakers in your private exercise room, then jump into an invigorating shower where multiple shower heads rejuvenate your tired muscles, and a steaming, cascading waterfall pulls all the stress from your body. You wrap yourself in a big fluffy bath sheet, toasty from the brass towel warmer as you step onto the ceramic tile floor that's been warmed by an underfloor radiant heating unit. You grab something comfortable from your lighted, walk-in closet, and then head out of your luxurious bathroom to the kitchen to help with dinner.

A master bath such as this, built in custom luxury homes fills a growing demand for private retreats replete with nurturing indulgences.

Master bathrooms are being rethought, with the emphasis shifting from form to function. These baths are still large, up to 400 square feet, but the space is organized differently. The newly defined master bath is actually an extension of the master suite, often including his and her walk-in closets, mirrored exercise space, (in remodeling projects, carved out of a spare bedroom) and separate areas for dressing, applying make-up, listening to music or making phone calls, or making coffee.

Large whirlpool tubs are often replaced with custom shower systems with built-in seats and steam capabilities, stylish alternatives like Victorian style claw-foot tubs, or smaller whirlpool tubs.

THE LUXURIOUS POWDER ROOM

A small space like a powder room can easily exude style, grace and superior quality. Stunning perfection shows in the details, like floors and counters of cultured marble, hand painted tile, or deeply colored solid surfacing, carefully placed lighting and gorgeous plumbing fixtures, and lots of distinctive accessories – decorative hardware, fancy soaps and towels and silk flowers.

Lighting is a major component of a successful bath, especially in a powder room. Consult with a lighting professional or your interior designer or bath designer, about appropriate lighting for the best results.

TAKING A TEST DRIVE

You wouldn't invest in a new car without taking it out for a test drive, so take the opportunity up front to test the individual fixtures and elements of a new kitchen or bath. Don't be hesitant to grab a magazine and climb into a bathtub, or to test sit a number of possible toilet choices or shower seats. Take your family to a showroom to evaluate counter heights and faucets. The more involved you can be in the planning, the more fun you'll have, and the better the end result will be.

451

UNIVERSAL DESIGN

One trend in the Chicago area luxury home market is "Universal Design." Interchangeable with accessible design or barrier-free design, this term refers to an emphasis on designing spaces for easy access and the utmost safety for everyone. As homeowners look forward in their lives, to the possibilities of starting a family, opening their home to aging parents, and staying in place as they themselves age, universal design concepts answer some of the concerns that come with these life changes. Some universal design concepts – wider door openings, varying vanity and countertop heights, lighting at appropriate height and strength, non-slip floors, and easy to use light switches and door, drawer, or window hardware.

452

THE REALITY OF REMODELING

Up scale kitchen and bath renovations are most often undertaken by homeowners who decide to invest in making their home aesthetically and functionally pleasing; or those who are so attracted to a particular part of town that they buy a home fully intending to update to meet their needs. As the median age for existing area homes reaches 30+ years, nowhere is the need for renovation and the desire for updating more obvious than in these two rooms.

These dollar smart homeowners know that in cost versus value surveys, kitchen renovations and bath additions or renovations yield a very high return on the original investment. Although these homeowners rarely embark on such remodeling projects with resale in mind, knowing their investment is a wise one gives them the freedom to fully realize their dreams of the ultimate sybaritic bath or the friendliest family kitchen that accommodates them now and well into the future.

Remodeling projects present a number of challenges and limitations to be addressed by your kitchen or bath designer.

Existing plumbing, electrical and ventilation systems will define what is and is not easily accomplished. Existing plumbing may not support luxury bath features, and ventilation systems dictate where cabinetry can be installed. The integrity of the original architecture is also an important defining parameter of the project.

Take your time in the planning stages. Decide if your budget will support raising floors to change plumbing or rewiring for refrigeration drawers in the kitchen, or luxury shower system in the bath. An extra few weeks at this point can save months and thousands of extra dollars, at the other end.

As soon as your contractor calls and says he's coming out to turn off your water and utilities to begin the remodeling process, your home life will be turned upside down. If possible, find alternate living quarters, and remove or carefully cover your furniture. In a kitchen remodel, set up a makeshift kitchen in a lower level family room or guest bedroom and expect to be using it for at least three or four months. Ask your contractor to schedule the work in the least disruptive way possible. Ask for a flowchart which allows you to understand the sequence of work to be done and the relationship of one trade to another's work schedule.

CONTEXTUALISM IN THE KITCHEN AND BATH

Like any other rooms in the home, continuity and contextualism in the kitchen and bath are important to the overall appearance of the home. This is an important point to consider in a remodeling project, especially in an historic home. There often are restrictions on the materials and structural changes that may be made in historic buildings. Your kitchen or bath designer should be aware of these kinds of restrictions.

A REMODELING CONTINGENCY FUND

Kitchen and bath remodeling projects are well known for unexpected, unforeseen expenses, so put a contingency fund in your budget from the beginning. This fund can cover anything from structural changes that need to be made to meet current building codes to your sudden desire to buy (and have installed) skylights in the kitchen or a little chandelier in the bathroom.

THE BEAUTY OF TOP QUALITY SURFACES

Luxury surfaces continue to add astonishing beauty to kitchens and baths in new and remodeled homes throughout the area. Solid surfaces now are available in a ever-widening range of colors, including a granite look, with high degrees of translucence and depth. Granite and stone add a beautiful, natural look, with an abundance of choices and finishes. Tile, stainless steel, laminates, and wood – even concrete – are other possibilities. Each surface has its benefits, beyond the inherent beauty it can add to your design. Your kitchen designer will advise you on the best choices for your project, based on overall design and budget. Use the professionals showcased in these pages to find the best quality materials and craftsmanship.

WHY EUROPEAN PRODUCTS COST MORE

1. European appliances and cabinets are built for a lifetime. When European families put their homes on the market, there's no question about whether the appliances are staying or going. They're going. So are the cabinets. These products are designed and built to be purchased and kept forever; therefore, the initial cost is higher.

2. Shipping tends to be more expensive, as are service parts.

453

KEEPING IT CLEAN

The beauty of high end fixtures, hardware, appliances, flooring and countertops can blind you from the practical considerations of maintenance and upkeep. Many new products are actually easier to keep clean. But before installing deeply colored countertops, ceramic tile backsplashes, or marble floors, make sure you're aware of the time and effort required to keep them in top condition.

LEAN AND LAVISH

The trend toward flush-mounted appliances and cabinetry is here. With built-in refrigerators, ovens and cooktops, kitchens gain a sleek, space-saving look. It's rich, elegant, smart design.

THE LUXURY OF BEAUTIFUL FIXTURES

Sinks, showers, tubs, faucets and hardware, are now top contributors to the true luxury and craftsmanship that homeowners are striving for in their new kitchens and baths. Today's sophisticated homeowners can be pampered by a wide variety of upgraded, special fixtures that offer luxury without sacrificing efficiency and function. Whirlpool tubs, unique surround spray shower enclosures and glamorous custom-designed vanities are in demand. Beautiful wall mounted faucets, float glass bathroom sinks and sleek industrial designs are hallmarks of high tech fixture style. Stainless steel sinks, and faucets are enjoying immense popularity in the kitchen, along with stainless steel appliances. But choices range into many unique colors of solid surface or quartz sinks, paired with elegant, multi-featured faucets and unusual drawer and cabinet hardware crafted from any number of materials.

To avoid construction delays, order your kitchen or bath fixtures according to the schedule on the contractor's timeline for your project. Allow yourself at least one month for shopping. There is such a wide variety of possibilities that you'll want to be able to give careful consideration to them all. You'll also want to have enough time to coordinate fixture colors and styles with the other design elements of the room. Don't hesitate to "test-drive" the fixtures, particularly bathroom fixtures. If a tub isn't a comfortable fit for your body, find out before you have it installed in your home. Once you've made your decision, plan on eight weeks between order and delivery. If you're building a new home, that means placing your fixtures order about the time when the roof goes on the house.

Establish your priorities and then set a good, working budget for your kitchen and bath fixtures and hardware, keeping an eye on your builder's allowance for these elements. Focus on the installed, not the retail cost. And remember, according to value versus cost studies, kitchens and bathrooms yield returns of over 100 percent at resale. ■

Kitchen & Bath
Designers

ARTISTIC KITCHEN DESIGNS ....**(630) 571-4567**
1600 W. 16th Street, Oak Brook — Fax: (630) 571-4572
See Add on Page: 477 — 800 Extension: 6014
Principal/Owner: Cindy Goodrich

BARRINGTON HOME WORKS ....**(847) 381-9526**
102 S. Hager Avenue, Barrington — Fax: (847) 381-9592
See Add on Page: 470 — 800 Extension: 1115
Principal/Owner: Jim Walker
e-mail: BHKC102@aol.com
Description: Kitchens and Bath's designed uniquely for you.

CABINETWERKS ....**(847) 821-9421**
185 Milwaukee Avenue Suite 110, Lincolnshire — Fax: (847) 821-9460
See Add on Page: 543 — 800 Extension: 1117
Principal/Owner: Dave Heigl
Website: www.pickellbuilders.com e-mail: dheigl@pickellbuilders.com
Description: CabinetWerks is an Orren Pickell Company.

CHICAGO KITCHEN & BATH ....**(312) 642-8844**
1521 N. Sedgwick Street, Chicago — Fax: (312) 642-2272
See Add on Page: 478, 479 — 800 Extension: 1245

CRYSTAL CABINET WORKS, INC. ....**(800) 347-5045**
1100 Crystal Drive, Princeton — Fax: (763) 389-3825
See Add on Page: 462, 463 — 800 Extension: 1077
Principal/Owner: Jeff Hammer / Mark Walsh
Website: ccworks.com e-mail: info@ccworks.com

CUCINE DEL VENETO ....**(312) 644-9520**
1344 Merchandise Mart, Chicago — Fax: (312) 644-9523
See Add on Page: 471 — 800 Extension: 1096
Principal/Owner: Jeffrey McDuffee
e-mail: jhmcduffee@earthlink.com

DESIGN STUDIO ....**(847) 234-0800**
709 N. Forest Avenue, Lake Forest — Fax: (847) 234-1166
See Add on Page: 482, 483 — 800 Extension: 1018
Principal/Owner: Mark Olmon
Description: Offering materials, design & installation services for your kitchen, den and library projects.

DREAM KITCHENS ....**(847) 933-9100**
3437 Dempster St., Skokie — Fax: (847) 933-9104
See Add on Page: 468 — 800 Extension: 1043
Principal/Owner: Rick Glickman
Website: www.dreamkitchens.com e-mail: rick@dreamkitchens.com
Description: Kitchens designed from a cook's perspective! Winner of US Chamber of Commerce's 2000 Blue CAAIP Award.

GLENCOE KITCHEN & DESIGN ....**(847) 242-9999**
661 Vernon Avenue, Glencoe — Fax: (847) 242-9909
See Add on Page: 461 — 800 Extension: 1137
Principal/Owner: John Kay
Website: www.glencoekitchens.com e-mail: info@glencoekitchens.com

455

continued on page **466**

CABINET WERKS

Unifitted Kitchens:

CabinetWerks, a division of Orren Pickell Builders, displays many elements of fine furniture in its "unfitted" kitchen vignettes. From the traditional feel Wood-Mode cabinets, to the uniquely defined, custom-built entertainment centers, cabinetry has become synonymous with quality furniture through the use of unlimited details!

AQUAWORKS

German Silver Sink:

The phrase "everything old is new again" is demonstrated by the reintroduction of the German Silver Sink. Originally designed in Germany in the late 1800's to wash fine china and crystal, this uniquely designed sink with its "S" compartments has been reengineered for the 21st Century, and now being handmade in this country by skilled craftsman. Each sink is numbered and registered and can be customized to your specifications.

TOMTEN, INC. CABINETRY DESIGNS

Pantry Cabinet:

The collaboration of functional and artistic designs breaks from tradition in this kitchen pantry cabinet. Instead of the usual approach to pantry storage, the use of "designing from the inside and outside at the same time" created this functional work of art. The cherry wood door panels were hand-carved from the designer's sketches, but the artist had freedom to interpret the drawings while working. The usual requirements for a pantry were incorporated to plan to overall size of the piece and interior features, which included easy-access shelving, interior setting space, pull-out baskets and interior lighting. After panels were carved and finished to match the cabinetry, the piece was assembled on-site and trimmed in keeping with the other kitchen cabinetry. The end result of this collaboration of art and function is a unique definition of a "pantry", enjoyable for its visual impact and design details.

Photo by John Luke Photography

456

Showroom

LAKEVIEW DISTRIBUTORS

Viking Designer Series Line:

Viking is introducing its new Designer Series line in early 2001. This is a complete line of integrated appliances with a stylish new appearance. Pictured here are the built-in oven products that include a micro-chamber, electric oven and warming drawer. The micro-chamber houses a microwave in Viking style. The oven offers several convection and conventional settings, and the warming drawer keeps a meal hot for up to two hours after preparation. The line also includes gas and electric cooktops, ventilation hoods, dishwashers, and refrigerators.

NUHAUS

Kitchen Hoods by Cheng Design:

Cheng Design introduces a new line of unique kitchen hoods for the style-savvy kitchens of tomorrow. This series of six distinctive designs is elegantly mastered with an artist's eye and a chef's sense for the demands of professional class cooktops. A singular blend of sleek modernism and organic warmth, Cheng hoods infuse today's high-style kitchen with a much welcome sense of home and hearth.

457

RUTT OF CHICAGO

The Millennium Kitchen:

The beauty of what we're calling the warm millennium kitchen is that it works in so many different design environments. The Diva range, from the French company Grande Cuisine, with its sleek, warm colors of wood, blends effortlessly with everything from traditional to contemporary décor. When complemented by Rutt cabinets, the design possibilities are endless. We've also introduced Allante marble and granite sinks. This is a unique look from Europe in which the whole sink is carved out of one piece of marble. Allante has a worldwide patent on the machine used to create the sinks, and up until now, has been unwilling to enter the American market. We're offering this product in a variety of options, including undermount sinks, farm sinks, vessel sinks and entire bath vanities.

Photo by Scavolini SPA

IDEA COMPANIES

Scavolini Cabinets:

Sleek, functional and smart as Scavolini brings a novel idea to cabinetry in their latest Melville design. Sliding cabinet doors with frosted glass panels, wood casing and metal accents, create the ultimate in modern appeal.

Designers of fine Cabinetry for the Home since 1965

KARLSON KITCHENS

1815 CENTRAL STREET • EVANSTON, ILLINOIS 60201
Tel: 847-491-1300 • Fax: 847-491-0100 • www.karlsonkitchens.com

studio**becker**

Designers of fine Cabinetry for the Home since 1965

KARLSON KITCHENS

1815 CENTRAL STREET • EVANSTON, ILLINOIS 60201
Tel: 847-491-1300 • Fax: 847-491-0100 • www.karlsonkitchens.com

Wood-Mode
FINE CUSTOM CABINETRY

The Finest in Kitchens and Baths

Award Winning Showroom!

GRABILL QUALITY CABINETRY

Winner of the National Kitchen and Bath Association's 2000
James H. Foster, Jr., CKD Memorial Award for excellence in desi

Downview Kitchens

SINCE 1967

NKBA The Finest Professionals in the Kitchen & Bath Industry
National Kitchen & Bath Association®

Showroom Hours:

M-T-W-F	10am-5pm
Th	10am-8pm
Sat	10am-4pm

Other hours by appointment

Associated with

PPI Professional Plumbing Inc.

RESIDENTIAL COMMERCIAL INDUSTRIAL

Kitchen & Bath Design Group, Ltd.
Showroom & Design Center

Expert Design • Professional Installation

1435 S. Barrington Rd • Barrington, IL 60010

tel: 847-381-7950
fax: 847-381-8004
www.insigniakitchenandbath.com

Exceptional custom cabinetry.

CRYSTAL
a fine name in cabinetry

www.ccworks.com

CHICAGO KITCHEN DESIGN GROUP
1332 The Merchandise Mart
Chicago, IL 60654
312-245-0100
fax 312-464-8941

KITCHEN & BATH DESIGN CONCEPT
1519 East Main Street
St. Charles, IL 60174
630-377-4059
fax 630-584-7817

BARRINGTON KITCHEN & BATH STUDIO
319 West Northwest Highway
Barrington, IL 60010
847-381-3084
fax 847-277-1406

LAMANTIA KITCHEN DESIGN
9100 Ogden
Brookfield, IL 60513
708-387-9900
fax 708-485-2023

WICKETS FINE CABINETRY
712 Vernon Avenue
Glencoe, IL 60022
847-835-0868
fax 847-835-7082

anyone in the world.

He chose Deborah Oertle and the staff at Rutt of Chicago. His requirements were simple. The designer and cabinetry had to be the best. The design team had to share Charlie's philosophy that even though the ingredients may be gathered from the same palette, each creation is new and unique.

Rutt of Chicago's owner Deborah Oertle has engaged clients for over 20 years with a unique business strategy. "We design the Mercedes for the first time every time. We've created an environment that serves as a demonstration kitchen for Charlie Trotter's restaurant and a television studio for Charlie's upcoming PBS cooking series." The kitchen has also been featured in numerous publications.

This same team is available to help you create the kitchen of your dreams. Call for an appointment, or stop by our showroom at the Merchandise Mart and see the kind of professionalism and attitude that met Charlie Trotter's high standards.

continued from page **455**

IDEA COMPANIES ....**(847) 998-1205**
1132 Waukegan Road, Glenview   Fax: (847) 998-8277
See Add on Page: 474   800 Extension: 6154
Principal/Owner: Frank Quintaro & Luis Torrese
Website: www.ideacompanies.com e-mail: idea@ideacompanies.com
Description: Also visit our Chicago showroom at 3812 N. Elston Avenue,
Chicago, IL 60618. Tel: 773-379-0050 Fax: 773-279-0060

INSIGNIA KITCHEN & BATH DESIGN GROUP, LTD................**(847) 381-7950**
1435 S. Barrington Road, Barrington   Fax: (847) 381-8004
See Add on Page: 460   800 Extension: 6159
Principal/Owner: Bryan Zolfo
Website: www.insigniakitchenandbath.com
e-mail: bzolfo@insigniakitchenand bath.com
Description: Winners of the National Kitchen and Bath Association James Foster,
CKD Memorial Award for Design Excellence for the year 2000 !

KARLSON KITCHENS ....**(847) 491-1300**
1815 Central Street, Evanston   Fax: (847) 491-0100
See Add on Page: 458, 459, 701   800 Extension: 1229
Principal/Owner: David Karlson
Website: www.karlsonkitchens.com e-mail: karlkit@wwa.com
Description: We have been designing and installing finer kitchens and master
bathrooms for over 30 years.

KITCHEN & BATH VISIONS, INC. ....**(847) 966-0091**
7911 W. Golf Road, Morton Grove   Fax: (847) 966-0173
See Add on Page: 467   800 Extension: 6188
Principal/Owner: Jack Wimer
Website: www.kbvisions.com e-mail: info@kbvisions.com
Description: BRAND NEW SHOWROOM !!

KITCHENS & ADDITIONS...**(847) 825-6622**
817 W. Devon, Park Ridge   Fax: (847) 825-6625
See Add on Page: 486   800 Extension: 1011
Principal/Owner: Terry Coldwell

KRENGEL & ASSOCIATES, INC...**(312) 644-4466**
1348 Merchandise Mart, Chicago   Fax: (312) 644-4465
See Add on Page: 472, 473   800 Extension: 6198
Principal/Owner: Ken Krengel
Website: www.woodmode.com e-mail: katherine@krengel.com

LEMONT KITCHEN & BATH, INC. ....**(630) 257-8144**
106 Stephen Street, Lemont   Fax: (630) 257-8142
See Add on Page: 475   800 Extension: 6209
Principal/Owner: Gary A. Lichlyter
e-mail: lemontkb@flash.net

HOWARD MILLER KITCHENS-BATHS-ADDITIONS ....**(847) 291-7050**
3026 Commercial Avenue, Northbrook   Fax: (847) 291-7075
See Add on Page: 469   800 Extension: 1100
Principal/Owner: Howard M. Miller
Website: www.howardmillerkitchens.com
e-mail: info@howardmillerkitchens.com
Description: Design/Build company specializing in kitchen and bath remodeling.
Northbrook showroom boosts a wide selection of materials.

NUHAUS..**(847) 831-1330**
1665 Old Skokie Road, Highland Park   Fax: (847) 831-1337
See Add on Page: 442, 443, 485   800 Extension: 6240
Principal/Owner: Doug Durbin
Website: www.nuhauscabinetry.com

continued on page **476**

Customer Service ❖ Design ❖ Sales

Installation and Project Management available

Kitchen & Bath
VISIONS INC.

*Where to go for the
service you expect...*

'9 West Golf Road, Morton Grove, IL 60053 Ph: 847.966.0091
www.kbvision.com   E-mail: info@kbvisions.com

Anything Less Could Cost You More!

Howard Miller
Kitchens • Baths • Additions

3026 Commercial Ave., Northbrook, IL 60062
(847) 291–7050

Showroom Hours
M – F 9 am – 5 pm and Sat 10 am – 2 pm
or by appointment

A wide range of services from design to complete
remodeling and installation or product only

One of the widest selections of kitchen and bath
products in the Chicagoland area since 1986

Authorized dealer of major brand names such as
Bertch,Ultracraft and Legacy cabinets, Dupont Corian,
Kohler, Jacuzzi, Elkay,Grohe, KWC and ARWA
plumbing products, flooring and ceramic tile

Call today to see how we can help on your project!

BARRINGTON HOMEWORKS

kitchens
designed
uniquely
for you.

(847) 381-9526
fax (847) 381-9592

cucine del veneto

innovative italian kitchens

Suite 1344   Merchandise Mart Plaza   Chicago

p 312.644.9520   f 312.644.9523

The basic function of a house is shelter. But there's an *art* to transforming a collection *of* rooms into a home. For instance, *making* a kitchen "yours" means designing it just for *you*. It means understanding how you *feel* when you're sipping that first morning cup, or sneaking a few scoops of Rocky Road *at* midnight. At best, it means creating a space that always welcomes you *home*. A tall order? Not for Wood-Mode. We've been doing it for over 55 years.

Visit one of our Chicago Showrooms:

Abruzzo Kitchen & Bath Studio, Inc.
7612 W. North Avenue
Elmwood Park
708-453-1000
www.AbruzzoKitchens.com

Better Kitchens, Inc.
7640 N. Milwaukee Avenue
Niles
847-967-7070
www.BetterKitchens.com

Cabinetwerks, Ltd.
185 Milwaukee Avenue, Suite 110
Lincolnshire
847-821-9421
www.Cabinetwerks.com

Distinctive Kitchen Designs
201-A S. Main Street
Wauconda
847-526-7822
www.DistinctiveKitchens.com

Karlson Kitchens
1815 Central Street
Evanston
847-491-1300
www.KarlsonKitchens.com

Lee Lumber
3250 N. Kedzie Avenue, Chicago
633 W. Pershing, Chicago
773-509-6700
www.LeeLumber.com

All Wood-Mode Cabinetry comes with a Lifetime Limited Warranty.

A potting area with mesh doors and apothecary drawers adds flair, function and convenience.

A casual, yet stylish hutch is the perfect accent piece, providing display space as well as storage.

A second island affords a beautiful solution for separating prep and clean-up areas.

Wood·Mode®
FINE CUSTOM CABINETRY

©2000 Wood-Mode, Inc.

SCAVOLINI

Lemont Kitchen & Bath
Inc

Quality is in the Details

Available exclusively at Lemont Kitchen & Bath

630.257.8144

lemontkb@flash.net

continued from page **466**

ROECKER CABINETS ....**(309) 266-5051**
850 N. Main Street, Morton   Fax: (309) 263-2454
See Add on Page: 480, 481   800 Extension: 1196
<u>Principal/Owner:</u> Kurt Schmidgall
<u>e-mail:</u> roecker@dpc.net

RUTT OF CHICAGO ....**(312) 670-7888**
200 World Trade Center - Merchandise Mart 13-160, Chicago   Fax: (312) 822-9223
See Add on Page: 464, 465   800 Extension: 1112
<u>Principal/Owner:</u> Deborah J. Oertle

TOMTEN, INC. CABINET DESIGNS ....**(630) 654-0051**
211 W. Burlington Avenue, Clarendon Hills   Fax: (630) 654-0092
See Add on Page: 487   800 Extension: 1220
<u>Principal/Owner:</u> Nels Anderson

"Outside of the chair,
the *teapot* is the most
ubiquitous and important
design element in
the domestic environment."

David McFaddon

476

ARTISTIC

KITCHEN DESIGNS

"Professional Design Through Complete Installation"

SHOWROOM

1600 W. Sixteenth Street
Oak Brook, IL

630.571.4567
fax 630.571.4572

Präzision.

Ours is a superior product that most of Chicago cannot offer. Kitchen and bathroom cabinetry elevated to fine furniture. The perfection of European design. The precision of German craftsmanship. Ergonomics elevated to art. Let us be your single contact from concept to realization of your vision.

_Perfektion.

ROECKER
CABINETS
INC.

Old World Craftsmanship
Since 1951

From traditional to ultra-modern contemporary,
Roecker Cabinets can design and build your
cabinetry and furniture needs where only
your imagination is our limitation.

NEW SHOWROOM
GATEWAY SQUARE: 777 NORTH YORK ROAD, SUITE 13
HINSDALE, IL 60521
630-789-9129 FAX 630-789-9169
FACTORY: 850 NORTH MAIN
MORTON, IL 61550
309-266-5051 FAX 309-263-2154

The Design Studio , Ltd.

Kitchens and Home Environs

Warm, inviting colors & textures flow seamlessly through our
Maple french Chateau Kitchen as well as in our
Traditional Soft Cherry designs.
~ ~ ~
You deserve your personal space.
Engage us now to fulfill your dreams.

The Design Studio, Ltd.

Kitchens and Home Environs

Creative use of countertop and backsplash materials
bring a calming sense of continuity to our
"family friendly" island kitchen designs.
~ ~ ~
You deserve your personal space.
Engage us now to fulfill your dreams.

Finally...
Chicago's Own
Home & Design
Sourcebook

The CHICAGO HOME BOOK, a comprehensive hands-on
design sourcebook to building, remodeling, decorating, furnishing
and landscaping a luxury home in Chicago and its suburbs,
is a "must-have" reference for the Chicagoland homeowner.
At over 700 pages, this beautiful, full-color hard cover
volume is quite simply the most complete, well-organized
reference to the Chicagoland home industry. It covers all aspects
of the process, with hundreds of listings of local home industry
professionals, accompanied by hundreds of inspiring photographs.
You will also find articles to assist in planning and completing a
project. The CHICAGO HOME BOOK tells you how to
find what you need when you need it.

Order your copy today!

CHICAGO
HOME
BOOK

Published by
The Ashley Group
1350 E. Touhy Avenue • Des Plaines, IL 60018
Toll Free 888-458-1750   Fax 847.390.2902
E-mail: ashleybooksales@cahners.com

Design and craftsmanship combined for excellence.

From Our Imagination...
    To Your Gourmet Kitchen...
        For the Heart of Your Home...
            Nels Anderson, Designer

 **Cabinetry Designs**

211 W. Burlington Avenue, Clarendon Hills, IL 60514
PH (630) 654-0051 FAX (630) 654-0092

 Design Connection: Barbara Young Interiors, Ltd.

Fixtures
& Hardware

AQUAWORKS ....**(847) 869-2111**
2308 Main Street, Evanston   Fax: (847) 869-2080
See Add on Page: 492, 493   800 Extension: 6011
Principal/Owner: Annette Carnow
Website: www.aquaworks.com   e-mail: home@aquaworks.com
Description: Everything to create the perfect bath, featuring a wide selection of
unique products from around the world.   Additional location at: Merchandise
Mart, Suite 1326, Chicago, IL 60654.   (866) 246-2111

BARTLETT SHOWER DOOR COMPANY ....**(773) 975-0069**
2219 N. Clybourn, Chicago   Fax: (773) 975-0099
See Add on Page: 489   800 Extension: 1098
Principal/Owner: John Klemptner

BATHHAUS ....**(847) 277-1313**
860 S. Northwest Highway, Barrington   Fax: (847) 277-7132
See Add on Page: 496   800 Extension: 1224
Principal/Owner: Jay Eiring
Website: bathhaus.com   e-mail: bathhaus@speakeasy.net

CRAWFORD SUPPLY CO. ....**(847) 967-0550**
8150 Lehigh Avenue, Morton Grove   Fax: (847) 967-2183
See Add on Page: 490, 491   800 Extension: 1046
Principal/Owner: Jeff Heksh

STONE GALLERY, INC. ....**(800) 733-4064**
1501 S. Michigan Ave., Chicago
See Add on Page: 494, 495   800 Extension: 1038
Principal/Owner: Shankar Vyyuru
Website: stonegalleryinc.com
Description: Importers and fabricators of natural stone. Exclusive distributors of
Rolex-Bain- Bath tubs; faucets; saunas, bidets.

488

"There are painters who
transform the sun into a yellow spot,
but there are others who, with the
help of their art and
intelligence, transform a yellow
spot into the sun."

Pablo Picasso

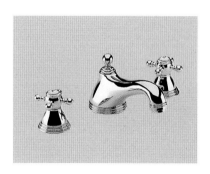

GROHE®

FAUCET TECHNOLOGY

Manufacturing specialists of stainless steel, and colored sinkware. The Kindred spirit shines, in over 100 models for residential and commercial applications.

KINDRED

ROLEX
BAIN

BY

STONE GALLERY INC.

1501 S. Michigan Ave.	6800 S. Rt.83
Chicago, IL 60605	Darien, IL 60561
phone 312.431.3800	phone 630.850.9651
fax 312.431.8700	fax 630.850.9661

Toll Free 1.800.733.4064

KALLISTA®

Kitchen & Bath
Surfaces

ANN SACKS ....**(312) 923-0919**
  501 North Wells Street, Chicago   Fax: (312) 913-0906
  See Add on Page: 499   800 Extension: 1059
  <u>Principal/Owner:</u> Debbie Winton
  <u>Website:</u> www.annsacks.com <u>e-mail:</u> dwinton@astsinc.com
  <u>Description:</u> Tile, Stone and exculsive kitchen/bath fixtures.

EXOTIC MARBLE & TILE ....**(847) 763-1863**
  8055 Monticello Ave., Skokie   Fax: (847) 763-1865
  See Add on Page: 498   800 Extension: 1068
  <u>Principal/Owner:</u> Angelo Angelon
  <u>Website:</u> www.exoticmarble.com

NORTH STAR SURFACES, LLC ....**(800) 383-9784**
  23 Empire Drive, St. Paul   Fax: (833) 378-9110
  See Add on Page: 614, 615   800 Extension: 1241
  <u>Principal/Owner:</u> Chuck Geerdes
  <u>Description:</u> Distributor of Avonite, Hi-Macs, Silestone, Transolid

PARKSITE, INC. ....**(630) 761-9490**
  1563 Hubbard Avenue, Batavia   Fax: (630) 761-6801
  See Add on Page: 500, 564, 565   800 Extension: 1174
  <u>Principal/Owner:</u> George Patee
  <u>Website:</u> www.parksite.com

EXOTIC MARBLE & TILE, INC
IMPORTERS - DISTRIBUTORS - MANUFACTURERS

MARBLE • GRANITE • LIMESTONE • TUMBLED STONE
BORDERS AND ACCENTS • COUNTERTOPS • FIREPLACES
PEDESTALS • COLUMNS • FLOORS • WALLS • DESIGN

8055 N. Monticello Ave.
Skokie, IL 60076
ph 847.763.1863   fax 847.763.1865
www.exoticmarble.com

Ann Sacks

501 N. Wells Street
Chicago, IL 60610
Phone: 312.923.0919
Fax: 312.923.0906
www.annsacks.com

tile   stone   plumbing

Appliances

DACOR DISTINCTIVE APPLIANCES ....**(630) 285-9065**
450 East Devon, Suite 140, Itasca   Fax: (630) 285-9067
See Add on Page: 512, 513   800 Extension: 6078
Principal/Owner: S. Michael Joseph / Anthony B. Joseph
Website: www.dacor.com
Description: An ISO 9001 Corporation. Family owned company based in
Pasadena, CA. All American made products.

LAKEVIEW APPLIANCE DISTRIBUTING ....**(630) 238-1280**
1071 Thorndale Avenue, Bensenville   Fax: (630) 238-1926
See Add on Page: 511   800 Extension: 1139
Principal/Owner: Philip Gafka

OAKTON DISTRIBUTORS, INC. ....**(847) 228-5858**
780 Lively Boulevard, Elk Grove Village   Fax: (847) 228-5803
See Add on Page: 502 - 510   800 Extension: 1074
Principal/Owner: Donny Danti
Website: www.oakton.com e-mail: sales@oakton.com
Description: Distributor of high-end kitchen products by Sub-Zero, Wolf
Gourmet, Gaggenau, Bosch, Best by Broan, Frank & Scotsman.

OAKTON
distributors, inc.

Representing:

Sub-Zero

Wolf

Gaggenau

Bosch

Best by Broan

Scotsman

Franke

780 Lively Boulevard
Elk Grove Village, IL 60007-1425
Phone 847/228-5858
Fax 847/228-5803
800/262-5866
www.oakton.com

Call us for a showroom appointment
or for a dealer close to you.

Live Kitchens
to experience.

Cooking
Demonstrations
by a Chef.

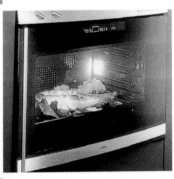

Showroom
Instructions.

Come see all
of the colors.

Or call and
ask questions.

An Affiliate of Sub-Zero Freezer Company, Inc.

The hottest commercial stoves available for your kitchen.

Knobs are also available in black.

INSTEAD OF GOING TO THE REFRIGERATOR, BRING THE REFRIGERATOR TO YOU.

he Sub-Zero 700 Series hides the refrigerator anywhere it's
eeded: in the workout room, near the home entertainment center,
ven next to the sink where you wash the vegetables. For more
leas, call for our free, beautiful full-line catalog, and the name
f your nearest dealer.

SUB-ZERO

The Ultimate Range Hood Designed And Hand Crafted By Italy

**STEAMING TOWARD PERFECT
RESULTS – WITHOUT PRESSURE.**

Gaggenau's new combination steam oven is the
first built-in appliance in the world to combine
the advantage of non-pressurized steaming and
convection. It brings professional-style steam
cooking into your home.

THE DIFFERENCE IS GAGGENAU.

THE PERFECT BLEND OF BEAUTY, PERFORMANCE, AND INNOVATION.

The Bosch dishwasher line has become the benchmark in kitchen designs. Not only does Bosch give you the most interior room, quietest operation, tops in efficiency, and unsurpassed quality, Bosch is also breaking new grounds with the new "Integra" design™. Whether your plans call for a complete remodeling project or to replace an existing dishwasher, the "Integra" design is your answer.

■ ■ ■ Because there's more to life than work, work, work. What would I do without my Franke?

Elements® undermount sink components are available through kitchen professionals. Sink and faucet catalog $3.

FRANKE®

Kitchen Sinks
Faucets
Water Dispensing Systems
Disposers
Custom Accessories

■ Technology   ■ Quality   ■ Design

I think I've died and gone to the kitchen.

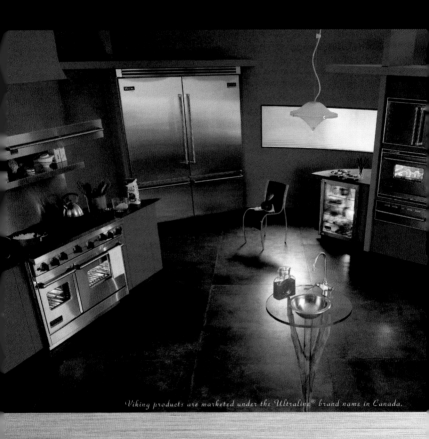

Viking products are marketed under the Ultraline® brand name in Canada.

The complete Viking kitchen is a chef's paradise. From the range to the refrigerator, every appliance offers the same superior performance and features you'd find in a professional kitchen.
And with 14 designer finishes to choose from,
your kitchen is sure to be a vision.
Ahhh, heaven.

VIKING®
www.vikingrange.com

LakeView
appliance distributing

For a showroom appointment or a dealer location close to you, call (630)238-1280 or toll-free 1-877-546-1280. 1071 Thorndale Avenue, Bensenville, IL 60106

The life of the kitchen™

A legendary leader in cooking technology for over 35 years! Furnishing the finest built-in contemporary & commercial-style appliances for your lifestyle.

"God is in the details."

Ludwig Mies van der Rohe

519

Elegant

Touches

Fine, handcrafted interior architectural elements are the details that distinguish the highest quality custom-designed and -built luxury homes and remodeling projects from all others. They lend richness and elegance, infusing a home with character and originality. Even an empty room can speak volumes about the personal taste and style of its owners with cabinetry, moldings, ceiling medallions, chair rails, staircases, mirrors and mantels created and installed by the best in the business. Windows, doors, and hardware must endure the rigors of regular use, synthesizing beauty and function into high quality design statements made to stand the test of time. Bring your eye for detail as you explore the finest in architectural elements on the following pages.

PRICING A POWER LIBRARY

• A 15 by 16 foot library, fully paneled in cherry, mahogany or oak, some cabinets, with moldings, desk with hidden computer,coffered ceilings: $20,000 to $30,000.

• In a 16 by 24 foot two-story study, less paneling and more cabinetry of cherry, mahogany or oak, heavy with moldings, and radius work, desk with more pull out and hidden compartments for fax machine, small copier, bar with leaded glass cabinet fronts and a marble top, built-in humidor, and heavily coffered ceilings with multiple steps: $40,000.

WALL TO WALL ELEGANCE

Nowhere is the commitment to elegant living through quality materials more apparent than in the selection of cabinets and millwork. Representing a significant percentage of the overall cost of a new or renovated home, sophisticated homeowners use this opportunity to declare their dedication to top quality.

Architectural millwork, made to order according to a set of architectural drawings, is becoming an increasingly popular luxury upgrade in new and remodeled homes. Creating a richly nostalgic atmosphere that reminds homeowners of the comfort and security of a grandparents' home, or the elegance of a club they've been in, the traditional styling of architectural features leads them to request drawings heavy on moldings and other fancy embellishments.

Elegant libraries, dens or sitting rooms dressed with fashionable raised panel cabinetry and special moldings are often included in the plans for new homes and remodeling projects. As a homeowner considering how and where to install millwork, ask yourself questions like these:

• How is the room used? Will a study be used for work or for solitude? Entertaining or a second office? Will it have to function as both a working office and an elegant room?

• How are the cabinets and shelves used? Books, collectibles, audio-video equipment, computer, fax or copy machines?

• What look do you want? You may want to consider "dressing" your rooms in different woods. You may like the rich look and feel of cherry paneling in your library, mahogany in the foyer, oak in a guest room and plaster in a dining room.

• Will the interior millwork choices work with the exterior architecture? A colonial home reminiscent of Mount Vernon should be filled with authentic details, like "dog-ear" corners, that create classic luxury. Using millwork inside a modern home can add interest and warmth to one or many rooms.

TIME IS OF THE ESSENCE

Hand-crafted high quality woodwork cannot be rushed. Millwork specialists encourage clients to contact them as early as possible with a clear idea of what kind of architectural statement they wish to make. The earlier you plan these details, the more options you'll have. Wainscoting with raised panels has to be coordinated with electrical outlets, window and door openings; beamed ceilings with light fixtures, and crown moldings with heating vents.

Hold a preliminary meeting before construction begins while it's early enough to incorporate innovative or special requirements into your plans. The more time you can devote to design (two to three weeks is recommended), the better your result will be. You're creating a custom millwork package that's never been designed for anyone before. Investments made on the front end are the most valuable. Ask about design fees, timelines and costs per revision. Keep your builder up to date on all of your millwork plans.

Drawings can be as detailed as you require. If you want to see the intricacies of a radius molding before you contract for it, let the millwork specialist know your requirements. Ask to see wood samples, with and without stain or paint.

Try to visit installed projects to get a firsthand feel for the quality of a specialist's work and to develop clearer ideas for your own home.

Changes made after an order is placed are costly. Therefore, if you're unsure, don't make a commitment. Add accessory moldings and other details as you see the project taking shape.

Expect a heavily laden room to take at least five to eight weeks to be delivered, about the time from the hanging of drywall to the installation of flooring. Installation takes one to three weeks, depending on the size and scope of the project.

THE ELEGANT REFINEMENT OF CUSTOM CABINETRY

Handcrafted custom cabinets are a recognizable standard of excellence which lend refinement and beauty to a home. Built in a kitchen, library, bathroom, or closet, or as a free-standing entertainment system or armoire, custom cabinets are a sophisticated signature statement.

There are no limits on the possibilities of custom cabinets. The requirements of any space, no matter how unusual, can be creatively met. The endless combinations of style and detail promise unique cabinetry to homeowners who are searching for an individual look, while the first class craftsmanship of experienced, dedicated woodworkers promises unparalleled quality.

DESIGNING HANDSOME CABINETRY

Cabinetry is a major element in your dream home, so let your imagination soar. Collect pictures of cabinets, noting the particular features you like. Cabinet makers appreciate visual examples because it's easier to interpret your desires from pictures than from words. Pictures crystallize your desires.

HOW TO RECOGNIZE CUSTOM CABINET QUALITY

1. Proper sanding which results in a smooth, beautiful finish.
2. Superior detail work, adding unexpected elegance.
3. Classic application of design features and architectural details.
4. Beautiful, functional hardware selections.
5. High quality hinges and drawer glides.
6. Superior overall functionality.

WHY YOU WANT A PROFESSIONAL DESIGNER

521

- They rely on experience to deliver you a custom product. Computer tools are great, but nothing replaces the experienced eye.
- They have established relationships with other trades, and can get top quality glass fronts for your cabinets, or granite for a bar top.
- Their design ability can save you significant dollars in installation.
- They know how to listen to their clients and help them get the results they dream of.

PRICING OF CUSTOM KITCHEN CABINETS

• **Deluxe Kitchen –Face frame style cabinets or oak, maple or pine, with raised panel doors; crown molding on upper cabinetry, decorative hardware, wood nosing (cap) around counter tops: $10,000 - $20,000**
• **Upgrade To – Shaker inset-style cabinets in cherrywood, painted finish: $20,000 additional.**

When you first meet with a cabinet maker, take your blueprints, and if possible, your builder, architect or designer. Be prepared to answer questions like:

• What is the exterior style of your home and do you want to continue that style inside?

• How will you the use the cabinets? Cutlery trays, pull-out bins? Shelves for books, CDs, computer software, collections?

• What styles and embellishments do you like? Shaker, Prairie, Country English, contemporary? Fancy moldings, wainscoting, inlaid banding? Use your Idea Notebook to communicate your preferences.

• Do you prefer particular woods? Cherry, oak, sycamore, or the more exotic ebony, Bubinga or Swiss pearwood? (Species must be selected on the basis of the finish you want.)

• Will cabinetry be visible from other rooms in the house? Must it match previously installed or selected flooring or countertops? (Take samples.)

MANAGING THE LENGTHY PROCESS OF A CUSTOM CABINET PROJECT

With plenty of unhurried time, you can be more creative, while allowing the woodworkers the time they need to deliver a top quality product. Take your blueprints to a cabinet maker early. Although installation occurs in the latter part of the construction, measuring usually takes place very early on.

If your project is carefully thought out, you won't be as likely to change your mind, but a contingency budget of ten to 15 percent for changes (like adding radiuses or a lacquered finish) is recommended.

Custom cabinets for a whole house, (kitchen, butler's pantry, library, master bath, and three to four additional baths) may take ten to 15 weeks depending on the details involved (heavy carving adds significant time). Cabinets for a kitchen remodeling may take two months.

THE DRAMATIC EFFECT OF EXCEPTIONAL STAIRCASES

Take full advantage of the opportunity to upgrade your new or remodeled home with a spectacular staircase, by contacting the stairmakers early in the design phase. Their familiarity with products, standards and building codes will be invaluable to you and your architect, contractor, or interior designer.

Visit a stair showroom or workroom on your own or with your architect, interior designer or builder, during the architectural drawing phase of your project. Discuss how you can achieve what you want at a cost conscious price. Choosing a standard size radius of 24 inches, in place of a custom 25 1/2 inch radius, for example, will help control costs.

Although your imagination may know no bounds in designing a staircase, hard and fast local building codes may keep your feet on the ground. Codes are not static, and stairmakers constantly update their files on local restrictions regarding details like the rise and run of a stair, and the size and height of rails.

THE STAIR-BUILDING PROCESS

The design of your stairs should be settled in the rough framing phase of the overall building project. If you work within this time frame, the stairs will be ready for installation after the drywall is hung and primer has been applied to the walls in the stair area.

Stairs can be built out of many woods. The most popular choice is red oak, but cherry, maple, walnut and mahogany are also used. If metal railings are preferred, you'll need to contact a specialist.

A top quality stair builder will design your stairs to your specifications. Consider the views you want of the house while on the stairs, and what kind of front entrance presentation you prefer. You may want to see the stairs from a particular room. An expert also can make suggestions regarding comfort and safety, and what styles will enhance the overall architecture.

Plans which are drawn on a computer can be changed with relative ease and can be printed at full size. This is very helpful to homeowners who want to see exactly what the stairs will look like in their home. The full-size plans can be taken to the job site, and tacked to the floor to be experienced firsthand.

THE POLISHED ARTISTRY OF CUSTOM GLASS AND MIRROR

A room can be transformed through the use of custom decorative glass and mirrors. Artists design intricately patterned, delicately painted glass to add light and architectural interest in all kinds of room dividers and partitions. Glass artistry can be based on any design, playing on the texture of carpet, the pattern of the brick, or repeating a fabric design. A glass block wall or floor panel can add the touch of distinction that sets a home above the others. Stained glass, usually associated with beautiful classic styling, can be designed in any style – from contemporary to art deco to traditional.

USING PLASTER DETAILING

Plaster architectural detailing and trim add a distinctive look to any home. Most often used in out of the way places, like in ceiling medallions or crown moldings, the high relief detailing is especially impressive.

PRICES OF CUSTOM STAIRS

Stairs can cost anywhere from $200 to $95,000, depending on size, materials and the complexity of design:
- Red Oak spiral staircase, upgraded railing: $10,000
- Red Oak circle stairs, standard railings on both sides and around upstairs landing: $13,000
- Six flights of Red Oak circle stairs stacked one atop the next, with landings at the top of each stair: $95,000
- Walnut or mahogany adds 50 percent to the overall cost.

DOOR #1, #2, OR #3?

• **Door #1 – Six panel oak door with sidelights of leaded glass: $1,700-$2,000**

• **Door #2 – Six panel oak door with lead and beveled glass: $3,000**

• **Door #3 – Oversized, all matched oak, with custom designed leaded glass and brass, sidelights, elliptical top over door: $15,000**

• **Allow $500 to $1,500 for doorknobs, hinges and other hardware.**

Top specialists, like those presented in the following pages, take great care in designing and delivering unique, top quality products. They work with top quality fabricated products, with the highest quality of beveling and edge work.

THE ARTISTIC PROCESS

Glass specialists will visit your home or building site to make recommendations and estimate costs and delivery time. Study their samples and if they have a showroom, go take a look. Perhaps you could visit an installed project. Seeing the possibilities can stimulate your imagination and open your eyes to new ideas in ways pictures simply cannot.

Allow a month to make a decision and four weeks for custom mirror work delivery, and ten to 14 weeks for decorated glass.

In order to have the glass or mirror ready for installation before the carpet is laid, decisions must be made during the framing or rough construction phase in a new home or remodeling job. Mirrored walls are installed as painting is being completed, so touch-ups can be done while painters are still on site.

Expect to pay a 50 percent deposit on any order after seeing a series of renderings and approving a final choice. Delivery generally is included in the price.

THE DRAMATIC EFFECT OF CUSTOM WINDOWS AND DOORS

Just as we're naturally drawn to establish eye contact with each other, our attention is naturally drawn to the "eyes" of a home, the windows, skylights and glass doors.

These very important structural features, when expertly planned and designed, add personality and distinction to your interior while complementing the exterior architectural style of your home.

After lumber, windows are the most expensive part of a home. Take the time to investigate the various features and qualities of windows, skylights and glass doors. Visit a specialty store offering top of the line products and service and take advantage of their awareness of current products as well as their accumulated knowledge.

Visit a showroom with your designer, builder or architect. Because of the rapidly changing requirements of local building codes, it's difficult for them to keep current on what can be installed in your municipality. In addition, the dizzying pace of energy efficiency improvements over the past five years can easily outrun the knowledge of everyone but the window specialist. Interior designers can help you understand proper placement and scale in relation to furnishings and room use.

As you define your needs ask questions about alternatives or options, such as energy efficiency, ease of maintenance, appropriate styles to suit the exterior architecture, and interior.

Top quality windows offer high energy efficiency, the best woodwork and hardware, and comprehensive service and guarantees (which should not be pro-rated). Good service agreements cover everything, including the locks.

Every home of distinction deserves an entry that exudes a warm welcome and a strong sense of homecoming. When we think of "coming home," we envision an entry door first, the strong, welcoming look of it, a first impression of the home behind it. To get the best quality door, contact a door or millwork specialist with a reputation for delivering top quality products. They can educate you on functionality, and wood and size choices and availability, as well as appropriate style. Doors are also made of steel or fiberglass, but wood offers the most flexibility for custom design.

Since doors are a permanent part of your architecture, carefully shop for the design that best reflects the special character of your home. Allow two to three weeks for delivery of a simple door and eight to 12 weeks if you're choosing a fancy front door. Doors are installed during the same phase as windows, before insulation and drywall.

FABULOUS HARDWARE ADDS DESIGN FLAIR

Door and cabinet hardware, towel bars and accessories add style and substance to interiors. Little things truly do make the difference – by paying attention to the selection of top quality hardware in long-lasting, great-looking finishes, you help define your signature style and commitment to quality in a custom home. There are hundreds of possibilities, so when you visit a specialty showroom, ask the sales staff for their guidance. They can direct you towards the products that will complement your established design style and help you stay within the limits of your budget. When a rim lock for the front door can easily cost $500, and knobs can be $10 each, the advice of a knowledgeable expert is priceless.

Most products are readily available in a short time frame, with the exception of door and cabinetry hardware. Allow eight weeks for your door hardware, and three to four weeks for cabinetry selections. Since accessory hardware is usually in stock, changing cabinet knobs, hooks and towel bars is a quick and fun way to get a new look. ∎

LUXURY GLASS & MIRROR

• **Mirrored Exercise Room:** Floor to ceiling, wall to wall mirrors, on two or three walls. Allow at least a month, from initial measuring, to squaring off & balancing walls, to installation. Price for polished mirror starts around $9 per square foot. Cut-outs for vent outlets cost extra.

• **Custom Shower Doors:** Frameless bent, or curved shower doors are popular luxury upgrades. Made of clear or sandblasted heavy glass–1/2" to 3/8" thick. $2,000 and up.

• **Stained Glass Room Divider:** Contemporary, clear on clear design, with a hint of color. Approximately 4' X 6', inset into a wall. $4,500.

• **Glass Dining Table:** Custom designed with bevel edge, 48" X 96" with two glass bases. $1,200.

THREE TIPS FOR DOOR HARDWARE

1. Use three hinges to a door–it keeps the door straight.
2. Match all hardware–hinges, knobs, handles, all in the same finish. use levers or knobs–don't mix.
3. Use a finish that will last.

Millwork

ARCHITECTURAL DISTRIBUTORS ....**(312) 661-1666**
13-161 Merchandise Mart, Chicago   Fax: (312) 661-1008
See Add on Page: 527   800 Extension: 1216
<u>Principal/Owner:</u> Michael Hoerl
<u>Website:</u> www.archdist.com

ARLEN- JACOB MANUFACTURING ....**(815) 485-4777**
2 H Ford Court, New Lenox   Fax: (815) 485-4782
See Add on Page: 531, 540   800 Extension: 1226
<u>Principal/Owner:</u> Dave Klein

BERNHARD WOODWORK, LTD. ....**(847) 291-1040**
3670 Woodhead Drive, Northbrook   Fax: (847) 291-1184
See Add on Page: 529   800 Extension: 1116
<u>Principal/Owner:</u> Mark Bernhard
<u>e-mail:</u> BernhardNB@aol.com
<u>Description:</u> Since 1965 Bernhard Woodwork, Ltd. manufactures, delivers and installs premium custom architectural woodwork for commercial, retail and residential clients.

PAOLI WOODWORK, INC. ....**(847) 928-2630**
10150 Franklin Avenue, Franklin Park   Fax: (847) 928-2631
See Add on Page: 530   800 Extension: 1175
<u>Principal/Owner:</u> Tom Paoli

PRAIRIE WOODOWORKING ....**(708) 386-0603**
343 Harrison Street, Oak Park   Fax: (708) 386-0603
See Add on Page: 532   800 Extension: 6262
<u>Principal/Owner:</u> Paul Pezalla
<u>Website:</u> www.bitsmart.com/radiator   <u>e-mail:</u> radiator@bitsmart.com

PREFERRED MILLWORK ....**(630) 293-4406**
980 Hawthorne Lane, West Chicago   Fax: (630) 293-4407
See Add on Page: 528, 560   800 Extension: 1202
<u>Principal/Owner:</u> Patrick Riccobene

WEATHER
SHIELD
WINDOWS & DOORS

PREFERRED MILLWORK
enterprises, inc.

Architectural Woodwork • *Windows* • *Doors*

980 Hawthorne Lane, West Chicago, IL 60185
(630) 293-4406 • Fax: (630) 293-4407

The Bernhard Solution

quality

performance

Solutions. Created with knowledge. Knowledge, earned by experience. The strength of our people.

As a leading source for architectural woodwork, our team of skilled craftsmen create beautiful, reliable, and high-impact custom products. Using precision, state-of-the-art technology to assure flawless execution of all design details. We build it right the first time. No call-backs and no hassles.

Our strategic partnerships with each client also assures that the finished project meets your specific needs.

Leading-edge, products built by experience– The Bernhard Solution.

experience

- Banks
- Offices
- Hospitals
- Corporate Headquarters
- High End Retail
- Custom Residential
- Museums
- Casinos
- Courtrooms
- Universities

people

BERNHARD WOODWORK LTD.
3670 Woodhead Drive, Northbrook, IL, 60062 Ph: 847-291-1040 Fx: 847-291-1184

Designers
&
Builders of

Fine

Architectural

Millwork,

Staircases

and

Ballustrades

Arlen - Jacob Manufacturing Co.

2-H Ford Court, New Lenox, IL 60451

PRAIRIE
WOODWORKING
Custom Wood Radiator Enclosures

At Prairie Woodworking
we custom design and handcraft
elegant hardwood radiator enclosures.

343 Harrison Street
Oak Park, Illinois 60304
708.386.0603
www.sitsmart.com/radiator

"EVERY TIME WE SAY LET THERE BE! IN ANY FORM, SOMETHING HAPPENS."

Stella Terrill Mann

The Ashley Group
Publishers of Fine Visual Reference for the Discerning Connoisseur
1350 Touhy Ave. • Des Plaines, Illinois 60018
888.458.1750 • FAX 847.390.2902
ashleygroup@cahners.com

Stairs &
Metalworking

ARLEN- JACOB MANUFACTURING ....**(815) 485-4777**
2 H Ford Court, New Lenox   Fax: (815) 485-4782
See Add on Page: 531, 540   800 Extension: 1045
<u>Principal/Owner:</u> Dave Klein

CREATIVE STAIRS ....**(630) 963-5050**
440-450 Odgen Ave., Lisle   Fax: (630) 963-3666
See Add on Page: 534, 535   800 Extension: 1056
<u>Principal/Owner:</u> Eliot Del Longo

CUSTOM WELDING ....**(630) 355-3696**
475 N. River Road, Naperville   Fax: (630) 355-3653
See Add on Page: 536, 537   800 Extension: 6077

LAKE SHORE STAIR ....**(847) 362-3262**
615 E. Park Avenue, Libertyville   Fax: (847) 362-3349
See Add on Page: 538, 539   800 Extension: 1024
<u>Principal/Owner:</u> Chris Jensen

NEIWEEM INDUSTRIES ....**(815) 759-1375**
21 Greenwood Drive, Oakwood Hills   Fax: (815) 759-1377
See Add on Page: 541   800 Extension: 1138
<u>Principal/Owner:</u> Kurt Neiweem

533

Creative Stairs
AND WOODWORKING INC.

Commitment to

Quality...

The staircase in a home will make a lasting impression and set the standard for quality and workmanship found throughout the home. The staircase should be a product of pride.

For 29 years Creative Stairs & Woodworking, Inc. has been creating staircases in the "Old World" tradition- not often or easily found today. Our designers and artisans painstakingly blend the beauty of rich woods, fine metals and other state-of-the-art materials with the precision, clean workmanship of "Old World" craftsman.

Creative Stairs & Woodworking, Inc. does it with "hands-on" involvement and attention to the smallest detail. Whether you choose a sweeping Victorian or a simple Contemporary design, we work closely with you from the planning stage to the final installation to create a warm, lovely staircase that will meet, or even exceed, your greatest expectations. To Creative Stairs & Woodworking, Inc. each staircase is a personal achievement, and the completed product is a true work of art. We take pride in what we do. . . and it shows.

At Creative Stairs & Woodworking, Inc. we see to it that you get what you pay for . . . a staircase that will last more than a lifetime. To learn more about our company and our products, visit our showroom at 440-450 Ogden Avenue, Lisle, Illinois, near Route 355 (North-South Tollway). Our knowledgeable sales staff is available to help you design your staircase and answer your questions.

If you want a Custom Staircase that is a true work of art, call Creative Stairs & Woodworking, Inc. at 630-963-5050. We look forward to working with you to enhance your home.

CUSTOM WOOD STAIRS, RAILINGS AND FIREPLACE MANTELS

SHOWROOM:
440-450 OGDEN AVE. LISLE, IL 60532
PHONE: (630) 963-5050
FAX: (630) 963-3666

Classic

Traditional

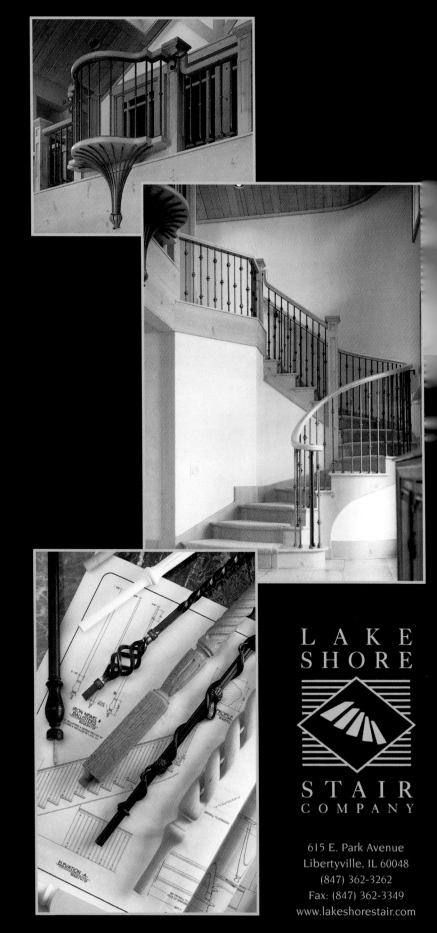

L A K E
S H O R E

S T A I R
C O M P A N Y

615 E. Park Avenue
Libertyville, IL 60048
(847) 362-3262
Fax: (847) 362-3349
www.lakeshorestair.com

Custom Builders of Fine Traditional & Contemporary
Ornamental Stair & Rails Systems.

Designers

&

Builders of

Fine

Architectural

Millwork,

Staircases

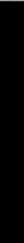

and

Ballustrades

Custom Cabinets

CABINETWERKS...**(847) 821-9421**
185 Milwaukee Avenue Suite 110, Lincolnshire   Fax: (847) 821-9460
See Add on Page: 543   800 Extension: 1117
<u>Principal/Owner:</u> Dave Heigl
<u>Website:</u> www.pickellbuilders.com   <u>e-mail:</u> dheigl@pickellbuilders.com
<u>Description:</u> CabinetWerks is an Orren Pickell Company.
SANDELL CABINETS INC...**(708) 754-0087**
323 W. 195th Street, Glenwood   Fax: (708) 754-8775
See Add on Page: 544   800 Extension: 1173
<u>Principal/Owner:</u> Thomas & Carol Miller

> "Cabinetry helps to define
> and develop the architectural
> qualities of the home."
>
> *Dave Heigl*

542

CabinetWerks
An Orren Pickell Company

185 Milwaukee Avenue, Suite 110, Lincolnshire, IL 60069
Phone: 847.821.9421   Fax: 847.821.9460
E-mail: dheig@pickellbuilders.com   Web: www.pickellbuilders.com

All work shown features

Photography by Linda Oyama Bryan

Sandell Cabinets, Inc.

CUSTOM MADE CABINETS

**323 W. 195th St.
Glenwood, IL 60425
(708) 754-0087 • Fax (708) 754-8775**

1-800-956-1199

Decorative
Glass & Mirrors

**CHARDONNAY DESIGNS, INC./
SGO OF THE NORTH SHORE**..**(847) 808-7272**
15 E. Palatine Road, Suite 118, Prospect Heights   Fax: (847) 808-7373
See Add on Page: 516, 517, 549   800 Extension: 1152
Principal/Owner: Charmaine Donnay Nilles
Website: chardonnaydesigns.com
Description: The Northshore's source for stained glass overlay. We also offer
complete interior design services to customize your home or business.

CIRCLE STUDIO ....**(773) 588-4848**
3928 N. Elston, Chicago   Fax: (773) 588-5333
See Add on Page: 546   800 Extension: 1052
Principal/Owner: Joseph Badalpour

CREATIVE MIRROR DESIGNS..**(630) 543-1166**
2141 W. Army Trail Road, Addison   Fax: (630) 543-1215
See Add on Page: 548   800 Extension: 1231
Principal/Owner: Mark Pritikin
Website: www.creativemirror.com   e-mail: mpritikin@creativemirror.com
Description: Specializing in custom mirrored walls, custom heavy glass, shower
doors and mirrored closet doors.

IMPERIAL GLASS BLOCK CO. ....**(847) 647-8770**
7412 Milwaukee Avenue, Niles   Fax: (847) 647-0922
See Add on Page: 547   800 Extension: 1041
Principal/Owner: Tom Pomykala

JOE'S GLASS & MIRROR WORKS ....**(708) 453-7496**
2637 N. Erie Street, River Grove   Fax: (708) 453-7498
See Add on Page: 550   800 Extension: 1157
Principal/Owner: Joe Corsei

545

The largest selection of glass block in the Midwest.
Add statement making form and function to your personal design.

IMPERIAL GLASS BLOCK CO.
7412 N. Milwaukee Avenue
Niles, Illinois 60714
847.647.8770
847.647.0922 FAX

Joe's Glass & Mirror Works, Inc.

2637 N Erie Street
River Grove, IL 60171

708-453-7496 bus
708-453-7498 fax

Custom Heavy Glass

Shower Enclosures

Glass Tabletops &
Countertops

Mirror Walls

Mirror Closet Doors

Store Fronts

*Call for further
information or
showroom
appointment.*

**Known for Custom
Quality Work**

Photography: Janet Zange

Hardware

BEMMCO ARCHITECTURAL PRODUCTS ....**(630) 960-5540**
1909 Ogden Avenue, Lisle   Fax: (630) 960-5574
See Add on Page: 554, 555   800 Extension: 6031
<u>Principal/Owner:</u> Ed Leon
CHICAGO BRASS..**(847) 926-0001**
7 Prairie Ave. (Half Day Rd.), Highwood   Fax: (847) 432-1178
See Add on Page: 552, 553   800 Extension: 1246
<u>Principal/Owner:</u> C.J. Schnakenberg
<u>Website:</u> www.chicagobrass.com   <u>e-mail:</u> info@chicagobrass.com

---

"This building is like a book. Its architecture is the binding; its text is in the glass and sculpture."

Malcolm Miller

551

CABINET
for your

At Crystal Cabinets nothing is more important tha
cabinetry styles and designs. Using only the fines
handcrafted, custom-designed and backed by a lif
Crafts to Ultra-Contemporary, your local Crystal d
room in the home as well as every lifestyle. ESPECIA

Y
ESTYLE

Val Constantin

g able to offer our customer a large variety of
·rials and the latest innovations, each cabinet is
limited warranty. From Old World to Arts &
offers a full line of cabinetry perfect for every
DURS.

BEMMCO
Architectural Products

1909 OGDEN AVE., LISLE, IL 60532
(630) 960-5540 FAX (630) 960-5574

Windows
& Doors

ASSURED CORPORATION ....**(708) 385-4079**
13013 S. Western Avenue, Blue Island   Fax: (708) 385-4039
See Add on Page: 558, 559   800 Extension: 1013
<u>Principal/Owner:</u> Mark J. Sala
<u>e-mail:</u> jsals@assuredcorp.com
<u>Description:</u> Manufacturer representative of elegant window; door products fabricated from steel, stainless steel, bronze and fine hardwoods.

FEATHER RIVER WOOD & GLASS......................................**(847) 920-0100**
1100 Central Avenue, Suite D, Wilmette   Fax: (847) 920-0150
See Add on Page: 561   800 Extension: 1002
<u>Principal/Owner:</u> Dick Cohen
<u>Website:</u> www.frwginc.com <u>e-mail:</u> dicksco@aol.com

KONSLER, LTD. ....**(847) 816-7979**
631 Park Avenue, Libertyville   Fax: (847) 816-7990
See Add on Page: 557   800 Extension: 1102
<u>Principal/Owner:</u> Connie Konsler

PREFERRED MILLWORK ....**(630) 293-4406**
980 Hawthorne Lane, West Chicago   Fax: (630) 293-4407
See Add on Page: 528, 560   800 Extension: 1203
<u>Principal/Owner:</u> Patrick Riccobene

HOPE'S

ASSURED CORPORATION

Steel, Stainless, Bronze and Fine
Hardwood Window and Door Systems
Design, Development, Distribution

MeGa WOOD
Fine Mahogany Windows and Doors

INFINITY ∞ BRONZE

Photography: Linda Oyama Br.
Courtesy of: Orren Pickell Build

Photography: Linda Oyama Bryan

Photography: Linda Oyama Br.

PREFERRED MILLWORK

enterprises, inc.

Architectural Woodwork • Windows • Doors

980 Hawthorne Lane, West Chicago, IL 60185
(630) 293-4406 • Fax: (630) 293-4407

Timeless Beauty

Quality
Craftsmanship

Distinctive
Products

for your
home by

1100 Central Avenue, Suite D
Wilmette, Illinios 60091
847-920-0100   FAX 847-920-0150

Finally...
Chicago's Own
Home & Design
Sourcebook

The CHICAGO HOME BOOK, a comprehensive hands-on design sourcebook to building, remodeling, decorating, furnishing and landscaping a luxury home in Chicago and its suburbs, is a "must-have" reference for the Chicagoland homeowner. At over 700 pages, this beautiful, full-color hard cover volume is quite simply the most complete, well-organized reference to the Chicagoland home industry. It covers all aspects of the process, with hundreds of listings of local home industry professionals, accompanied by hundreds of inspiring photographs. You will also find articles to assist in planning and completing a project. The CHICAGO HOME BOOK tells you how to find what you need when you need it.

Order your copy today!

Published by
The Ashley Group
1350 E. Touhy Avenue • Des Plaines, IL 60018
888-458-1750
E-mail: ashleybooksales@cahners.com

Photo courtesy of:
Oscar Isberian Rugs

FLOORING & COUNTERTOPS

the possibilities are endless...

CORIAN®

SOLID SURFACES

by DuPont®

FLOORING &
COUNTERTOPS

"Things are pretty, *graceful*, rich, *elegant*, handsome, but, until they speak *to the imagination*, not yet *beautiful*."

Ralph Waldo Emerson

567

Tops 'N Bottoms

The solid surfaces of a home, the floors and countertops, are show-stopping design elements that add beauty and distinction to each room. From exquisite marble slabs, richly polished woods, and luxurious area and wall-to-wall carpets, to fabulous granites, seamless, durable solid surfaces and highly unique ceramic tiles, the possibilities for color, style and combination are unlimited.

Chicago area custom homeowners are well traveled and sophisticated in their tastes and preferences, as shop owners and craftsmen who cater to this clientele will attest. Their strong desire for quality and beauty, and their interest in understanding the benefits and unique beauty of each choice, make for educated and appropriate choices that add value and personality to the home.

The following pages will introduce you to some of the most distinguished suppliers and artisans working with these products in the Chicago area.

FLOOR COVERINGS OF DISTINCTION...CARPETS & RUGS

From a room-sized French Aubusson rug to a dense wool carpet with inset borders, "soft" floor treatments are used in area homes to make a signature statement, or blend quietly into the background to let other art and furnishings grab the attention.

Selecting carpeting and rugs requires research, a dedicated search, and the guidance of a well established design plan. Because the floor covers the width and depth of any room, it's very important that your choices are made in concert with other design decisions–from furniture to art, from window treatments to lighting.

Your interior designer or a representative at any of the fine retail stores featured in the following pages is qualified to educate you as you make your selections.

Rug and carpet dealers who cater to a clientele that demands a high level of personal service (from advice to installation and maintenance) and top quality products, are themselves dedicated to only the best in terms of service and selection. Their accumulated knowledge will be a most important benefit as you select the right carpet for your home.

THE WORLD AT YOUR FEET

Today's profusion of various fibers, colors, patterns, textures, and weights make carpet selection exciting and challenging. Your search won't be overwhelming if you realize the requirements of your own home and work within those boundaries.

Begin where the carpet will eventually end up – that is, in your home. Consider how a carpet will function by answering questions like these:

• What is the traffic pattern? High traffic areas, like stairs and halls, require a stain resistant dense or low level loop carpet for top durability in a color or pattern that won't show wear. Your choices for a bedroom, where traffic is minimal, will include lighter colors in deeper plush or velvets.

• How will it fit with existing or developing decors? Do you need a neutral for an unobtrusive background, or an eye-catching tone-on-tone texture that's a work of art in itself?

• Will it flow nicely into adjoining rooms? Carpet or other flooring treatments in the surrounding rooms need to be considered.

• What needs, other than decorative, must the carpet fill? Do you need to keep a room warm, muffle sound, protect a natural wood floor?

• How is the room used? Do teenagers and toddlers carry snacks into the family room? Is a finished basement used for ping-pong as well as a home office?

ORIENTAL RUGS

The decision to invest in an Oriental rug should be made carefully. Buying a rug purely for its decorative beauty and buying for investment purposes require two different approaches. If you're buying for aesthetics, put beauty first and condition second. Certain colors and patterns are more significant than others; a reputable dealer can guide you. Check for quality by looking at these features:

• Regularity of knotting.
• Color clarity.
• Rug lies evenly on the floor.
• Back is free of damage or repair marks.

568

THE ARTISTRY OF RUGS

Nothing compares to the artful elegance of a carefully selected area rug placed on a hard surface. Through pattern, design, texture and color, rug designers create a work of art that is truly enduring. If you have hardwood, marble or natural stone floors, an area rug will only enhance their natural beauty. From Chinese silk, to colorful Pakistanis, to rare Caucasian antiques, the possibilities are as varied as the world is wide.

If you're creating a new interior, it's best to start with rug selection. First, it's harder to find the 'right' rug than it is to find the 'right' fabric or paint: there are simply fewer fine rugs than there are fabrics, patterns or colors. However, don't make a final commitment on a rug until you know it will work with the overall design. Second, rugs usually outlive other furnishings. Homeowners like to hang on to their rugs when they move, and keep them as family heirlooms.

In recent years, many rug clients have been enjoying a bounty of beautiful, well-made rugs from every major rug-producing country in the world. As competition for the global market intensifies, rugs of exceptionally high caliber are more readily available. Getting qualified advice is more important than ever.

Fine rug dealers, like those showcased in the following pages, have knowledgeable staff members who are dedicated to educating their clientele and helping them find a rug they'll love. Through careful consideration of your tastes, and the requirements of your home, these professionals will virtually walk you through the process. They'll encourage you to take your time, and to judge each rug on its own merits. They'll insist on you taking rugs home so you can experience them in your own light (and may also provide delivery). And their companies will offer cleaning and repair service, which may well be important to you some day.

ELEGANCE UNDERFOOT: HARDWOOD

A hardwood floor is part of the dream for many custom homeowners searching for a warm, welcoming environment. Highly polished planks or fine parquet, the beauty of wood has always been a definitive part of luxurious homes and as the design "warming trend" continues, a wood floor figures prominently in achieving this feeling.

With new product options that make maintenance even easier, wood floors continue to add value and distinction in upscale homes throughout the area and the suburbs. Plank, parquet, and strip wood come in a wide variety of materials, and scores of styles and tones. Consider what effect you're trying to achieve.

FOR SUCCESSFUL CARPET SHOPPING

1. Take along blueprints (or accurate measurements), fabric swatches, paint chips, & photos.
2. Focus on installed, not retail price.
3. Take samples home to experience in the light of the room.
4. Be aware of delivery times; most carpet is available within weeks; special orders or custom designs take much longer.
5. Shop together. It saves time in the decision-making process.

569

BUDGETING FOR WOOD FLOOR*

2 1/4" strip oak –$10/sq. ft. Wider plank or parquet, glued & nailed–$15/sq.ft. Fancy parquet, hand-finished plank or French patterns (Versailles, Brittany)–$30/sq. ft. and up.
* Estimates include finishing and installation; not sub-floor trim.

THE NUMBER ONE WAY TO DECIDE ON A RUG

Do you like the rug enough to decorate around it? There's your answer.

CERAMIC TILE AS STONE

With textured surfaces and color variations, ceramic tile can look strikingly like stone. You can get the tone on tone veining of marble, or the look of split stone, in assorted shapes, sizes and color.

Plank wood complements a traditional interior, while parquet wood flooring offers a highly stylized look. Designs stenciled directly on to floorboards create an original Arts and Crafts feel.

The more exotic woods used for flooring, like Brazilian cherry wood, are often harvested from managed forests.

VINYL AND LAMINATES

Vinyl or laminated floor coverings are no longer considered candidates for immediate rehab. – as a matter of fact, they're among the most updated looks in flooring. Stylish laminates are made to convincingly simulate wood, ceramic tile and other natural flooring products, and are excellent choices for heavy traffic areas. They come in hundreds of colors and patterns, and offer great compatibility with countertop materials.

THE RENAISSANCE OF CERAMIC TILE

Ceramic tile has literally come out of the back rooms and into the spotlight with its color, beauty and unique stylistic potential. As sophisticated shoppers gain a better understanding of the nature and possibilities of tile, its use has increased dramatically. Homeowners who want added quality and value in their homes are searching out hand painted glazed tiles for the risers of a staircase, quirky rectangular tiles to frame a powder room mirror, and ceramic tiles that look exactly like stone for their sun porch or kitchen. From traditional to modern, imported to domestic, ceramic tile offers a world of possibilities.

It is the perfect solution for homeowners who want floor, walls, countertops or backsplashes made of top quality, durable and attractive materials. A glazed clay natural product, ceramic tile is flexible, easy to care for, and allows for a variety of design ideas. It is easily cleaned with water and doesn't require waxing or polishing. And, like other natural flooring and counter products, ceramic tile adds visible value to a luxury home.

SELECTING CERAMIC TILE

Not all tile works in all situations, so it's imperative that you get good advice and counsel when selecting ceramic tile for your home. Ceramic tile is wear-rated, and this standardized system will steer you in the right direction. Patronize specialists who can provide creative, quality-driven advice. Visit showrooms to get an idea of the many colors, shapes and sizes available for use on floors, walls and counters. You'll be in for a very pleasant surprise.

If you're building or remodeling, your builder, architect, and/or interior designer can help you in your search and suggest creative ways to enliven your interior schemes. Individual hand-painted tiles can be interspersed in a solid color backsplash to add interest and individuality. Tiles can be included in a glass block partition, on a wallpapered wall, or in harmony with an area rug.

Grout, which can be difficult to keep clean, is now being addressed as a potential design element. By using a colored grout, the grout lines become a contrast design element – or can be colored to match the tile itself.

THE SOPHISTICATED LOOK OF NATURAL STONE

For a luxurious look that radiates strength and character, the world of natural stone offers dazzling possibilities. As custom buyers look for that "special something" to add to the beauty and value of their homes, they turn to the growing natural stone marketplace. A whole world of possibilities is now open to involved homeowners who contact the master craftsmen and suppliers who dedicate their careers to excellence in stone design, installation and refurbishing.

Marble and granite, which have always been options for homeowners are more popular than ever. With luxurious texture and color, marble is often the choice to add dramatic beauty to a grand entryway or a master bath upgrade. Granite continues to grow in popularity especially in luxury kitchens – there is no better material for countertops. It's also popular for a section of countertop dedicated to rolling pastry or dough. Rustic, weathered and unpolished, or highly polished and brilliant, granite brings elegance and rich visual texture that adds easily recognizable value to a home. Beyond marble and granite, the better suppliers of stone products also can introduce homeowners to slates, soapstone, limestone, English Kirkstone, sandstone, and travertine, which can be finished in a variety of individual ways.

PRICING FOR NATURAL STONE

As with all flooring and countertop materials, get an installed, not a retail quote. Installation can drive the cost up significantly. Preparing a realistic quote may take days of research, due to the tremendous variety of factors that can influence price. As a general guideline, the installed starting price per square foot:
• Granite: $30
• Tumbled marble, limestone, slate: $20
• Engineered stone/quartzite: $25
• Antique stone, with intricate installation: $75
• Granite slab countertop: $70

571

MAKE IT CONCRETE

This material is a versatile and indestructible choice, available in a variety of colors and textures. Sealed concrete can be made with creative borders, scored, sandblasted or stained. A strong, natural material, it can be made to look like other materials and natural stone.

SOLID SURFACING SHOWS UP ON TILES

Durable, non-porous solid surface materials are now being used to make decorative wall tiles. Check with your countertop supplier for information and ideas.

ADJUSTING TO STONE PRODUCTS IN THE HOME

Like Mother Nature herself, natural stone is both rugged and vulnerable. Each stone requires specific care and maintenance and homeowners often experience a period of adjustment as they become accustomed to the requirements of caring for their floors or countertops.

Ask an expert about the different requirements and characteristics. Soapstone, for example, is a beautiful, soft stone with an antique patina many people love. Accumulated stains and scratches just add to the look. Granite, on the other hand, will not stain.

A professional can educate you about the specific characteristics of each stone product so you make an informed decision on what products will best serve the lifestyle of your family.

CHOOSING STONE – A UNIQUE EXPERIENCE

Once a decision to use a natural stone is made, begin your search right away. By allowing plenty of time to discover the full realm of choices, you'll be able to choose a stone and finish that brings luster and value to your home, without the pressure of a deadline. If you order imported stone, it can take months for delivery. Be prepared to visit your supplier's warehouse to inspect the stone that will be used in your home. Natural stone varies – piece to piece, box to box – a slab can vary in color from one end to the other. If you understand this degree of unpredictable irregularity is unavoidable, it will help you approach the selection in a realistic way.

STRONG AND ELEGANT COUNTERTOPS

The quest for quality and style does not stop until the countertops are selected. Today's countertop marketplace is brimming with man-made products that add high style without sacrificing strength and resiliency.

As the functions of kitchens become broader, the demand for aesthetics continues to increase dramatically. For lasting beauty with incredible design sensibilities, man-made solid surfaces are a very popular choice. The overwhelming number of possibilities and combinations in selecting countertops makes it vital to work with specialists who are quality-oriented. Countertops represent a significant investment in a custom home, and quality, performance and style must be the primary considerations in any decision. Established professionals, like those introduced in your Home Book, have a reputation for expert installation and service of the top quality products that define luxury.

MAKE COUNTERTOP CHOICES EARLY

Since decisions on cabinetry are often made far in advance, it's best to make a countertop choice concurrently.

Expect to spend at least two weeks visiting showrooms and acquainting yourself with design and materials. Take along paint chips, samples of cabinet and flooring materials, and any pictures of the look you're trying to achieve. Expect a solid surface custom counter order to take at least five weeks to arrive.

A WEALTH OF COUNTERTOP OPTIONS

You'll face a field of hundreds of colors and textures of solid surfacing, laminates, ceramic tile, natural stone, wood and stainless or enameled steel. Poured concrete counters also are finding their way into luxury kitchens in the area.

Laminate or color-through laminate offer hundreds of colors, patterns and textures, many of which convincingly mimic the look of solid surfacing or granite. Enjoying growing popularity in countertop application, are the natural stones, those staggeringly gorgeous slabs of granite, marble or slate, which offer the timeless look of quality and luxury. Naturally quarried stone is extremely durable and brings a dramatic beauty and texture to the kitchen or bath. For endless color and pattern possibilities, ceramic tile is a highly durable option. Man made resin-based solid surfacing materials offer many of the same benefits as stone. These surfaces are fabricated for durability and beauty, and new choices offer a visual depth that is astounding to the eye. It can be bent, carved, or sculpted. Elaborate edges can be cut into a solid surface counter and sections can be carved out to accommodate other surface materials, such as stainless steel or marble. Best known for superior durability, solid surfaces stand up to scratches, heat and water.

FINDING THE BEST SOURCE FOR MATERIALS

If you're building or remodeling your home, your designer, builder or architect will help you develop some ideas and find a supplier for the material you choose. Reputable suppliers like those featured in the Home Book, are experienced in selecting the best products and providing expert installation. Go visit a showroom or office – their knowledge will be invaluable to you. The intricacies and idiosyncrasies of natural products, and the sheer volume of possibilities in fabricated surfaces, can be confounding on your own. ■

BEYOND TRADITIONAL

Solid surfacing is now being used to make custom faucets, decorative wall tiles, and lots of other creative touches for the home. Their rich colors (including granite), famed durability and versatility are perfect for bringing ideas to life. Check with your countertop supplier for information and ideas.

BE CREATIVE!

Mix and match counter top materials for optimum functionality and up-to-date style. Install butcher block for chopping vegetables and slicing breads, a slab of marble for rolling pastry and bakery dough, granite on an island for overall elegance, and solid surfaces for beauty and durability around the sinks and cooktop areas.

573

Carpeting & Rugs

CARLSON'S FLOORS, INC. .... **(630) 232-4964**
728 W. State Street, Geneva   Fax: (630) 232-4350
See Add on Page: 578   800 Extension: 1252
<u>Principal/Owner:</u> Lisa Nelson
<u>e-mail:</u> carlsonsfloors@aol.com

CASPIAN ORIENTAL RUGS .... **(312) 664-7576**
770 N. LaSalle Street, Chicago   Fax: (312) 664-3490
See Add on Page: 580, 581   800 Extension: 1250
<u>Principal/Owner:</u> Jim Soomekh
<u>Description:</u> Chicagoland's largest direct importer of fine oriental rugs. Modern, antique, aubusson and decorative. Professional cleaning, repair and appraisal.

ILOULIAN ANTIQUE & DECORATIVE CARPETS .... **(847) 266-1000**
1783 St. Johns Avenue, Highland Park   Fax: (847) 266-1055
See Add on Page: 585   800 Extension: 1055
<u>Principal/Owner:</u> Nader Iloulian

OSCAR ISBERIAN RUGS .... **(847) 475-0010**
1028 Chicago Avenue, Evanston   Fax: (847) 475-0020
See Add on Page: 582, 583   800 Extension: 1218
<u>Description:</u> Chicago's finest selection of Oriental Rugs since 1920.

LEWIS CARPET ONE .... **(847) 835-2400**
1840 Frontage Road, Northbrook   Fax: (847) 835-1614
See Add on Page: 579   800 Extension: 6213
<u>Principal/Owner:</u> Steven Lewis
<u>Website:</u> www.carpetone.com/lewiscarpetone   <u>e-mail:</u> burgooking@aol.com

MATERIAL CULTURE .... **(312) 467-1490**
401 N. LaSalle, Chicago   Fax: (312) 467-1491
See Add on Page: 584, 665   800 Extension: 1054
<u>Principal/Owner:</u> Tony Trotalli

PEDIAN RUG INC. .... **(847) 675-9111**
6535 N. Lincoln, Lincolnwood   Fax: (847) 675-9120
See Add on Page: 575 - 577   800 Extension: 1232
<u>Principal/Owner:</u> H. Pedian, V. Pedian, A. Pedian
<u>Description:</u> Pedian Rug Co. has been providing the highest quality installations and the finest selection of floor covering in the Chicago area for over 95 years.

ROUZATI RUGS .... **(847) 328-0000**
1907 Central Street, Evanston   Fax: (847) 328-2306
See Add on Page: 586, 587, 719   800 Extension: 1208
<u>Principal/Owner:</u> Jafam Rouzati

Pedian Rug

THE FLOOR STORE

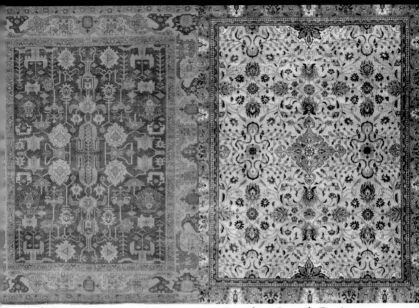

Oushak Design

Ferrahan Sarouk Design

SAFAVIEH

Tabriz Floral Design

Himalayan Design

For the finest selections visit our showrooms:

Lincolnwood
- 6535 N. Lincoln Ave. (847) 675.9111

Oakbrook Terrace
- 17 W. 504 22nd St. (630) 833.5410

Arlington Heights
- 1215 N. Rand Rd. (847) 394.5500

Pedian's World
CARPETING
ORIENTAL RUGS
CUSTOM FLOORS

Pedian Rug & Tile
THE FLOOR STORE

Pedian Rug & Tile

THE FLOOR STORE

For the finest selections visit our showrooms:

Lincolnwood
- 6535 N. Lincoln Ave. (847) 675.9111

Oakbrook Terrace
- 17 W. 504 22nd St. (630) 833.5410

Arlington Heights
- 1215 N. Rand Rd. (847) 394.5500

The

Grou

THE ASHLEY GROUP

The Ashley Group is the largest provider of home
quality designing, building, and decorating information and
For more information on the many products of **The Ashley**
Cahners Business Information (www.cahners.com)
U.S. provider of business information to 16
manufacturing and retail. Cahners' rich content portfolio
Publishers Weekly, Design News and 152 other

RESOURCE COLLECTION

visual resource images, and strives to provide the highest
resources available, to upscale consumers and professionals.
Group, visit our website at www.ashleygroup@cahners.com.
a member of the Reed Elsevier plc group, is a leading
vertical markets, including entertainment,
encompasses more than 140 Web sites as well as *Variety*,
market-leading business-to-business magazines

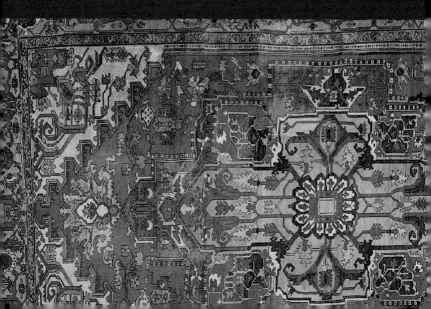

Isberian Rugs

National Rug Retailer of the Year

Evanston:
1028 Chicago Avenue
847/475–0010

Chicago:
122 West Kinzie St.
312/467–1212

Barrington: at Richard Honquest
1455 S. Barrington Rd.
847/382–1700

www.isberian.com

CHICAGO'S CARPET BOUTIQUE

We Stand Behind
Our Rugs 110%

Rouzati Oriental Rugs, Inc.

1907 Central Street
Evanston, IL 60201
847.328.0000 Fax 328.2306

Flooring

ACE FLOORING CO. INC. ....**(847) 696-2800**
1024 Busse Highway, Park Ridge   Fax: (847) 696-2824
See Add on Page: 592   800 Extension: 1000
Principal/Owner: Annie Ursache

APEX WOOD FLOORS...**(630) 963-9322**
1326 Ogden Avenue, Downers Grove   Fax: (630) 963-9370
See Add on Page: 590   800 Extension: 1065
Principal/Owner: John Lessick
Description: In business 20 yrs, specializing in inlay borders, medallions, custom stains + handscraping.

ERICKSON DECORATING PRODUCTS, INC. ....**(773) 539-7555**
6040 N. Pulaski Road, Chicago   Fax: (773) 539-9694
See Add on Page: 591   800 Extension: 1124
Principal/Owner: John Erickson
Website: http://www.onlinefloorstore.com e-mail: info@onlinefloorstore.com
Description: Erickson's is one of the Midwest's largest hardwood flooring distributors, stocking full line's of abrasives, finishes, equipment, cleaners and flooring.

FLOORGUARD, INC....**(630) 231-9070**
1130 Carolina Drive, West Chicago   Fax: (630) 231-3836
See Add on Page: 589   800 Extension: 1037
Principal/Owner: Gus Schuberth
Website: www.floorguard.com e-mail: info@floorguard.com
Description: Don't confuse Floorguard with cheap paints or look alikes that flake or peel. Floorguard is the ultimate residential Garage flooring system.

HERITAGE FLOORING ....**(847) 940-7440**
444 Lake Cook Road, Suite 16, Deerfield   Fax: (847) 940-7472
See Add on Page: 593   800 Extension: 6145
Principal/Owner: H. Scott Norris
e-mail: scott@heritagefloors.com
Description: From custom installation and design of new wood floors to refinishing, restoration and maintenance of existing wood floors, we provide a full range of services. Our quality and craftsmanship are second to none.

onlinefloorstore.com

Drive to the floor store, or drive here?

Why spend your valuable time , waiting in line, when you can order from one of the biggest hardwood flooring distributors in the Midwest, Online.

Finishes * Flooring * Cleaners * Abrasives * Equipment

Erickson Decorating Products, Inc.
web: www.onlinefloorstore.com
email: Info@onlinefloorstore.com
6040 North Pulaski Rd.
Chicago, IL 60646
773.539.7555
800.539.7550
773.539.9698 Fax

"IT STARTS
WITH IDEAS...
BIG OR SMALL, IN
WORDS OR PICTURES,
IN COLORS OR SHAPES....
CRYSTAL CLEAR
OR BARELY THERE.
THAT'S HOW IT STARTS"

Paul A Casper & Carolyn Nichols

Heritage Flooring

"The finest in distinctive hardwood floors"

Contact us now for a private, in home consulatation

Heritage Flooring, Inc.
444 Lake Cook Road • Suite 16
Deerfield, Illinois 60015
(847) 940-7440

Ceramic Tile

FRANK ZANOTTI TILE CO. INC. ....**(847) 433-3636**
6 Walker, Highwood   Fax: (847) 433-8950
See Add on Page: 595   800 Extension: 1114
<u>Principal/Owner:</u> Frank Zanotti

"Old-world charm can be evoked with materials such as limestone, slate or tumbled marble, while the edginess of stainless steel or glass blends *beautifully in a high tech home."*

FRANK ZANOTTI TILE & STONE CO., INC.
6 WALKER HIGHWOOD, IL 60040
847-433-3636   FAX 847-433-8950

Marble & **Granite**

ADVANCED STONE TECHNOLOGIES, INC...............................**(863) 467-8944**
2455 NW 16th Blvd., Okeechobee Fax: (863) 467-5857
See Add on Page: 602, 603 800 Extension: 1260
Website: www.advancedstonetechno.com
e-mail: inquiry@advancedstonetechno.com
Description: Contractors of custom mosaic work in marble and granite.
Unlimited design possibilities. Minimal delivery time. Created in the USA.

ARC STONE IV ....**(847) 299-6660**
520 Santa Rosa Drive, Des Plaines Fax: (847) 299-6669
See Add on Page: 608, 609 800 Extension: 1239
Principal/Owner: Giuseppe Capozza/ Danny Coiro
Website: www.arc-stone.com

CHICAGO GRANITE & MARBLE INC. ....**(888) 334-4808**
415 Busse Road, Elk Grove Village Fax: (847) 806-7002
See Add on Page: 612 800 Extension: 1009
Website: www.universalgranite.com e-mail: universeg@aol.com
Description: Please contact us for top quality workmanship, elegant finish and
prompt after sales service.

GRANITE & MARBLE RESOURCES...**(312) 670-4400**
1374 Merchandise Mart, Chicago Fax: (312) 670-0158
See Add on Page: 597 - 599 800 Extension: 1243
Principal/Owner: Robert Briggs
Website: www.granite-marble.net e-mail: info@stoneandkitchen.com

GRANITE PRO ....**(312) 432-1122**
1826 S. Clinton, Chicago Fax: (312) 432-9842
See Add on Page: 604 800 Extension: 1160
Principal/Owner: Greg Siwek

GRANITEWERKS ....**(773) 292-1202**
2218 North Elston, Chicago
See Add on Page: 600, 601 800 Extension: 1161
Principal/Owner: Michael Crane/ John Bozck
Website: www.granitewerks.com e-mail: granitewerks@mindspring.com
Description: We import, fabricate and install natural stone and Silestone (R),
engineered stone. Residential, commercial interior and hospitality markets.
Serving the Midwest.

ITALDECOR IMPORTS ....**(847) 290-0601**
1480 Landmeier Road, Elk Grove Village Fax: (847) 290-0031
See Add on Page: 607 800 Extension: 6164
Principal/Owner: Vito Guarino & Claudio Turano
Website: www.italdecor.com

STONECUTTERS...**(847) 657-9000**
2014 Lehigh Avenue, Glenview Fax: (847) 657-9300
See Add on Page: 605 800 Extension: 6306
Principal/Owner: Howard Goldstein
Website: www.stonecutters.com e-mail: email@stonecutters.com

continued on page **606**

Stone &
Kitchen Salon
(A division of Granite and Marble Resources)

Pub / Wine Cellar
To your taste. Carved and knotty pine panels. Tumbled chocolate Travertine floor with a German Limestone Countertop.

Chicago Showroom

1374 Merchandise Mart, Chicago
Ph: 312.670.4400 Fax: 312.670.0158
email: info@stoneandkitchen.com

**Warehouse-Fabrication
& Installation**

North Shore Showroom
8027 N. Lawndale, Skokie
Ph: 847.674.7926 Fax: 847.674.7927

Antique Maple Kitchen

Old-world style cabinet with inset doors. Time worn distressed finishing and architectural detailing. Custom colored and ten-step finishing process. Custom Granite top with natural stone designed back-splash. Antique Jerusalem limestone floor.

Carved Marble Fountain

Intricate sculpture from our joint-venture studio in China. Italian quality for the price of plaster or cement. "Seeing and touching is believing."

Carved Marble Fireplace

Limitless in design. Send us your spec. Nothing is too complex! Our art is your form and function.

MOSAICS
By
Boz Art

ARTISTIC MOSAICS IN M

Opus Sectile - Pebble -
Medallions - Inlays - Borders - W
Unlimited Design Possibil
CREATED

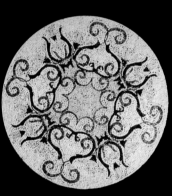

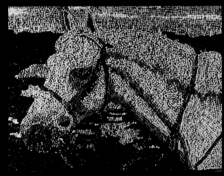

RBLE, GRANITE & STONE

GRANITE PRO

CUSTOM GRANITE & MARBLE FABRICATORS

1826 SOUTH CLINTON • CHICAGO, IL 60616
PHONE 312-432-1122
FAX 312-432-9842
WWW.GRANITEPRO.COM

continued from page **596**

TERRAZZO & MARBLE SUPPLY COMPANIES..........................**(847) 353-8000**
77 South Wheeling Road, Wheeling   Fax: (847) 353-8010
See Add on Page: 610, 611   800 Extension: 1032
<u>Principal/Owner:</u> Joel Rotondo
<u>Website:</u> tmsupply.com   <u>e-mail:</u> tmsupply@aol.com
<u>Description:</u> One of the largest distributors of natural stone. Designer
Showroom - Specialty Stones

"Nothing compares to the
artful elegance of a carefully
selected area rug placed
on a hard surface."

ARC
STONE IV

SERVING THE MARBLE AND GRANITE INDUSTRY

One of the East coast's largest stone suppliers is now in the Midwest. Suppliers of granite, marble, slate, travertine, limestone and tumbled stone. Come visit our new Des Plaines showroom.

520 Santa Rosa Dr., Des Plaines, IL 60018
800.664.8453   847.299.6669

New Jersey
201.531.0600

Maryland
301.931.1600

Florida
561.478.8805

www.arc-stone.com

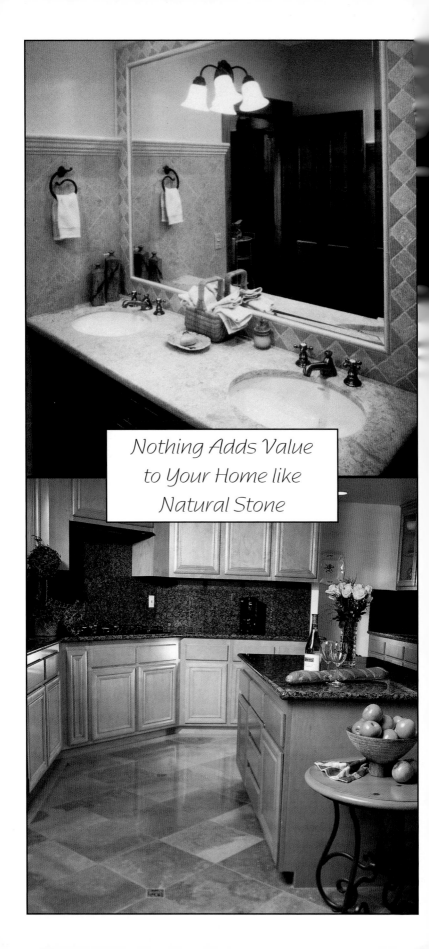

Nothing Adds Value to Your Home like Natural Stone

More home owners trust u do their kitcher counter tops everyday.

More professio als trust us wi their client's ho than ever befor

It might be something in the air. But we think it is because we deliver better value, better quailty all the time. And everyone knows it.

Solid Surfaces

NORTH STAR SURFACES, LLC ....**(800) 383-9784**
23 Empire Drive, St. Paul
See Add on Page: 614, 615
<u>Principal/Owner:</u> Chuck Geerdes
<u>Description:</u> Distributor of Avonite, Hi-Macs, Silestone, Transolid

Fax: (833) 378-9110
800 Extension: 1241

"For a luxurious look that radiates
strength and character, the
world of natural stone
offers dazzling possibilities."

613

STRENGTH & ELEGANCE

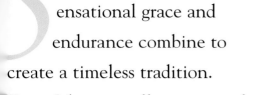

Sensational grace and endurance combine to create a timeless tradition. We at Silestone offer you a surface that will stand the same test of time. We bring the elegance of natural tone with added strength and durability to your home.

Silestone. Strength and elegance even nature can't beat.

Crafted from the finest quartz, Silestone is an engineered stone that is more durable than plastic solid surface or any natural material...including granite. Stain, heat and scratch resistant, Silestone is your low maintenance countertop for today's kitchen and bath.

With a luxurious array of colors, Silestone will compliment your kitchen, whether you are classically traditional or contemporarily modern.

SILESTONE®

THE LEADER IN QUARTZ SURFACING

North Star Surfaces
Toll Free 800.383.9784
www.silestoneusa.com

Stone
Slate & Concrete

OLD WORLD STONE, INC. ....**(847) 787-0166**
2435 Brickvale Drive, Elk Grove Village   Fax: (847) 787-0267
See Add on Page: 620   800 Extension: 1221
<u>Description:</u> Showroom: 200 W. Superior, Chicago, IL 60610
Tel: 312-661-7140 Fax: 312-329-9431

SELECT STONE COMPANY ....**(847) 350-0800**
2424 N. Pam Am Blvd., Elk Grove Village   Fax: (847) 350-2977
See Add on Page: 617   800 Extension: 1204

STONECRAFTERS ....**(847) 526-9594**
388 Hollow Hill Drive, Wauconda   Fax: (847) 526-9507
See Add on Page: 618, 619   800 Extension: 6305
<u>Principal/Owner:</u> David Hammerl

THE SELECT STONE COMPANY
IMPORTER AND DISTRIBUTOR OF LIMESTONE, MARBLE, GRANITE AND SLATE

Specialists in Exclusive Stone

2424 N. Pan Am Blvd., Elk Grove Village, IL 60007
(847)350-0800 Fax (847)350-2977

Your Vision...

...our Craft.

A Natural Combination.

Stonecrafters

FINE HANDCRAFTED GRANITE & MARBLE

388 HOLLOW HILL DRIVE
WAUCONDA, IL 60084

PHONE   847.526.9594
FAX LINE 847.526.9507

NATIONAL KITCHEN
NKBA
& BATH ASSOCIATION

Stonecrafters

FINE HANDCRAFTED GRANITE & MARBLE

HOME

FURNISHINGS

& DECORATING

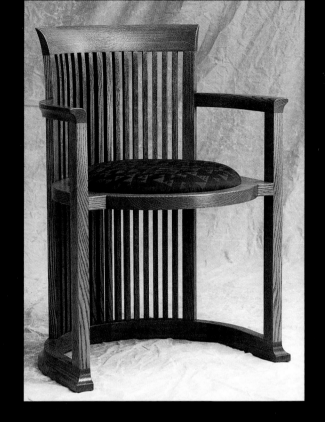

Prairie in the Round

"One may do
whate'er one likes

In Art:
the only thing is,

to make sure

That one does

like it. "

Robert Browning

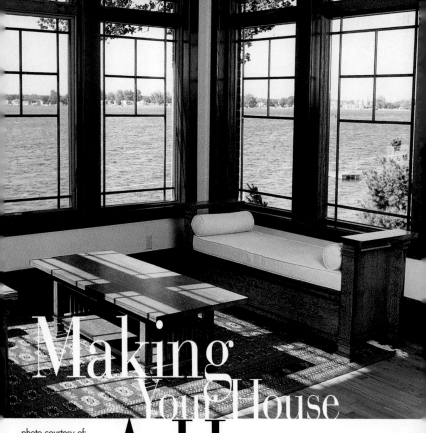

Making Your House A Home

photo courtesy of:
**Swartzendruber
Hardware**

625

A beautifully designed, meticulously planned house becomes a home when the furnishings are set in place. Comfortably upholstered sofas and chairs in the family room, a unique faux-finished foyer, richly appointed windows in the dining room, all give a home its individual flair and welcoming livability.

Today's homeowners, whether they're in their first or final home, have the elevated taste that comes from exposure to good design. They know what quality furniture looks and feels like and they want it in their homes.

In the home furnishing industry, one item is more outrageously gorgeous than the next, and anything you can imagine can be yours. This freedom can be overwhelming, even intimidating, if you don't keep a sharp focus.

By visiting the finest stores, specialty shops, and artisans, like those presented in the following pages of the Home Book, you can be certain your desire for top quality is already understood and that knowledgeable people are ready to guide you. Enjoy.

MODERN IDEAS

With an evolutionary array of styles, contemporary furnishings add excitement, elegance and personality to a home. From Bauhaus, Retro, and Deco, to pure modern, these artful furnishings satisfy the desire for unique, individual expression.

KEEP IT ALIVE!

Regardless of your budget, you needn't sacrifice quality or style. Set your priorities and let your home take on a dynamic, ever-changing feel as you add or replace furnishings over a period of time.

ACCEPT ONLY THE BEST IN HOME FURNISHINGS

When you want only the best home furnishings, scout the stores offering top quality products and superlative service. These retail stores have knowledgeable staff, sometimes including trained and licensed interior designers, to help you make your selections. (Some may ask nominal fee, which is applied to later purchases, for the designer to help you develop thorough plans.) With a wealth of accumulated knowledge and an unwavering commitment to the highest level of customer service, these experts can advise you on combining optimum comfort with superior quality and fabulous style.

TAKE TIME TO CHOOSE FURNITURE

Your interior designer, or qualified store personnel, can direct your search and keep you within the scale of your floor plan. Their firsthand knowledge of pricing, products and features will help you find the best quality for your money.

To save time, take along your blueprint or a detailed drawing with measurements, door and window placements, and special architectural features. If your spouse or anyone else will be involved in the final decision, try to shop together to eliminate return trips. Most stores can deliver most furniture within eight weeks, but special custom pieces may take up to 16 weeks.

When furnishing a new room, concentrate on selecting one important piece to create a focus, like a Chinese Chippendale-style daybed or an original Arts & Crafts spindle table. Select around whatever special pieces you already own.

Ruthlessly assess your current interior. Clear out pieces that need to be replaced or no longer work with your lifestyle, even if you have no clear idea of what you'll be replacing them with. Sometimes empty space makes visualizing something new much easier.

Be open-minded and accept direction. Salespeople at top stores can help you find exactly what you're seeking, and, if you ask them, can guide you away from inappropriate decisions, towards more suitable alternatives.

THINKING ABOUT FURNISHINGS

Beautiful furnishings complete your vision of "home." If you've been working with an interior designer, kitchen and bath designer, or an architect, you're familiar with the process of defining your personal style. Nowhere is that ability more important than in the selection of furnishings, the most visible and functional contributors to your home interior. Continue to refine your own sense of style. In addition to the Home Book, there are dozens of shelter magazines that showcase beautiful interiors in many styles, and ways to mix them together. Visiting model homes, loft or condominium developments, designer showhouses, or house walks, will help you define your own style preference. By walking through these settings, you'll get a good idea of what furniture arrangements really feel like in a home environment. As you browse through the endless possibilities, keep these thoughts in mind:

• What are your priorities? Develop a list of "must have," "want to have," and "dreaming about."

• Do you want your furnishings to follow the architecture? This always proves a good starting point.

• What colors or styles are already established through the flooring, walls, windows, or cabinetry?

• Can you get the furnishings through the doorway, up the elevator, or down the stairs?

• Does the piece reflect your tastes? Don't be influenced too strongly by what looks great in a showroom or designer house.

• What major pieces will be with you for a long time? Allow a lion's share of your budget for these.

• Does the piece fit the overall decorating scheme? Although the days of strict adherence to one style per room are over it's still necessary to use coordinated styles.

• Do you have something (a lamp, antique candlesticks, a framed picture) you can put on the table you're considering? If not, choose accessories when you choose the table.

• Will a piece work for your family's lifestyle? Chose upholstery fabrics, colors and fixtures that will enhance, not hinder, your everyday life.

• Is the piece comfortable? Before you buy, sit on the chair, recline on the sofa, pull a chair up to the table.

THREE IS THE MAGIC NUMBER

In accessorizing a home, thinking in "threes" is a good rule of thumb: Three candlesticks with candles of three different heights. Three colors of pottery grouped together, one less vibrant to highlight the others. Three patterns in a room.

LOFT LIGHTING

Lofts do have large windows, but they're usually on one wall. That presents a lighting challenge that is often met with new low voltage systems. The transformer is hidden in a closet of soffit; decorative transformers are mounted on a wall. The halogen bulbs last thousands of hours – very important given the height of loft ceilings.

A BRIGHT IDEA

Buy a few clip-on lights with 50-watt bulbs and take them home with you to pinpoint your needs and favorite lighting looks. Experiment with them to create different effects. See if you like up- or downlights to highlight an architectural feature. Get an idea of how much light it takes to illuminate a room.

CONSIDERING CUSTOM FURNITURE

Our area is home to many talented, accessible furniture designers who can create whatever you need to fill a special space in your home, and to satisfy your desire for owning a unique, one-of-a-kind object.

Contacting a furniture designer is the first step toward attaining a fabulous piece of individualized art for your home. Some of the best known designers working here today are listed in the following pages of the Home Book. You can contact them directly, or through your interior designer.

The second step is an initial meeting, during which you'll see examples of the designer's work and answer questions like:

What kind of piece do you want? Free standing entertainment system, dining table, armoire?

What functions must it serve? It is a piece of art, but the furniture still must function in ways that make it practical and usable. Explain your needs clearly.

Do you have favorite woods, materials or colors? As with ordering custom woodwork, the possibilities are almost unlimited. Different woods can be painted or finished differently for all kinds of looks. Have some ideas in mind.

Are you open to new ideas and approaches? If you'd like the designer to suggest new ways of reaching your goal, let him or her know.

If the designer's portfolio excites you, the communication is good, and you trust him or her to deliver your project in a top quality, professional manner, then you're ready to begin. Ask the designer to create a couple of design options. Make sure you and the designer are in agreement regarding finishes, materials, stain or paint samples you want to see, and a completion date. Most charge a 50 percent deposit at the beginning with the balance due upon completion. If you decide not to go ahead with construction of a piece, expect to be billed a designer's fee. A commissioned piece of furniture requires a reasonable amount of time to get from start to finish. If you want an entertainment system for Super Bowl Sunday, make your final design decisions when you take down the Halloween decorations. Keep in mind that the process cannot be rushed.

FILL YOUR HOME WITH SPIRIT...ACCESSORIZE

It is through a table full of delightfully framed family photographs, treasured collectibles on the mantle, or stacks of favorite books in an armoire, that your personality will come shining through. Accessorizing is critical to successful furnishing, because it adds the special touches which make you feel truly at home.

Accessorizing often starts with collections or photographs. Take a handful of your favorite family photos to a fine accessory store, or to your interior designer, to get help in choosing interesting frames that will do justice to the pictures and add flair to any room. Add to an old collection or start a new one. It can be anything – quilts, candlesticks, antique books, or baseballs.

The best thing about accessories is their flexibility. By changing them, or simply moving them around the room or the house, you can create a fresh, new look anytime. By recognizing the great impact of the smaller items in your home, you'll have the ability to refresh and invigorate your interiors to reflect your changing interests and lifestyle.

THE LITTLE THINGS MEAN A LOT

A decor doesn't always start with rugs, furniture and lighting. Many area homeowners are making the decision to give their collections, their interests or their families priority when decorating the home. When a collection of turtles, a passion for music, or a love for flowers is allowed to take front and center in a decorating process, the result will always be intensely personal and fulfilling.

Accessorizing is artful, and an interior designer or salesperson at a fine store will help you establish ways to display your treasures in the most appropriate way. Some people love a "cluttered" tabletop; others prefer a more ordered composition.

THE GLOBAL MARKET-PLACE

There are so many exciting lighting designs available from all over the world, a lighting retailer can't possibly show you even half of them in the showroom. Allow yourself enough time to pour over the catalogs of beautiful chandeliers, luminaries (lamps), and other lighting fixtures available to you. A special order may take up to eight weeks, but it may net you the most beautiful piece of art in your room!

629

LIGHTING YOUR ENTERTAINMENT ROOM

One suggestion for properly lighting a 20-foot by 20-foot room to be used for watching television, listening to music and entertaining friends:
• General lighting provided by recessed fixtures
• A wall-mounted dimming package, with remote control
• A decorative ceiling fixture for more lighting when entertaining.

FABULOUS FABRICS!

You can design an entire room based on a fabulous fabric choice for a pillow, tableskirt, window treatment, or furniture. Evocative color and rich texture are added to any decor through the choices of fabrics and upholstery. Choose what you find enjoyable and comfortable. Always take a swatch home to test it in your light, with the rest of your decorative scheme.

SPOTLIGHT ON LIGHTING

Lighting can be the focal point of a room, or it can be so subtle that it's almost invisible. The trick is knowing what you want to accomplish.

Indeed, when we remember a place as cozy, elegant, or dramatic, or cold and uncomfortable, we're feeling the emotional power of illumination.

This is an exciting time to be choosing a lighting scheme for your home. You will be selecting from an array of imported and domestic products which, when properly used, enhance your furnishings and artwork as well as the comfort level of your daily life. It's critical to make correct lighting decisions.

The industry is filled with options and combinations, from fixtures and bulbs to dimmers and integrated systems. Top lighting retailers in the area employ in-house design consultants to guide you. Or you can employ a residential lighting designer.

To deliver a superior lighting scheme, a designer must know:

• What is your budget? One of the biggest mistakes custom home owners make is under budgeting for their lighting program.

• What are your needs? Lighting falls into three categories – general, task, and atmospheric. A study/work area, a cozy nook, and a kitchen each require different lighting.

• What feeling are you trying to create?

• What "givens" are you working with? Where are your windows or skylights? The use of artificial, indoor light depends to a great degree on the natural light coming in.

• What materials are on the floor and what colors are on the walls and ceiling? This affects reflectance.

• Where is your furniture placed, and how big are individual pieces? This is especially important when you're choosing a dining room chandelier.

• If you're replacing something, why are you replacing it? Know the wattage, for instance, if a current light source is no longer bright enough.

• Are there energy/environmental concerns? Lighting consumes 12 to 15 percent of the electricity used in the home. An expert can develop a plan that maximizes energy efficiency.

• Who lives in the house? Will footballs and frisbees be flying through the kitchen? Pass on the hanging fixture and choose recessed lighting instead.

Finally, try to shop together. The reason for almost all returns is that "my husband or wife didn't like it!" This can tack weeks on to the process of finishing a room. Special orders take up to eight weeks. Your builder will let you know at what point you need to supply fixtures for installation.

THE WELCOME LIVABILITY OF CASUAL FURNISHINGS

As more homeowners opt for a casual, yet elegant ambiance, casual furnishings continue to grow in popularity. In fact, the viability of the trend has recently been recognized within the industry, which has created a separate casual furnishings classification.

Casual furniture is simply less formal in style and function than traditional furniture and is usually found in the family room, sunroom, breakfast room, and bedroom. More often now, these pieces are in the living room. Iron and glass tables, Baker's Racks of pewter and wood, rattan dressers, wicker chairs, and futons are all examples of casual furniture. Sometimes found in traditional furniture stores as accent pieces, full lines of innovative, functional casual furnishings, including accessories, are available at casual furniture specialty stores like those presented in these pages.

"DECKED OUT" FOR OUTDOOR LIVING

As homeowners strive to expand comfortable living space into their yards, top quality outdoor furniture responds with new and innovative styles. Before you go looking at outdoor furniture, think about:

• What look do you like? The intricate patterns of wrought iron? The smooth and timeless beauty of silvery teak wood? The sleek design of sturdy aluminum, which comes with straps, slings or cushions?

• What pieces do you need? Furnishing larger decks and terraces requires careful planning. Area homeowners are buying more seating and end tables and phasing out umbrellas. Ask your landscape architect, deck contractor, or casual furniture store personnel for ideas.

• Can you store the furniture in the winter or will it stay outdoors under cover?

• Can you see the furniture from inside? Make sure the outdoor furnishings won't distract from established design inside or outside.

STAYING IN TUNE

Local piano dealers report that new pianos must be tuned three or four times within the first year. After that, once or twice a year is plenty.

631

'FAUX' FINISH TROMPE L'OEIL?

Any painting technique replicating another look is called a 'faux.' (fake) finish. There are many methods to achieve wonderful individual effects. Trompe l'oeil (fool the eye) is a mural painting that creates illusion through perspective. A wall becomes an arched entry to a garden.

• What is the level of maintenance? If you invest in a top quality product and maintain it well, you can expect it to last you at least 20 years.

THE SPECIAL QUALITY OF PIANOS

A new or professionally reconditioned piano makes an excellent contribution to the elegance and lifestyle of a growing number of area homes. Pianos add a dimension of personality that no ordinary piece of furniture can match. They are recognized for the beauty they add, visually and acoustically.

First time piano buyers may be astonished at the range of choices they have and the variables that will influence their eventual decision. Go to those showrooms that carry the best brand name pianos. Not only will you be offered superior quality instruments, but you'll also get the value of the sales staff's professional knowledge and experience. Questions that you need to answer will include:

• Who are the primary players of the instrument?

• What level of players are they (serious, beginners)?

• Who are their teachers?

• What is the size of the room the piano will placed in?

• What are your preferences in wood color or leg shape?

• Are you interested in software packages that convert your instrument into a player piano?

Pianos represent a significant financial investment, one that will not depreciate, and may actually appreciate over time. If a new piano is out of your financial range, ask about the store's selection of reconditioned instruments that they've acquired through trades. The best stores recondition these pieces to a uniformly high standard of excellence, and are good options for you to consider. These stores also hold occasional promotions, when special pricing will be in effect for a period of time.

FROM SONATA TO SYMPHONY

Even if you don't play a note, you can enjoy the rich sound of live piano music in your home today. Any good quality piano can be turned into a player piano with the installation of a state of the art software package. These packages offer high quality sound reproduction, including all nuances of live performance. You can also manipulate the performance — speeding it up or slowing it down — and even make your own discs. Upgrades include an orchestra attachment, so you can get the effect of an entire orchestra playing along with the piano — or with you — in perfect synchronicity.

ART–OUT OF THE FRAME

Through their travels, reading and exposure to art and design, sophisticated homeowners are aware of the beauty that can be added to their homes with specialty decorative painting. They see in walls, furniture, and fabrics the perfect canvases for unique works of art. The demand for beautiful art applied directly to walls, stairs or furniture has created a renaissance in decorative painting. Faux finishes, trompe l'oeil and murals have joined the traditional finishes of paint, wallpaper and stain for consideration in outstanding residential interiors.

Decorative painting is often applied in kitchens, entryways, and great rooms, where families and guests will get the most enjoyment from this special touch. Faux finishes on walls are intensely original and creative, an outlet for your desires for artistic expression in your own home. Completely custom in color and texture, it has no seams and is generally more durable than wallcovering.

Elegance, drama, whimsy – whatever your style, it's important to find an artist whose vision can translate your desire for something "fantastic" into reality. Specialty painters of the highest caliber, such as those on these pages, can help you fine-tune your idea, or develop a concept from scratch. At your initial meeting, discuss your ideas, whether they're crystal clear or barely there. Don't be apprehensive if you don't have a clear idea. Artists are by profession visually creative, and by asking you questions and showing you ideas, you can develop a concept together.

Ask to see samples of his or her other work, and if possible, visit homes or buildings where the work is installed. Ask for, and call, references. Find out if the work was completed on time and on budget. Based on your initial conversations, a painter can give you a rough estimate based on the size of the room and the finish you've discussed.

LIGHTBULB POWER

New and improved lightbulbs are hot news in the late 1990's. Newly engineered light sources now bring natural sunshine-quality light into area homes. Energy efficiency and life expectancy are both way up. Ask your lighting provider for information.

633

THE PRICE OF GETTING ORGANIZED

• An eight-foot closet, round steel chrome-plated rods, double and single hang, with a five-drawer unit : $800 to $1,000

• His and Hers walk-in closet, full length and double hang rods, two five-drawer units, foldable storage space, mirrored back wall, shoe rack: $1,000 to $4,000

• Conversion of a full-size bedroom into closet area with islands, custom designed cabinets with full extension drawers and decorative hardware, mirrors, jewelry drawers, and many other luxury appointments: $15,000

• Customized desk area, with file drawers, computer stand and slide shelves for printer and keyboard and mouse pad, high pressure surface on melamine with shelves above desk: $1,000

•Average garage remodel, with open and closed storage, sports racks for bikes and fishing poles, a small workbench, and a 4 by 8-foot pegboard, installed horizontally: $2,500

A deposit is generally required, with balance due at completion. Discuss payment plans in the initial meeting. Surface preparation, such as stripping and patching, is not usually done by the specialty painter. Ask for references to do this work if you don't have a painter you already use.

Before painting is begun in your home, the artist should provide you with a custom sample large enough to provide a good visual sense of what the technique will look like in your home, with your fabrics and cabinets.

In trompe l'oeil or any type of mural, don't look for smooth perfection. The effect of trompe l'oeil, which means "fool the eye," is very natural and artistic. If vines, for example, look uniform, it's more likely stenciling has been used. Stencils may be used to lay the groundwork for murals, or when a uniform look is desired.

You can expect the artist to get back to you with sample drawings, showing color and technique, usually within a week. One suburban artist averages two meetings with clients before painting begins. If all decision-makers can attend these meetings, the process will move along more quickly.

Specialty painting is done last, after carpet, trim and other finishing touches are installed. Faux painting of an average-sized room, around 15 by 15 feet, should take two days, depending on the experience of the painter. A vine-covered shelf may take two to three days.

THE HOME OFFICE ARRIVES

At the end of the 20th Century, the home office is a "must-have" room for many area homeowners. More businesses are being operated from home, and increasing numbers of companies are allowing, even encouraging, telecommuting. Spreading out on the dining room table or kitchen table is no longer anywhere near efficient. To answer the demand for home office furnishings and design, many of the top home furnishings stores, like those showcased in the following pages, are dedicating floor space and development resources to providing workable furnishings without sacrificing style or quality. Ergonomically correct desks, keyboard shelves, and chairs are all crucial to high performance home office furniture.

Because the home office requires specific wiring and lighting, be sure your architect, designer and builder are involved in the planning process. If you're simply outfitting an existing room to be your home office, designers on staff at fine furniture stores can guide you. However, it's still most practical to get some architectural input for optimum comfort and functionality of the space.

Unless you're designing a home office that will be architecturally separated from the rest of your home (like a 'loft' office over the garage) it's a challenge to effectively separate work and home. As you plan a home office, ask yourself these questions:

• How do I work best? Close to the action or tucked away where it's quiet?

• How much space do I need? More than one desk, space for computer equipment and other technology, or reference books and files? Space for seeing clients?

• How many phone lines are needed? Get more than you currently need. Do you like a window view? Consider natural light as well as artificial light.

• How will you furnish the office? Will the space also serve as a library or guest room?

Spend some time testing desks and chairs for the most comfortable fit. Top quality office furnishings are now being produced in "scaled down" versions for home use. Make the space attractive and comfortable by using accessories and personal touches. ■

635

ALCHEMIST WOODWORKS

Granite/Wood Tables: Combinations of disparate materials provide interesting contrasts within the arts and crafts context. Highly polished granite offers a counterpoint to the warm look and feel of natural wood in this example. Client preferences for color and texture can be readily accommodated using similar techniques applied to a variety of unique furniture forms.

CHAMPAGNE FURNITURE GALLERY, INC.

Oriental Bar Cabinet: This Oriental bar cabinet features a black and silver crackled finish with glazed silver base, mirrored back and glass shelves with interior lighting.

PENNY & GENTLE MERCANTILE COMPANY

Framed Mirrors: A vast assortment of framed ornamental beveled mirrors is available at Penny & Gentle. The selection of frames ranges from ornate Baroque to simplistic profiles, all wonderfully reflecting the décor and style of your home. The choices are unlimited.

HESTER DECORATING

Faux Finishes:

Subtle nuances in color and texture can dramatically impact the feeling in a room. One of the hottest trends in faux finishes is achieved through a Venetian plaster effect that is available in any color imaginable. This Old World look is popular particularly with clients who want their homes to have a warm, comfortable feel. Color and texture options also play a key role for clients seeking a more contemporary feel. We can create the illusion of floating metallic crystals by adding metal flakes to a clear glaze and then applying that over a two-toned glaze. Again, because any color can be achieved, the possibilities are limitless.

637

MATERIAL CULTURE

Tibetan Rugs:

This Tibetan rug is from a new collection of carpets hand-knitted in Nepal using vegetable dyes and hand-spun wool.

CANNON/BULLOCK

Occasional Furniture Collection:

From Cannon/Bullock's collection of occasional furniture, our drum-like side table is hand carved and planed hardwood with sides wrapped in one of our handmade Lokta papers from Nepal. A variety of wood finishes are available, and the full range of our Caravan Collection papers are available to choose from for wrapping.

SWARTZENDRUBER HARDWOOD CREATIONS

French Country Dining Room:

Fresh from the drawing board to be custom built for you by our craftsmen, the luxurious curves of the French Country dining table and chairs are sensuous to the touch and inviting to the eye. Available in mahogany, we also can fashion this dining set from the hardwood of your choice.

638

HARDWOOD FURNITURE & DESIGN

American Black Walnut Furniture:

The newest star in the world of custom designed hardwood furniture is authentic American black walnut. As delicately grained as cherry, premium black walnut has a rich brown color that cannot be replicated and mellows with age to become even deeper and richer in hue. Look for handcrafted black walnut creations enhanced with hand-rubbed wax finishes in our workshop showroom.

SCANDINAVIAN DESIGN

Partout Modular Collection:

This handsome modular series by TM Line offers design, quality, function and, most importantly, flexibility. Combine Partout pieces to form a wine wall, a curio cabinet or a sideboard, or use your imagination – the possibilities are endless. These modular pieces are available in birch and cherry.

Showroom

see who and what everyone will be talking about.

KARLSON KITCHENS
*Studio Becker
Wardrobe System*
Never enough room for everything? The Studio Becker Wardrobe System could be the answer. Clothing, jewelry and shoes are all organized to maximize the dressing and storage experience. Truly luxurious, this custom-created wardrobe system is designed to benefit individual wardrobe differences while reflecting a variety of space considerations. Handcrafted leather pulls and natural maple cabinetry with contrasting inlays will enhance the beauty of your home.

639

SAWBRIDGE STUDIOS
Buechley Dining Set:
The La Junta table and Alpha chairs from renowned Santa Fe designers Larry and Nancy Buechley celebrate the open look and fluid lines for which this couple is known. A perfect marriage of walnut, maple, leather and glass, these select, hand-fashioned pieces are truly one of a kind.

Custom Furniture Portfolio

SWARTZENDRUBER HARDWOOD CREATIONS,
Carol Simmons:
"Walk through the showroom located in the historic Old Bag Factory and see handcrafted furniture in the Prairie, Arts and Crafts, French Country and Contemporary styles. Step out on the observation deck and watch the pieces being built right before your eyes. Each piece is built to order, giving you an endless palette of possibilities."

ALCHEMIST WOODWORKS,
David Bancroft:
"The designs of Frank Lloyd Wright and his Prairie School contemporaries offer an excellent starting point for variations and adaptations. The plant stand is actually an adaptation of a lamp designed by Wright that works well as a platform for displaying a variety of objects."

Swartzendruber

Home Furnishings

ARVIN DESIGNS ....**(219) 357-4450**
  1003 N. Randolph Street, Garrett   Fax: (219) 357-0947
  See Add on Page: 657   800 Extension: 1087
  <u>Principal/Owner:</u> Sandra Arvin

CANNON/ BULLOCK ....**(323) 221-9286**
  4975 Valley Blvd., Los Angeles   Fax: (323) 221-9287
  See Add on Page: 646, 647   800 Extension: 1029
  <u>Principal/Owner:</u> Richard Bullock & Richard Cannon
  <u>Website:</u> www.cannonbullock.com <u>e-mail:</u> mail@cannonbullock.com

CHAMPAGNE FURNITURE GALLERY, INC. ....**(312) 923-9800**
  65 W. Illinois Street, Chicgao   Fax: (312) 923-9802
  See Add on Page: 367, 670   800 Extension: 1026
  <u>Principal/Owner:</u> Patricia Champagne, IIDA
  <u>Website:</u> champagnefurniture.com <u>e-mail:</u> sales@champagnefurniture.com
  <u>Description:</u> Retail store exhibiting six elegantly furnished, fully accessorized
  rooms; offering full service interior design.

CHEN & CHEN ORIENTAL FURNITURE ....**(847) 432-2828**
  1848 First Street, Highland Park   Fax: (847) 432-8787
  See Add on Page: 658   800 Extension: 1006
  <u>Principal/Owner:</u> Lily Chen
  <u>Website:</u> www.chenandchen.com
  <u>Description:</u> Chen & Chen provides rare, authentic one-of-a-kind handcrafted
  oriental furniture. Art. History. Value. All in one!

DARLEEN'S INTERIORS ....**(630) 357-3719**
  2852 W. Ogden Avenue, Naperville   Fax: (630) 357-9724
  See Add on Page: 364, 660   800 Extension: 1256
  <u>Principal/Owner:</u> Darleen McFarlan

GIEMME USA, LLC ....**(336) 882-1880**
  502 N. Hamliton Street, Highpoint   Fax: (336) 882-0322
  See Add on Page: 670   800 Extension: 1172
  <u>Principal/Owner:</u> Woods Delay Dixon
  <u>Website:</u> www.giemme-stile.it <u>e-mail:</u> giemme@aol.com
  <u>Description:</u> Giemme is an Halian manufacturer of high-end casegood furniture
  offering bedroom, dining room, occasional and office furniture in a wide variety
  of styles and woods.

continued on page **648**

640

"I had three chairs in
my house; one for *solitude,*
two for *friendship,* three for *society.*"
Henry David Thoreau

furnishings for the inspired home

JAYSON
HOME & GARDEN

LE STYLE

ligne roset

DE VIE.

Distinctive, understated furniture, lighting, and
home accessories crafted in France.

KREISS
COLLECTION®

CANNON/BULLOCK

INTERIOR DESIGN   **ARCHITECTURAL DESIGN**   **DESIGN PRODUCT**

WALLCOVERINGS

LIGHTING

WINDOW SHADES

TASSELS + TRIMS + FABRICS

FURNITURE

RUGS

ACCESSORIES

SUSPENSIONS LAMINATE

www.CANNONBULLOCK.com

(323) 221-9286 - Fax (323) 221-9287
e-mail: mail@cannonbullock.com

LOS ANGELES   NEW YORK   CHICAGO   ATLANTA   BOSTON
KANSAS CITY   LAGUNA NIGUEL   LAS VEGAS
LONDON   SYDNEY   MONTREAL
AUCKLAND   ISTANBUL

DALLAS   DANIA   DENVER   HONOLULU   HOUSTON
PORTLAND   SAN FRANCISCO   SEATTLE
TORONTO   VANCOUVER   TOKYO
SINGAPORE   MEXICO CITY

Home Furnishings & Decorating

continued from page **640**

HUFFORD FURNITURE ....**(312) 236-4191**
   310 W. Washington, Chicago   Fax: (312) 236-0559
   See Add on Page: 662, 663   800 Extension: 1021
   <u>Principal/Owner:</u> John Clarkson
   <u>Website:</u> www.huffordfurniture.com
   <u>Description:</u> As one of Chicago's oldest independent furniture stores, Hufford
has served discriminating Chicagoans since 1899.

JAYSON HOME & GARDEN ....**(773) 525-3100**
   1885 & 1911 N. Clybourn Ave., Chicago   Fax: (773) 525-3151
   See Add on Page: 641   800 Extension: 1057
   <u>Principal/Owner:</u> Jay Goltz
   <u>Website:</u> jaysonhome-garden.com <u>e-mail:</u> home@jaysonhome-garden.com

KREISS COLLECTION ....**(312) 527-0907**
   415 N. La Salle Street, Chicago   Fax: (312) 527-5347
   See Add on Page: 645   800 Extension: 1094
   <u>Principal/Owner:</u> Michael Kreiss
   <u>Website:</u> www.kreiss.com <u>e-mail:</u> chicago@kreissshowrooms.com
   <u>Description:</u> A world-class look, featuring an international mix of custom, handmade furniture, unique accessories, professional design consulting, exclusive
fabrics and luxury bed linens.

LES TISSUS COLBERT ....**(630) 232-9940**
   207 W. State Street, Geneva   Fax: (630) 232-9946
   See Add on Page: 661   800 Extension: 6212
   <u>Principal/Owner:</u> Kathy Hanley
   <u>e-mail:</u> lestissuscolbert@aol.com

LIGNE ROSET ....**(314) 965-1991**
   12412 Powerscourt Drive, Suite 175, St. Louis   Fax: (314) 965-8848
   56 E. Walton Street, Chicago   (312) 967-1207
   See Add on Page: 644   800 Extension: 1050
   <u>Principal/Owner:</u> Jon Panullo

MATERIAL CULTURE ....**(312) 467-1490**
   401 N. LaSalle, Chicago   Fax: (312) 467-1491
   See Add on Page: 584, 665   800 Extension: 1111
   <u>Principal/Owner:</u> Tony Trotalli

THE MERCHANDISE MART ....**(312) 527-4141**
   200 World Trade Center, Suite 470, Chicago   Fax: (312) 527-7782
   See Add on Page: 668, 669   800 Extension: 1156
   <u>Website:</u> www.mmart.com

continued on page **656**

"A beautifully designed, meticulously
planned house becomes a *home*
when the furnishings are set in place."

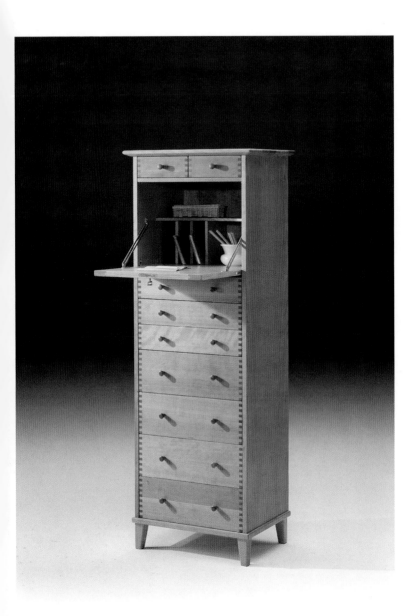

...furniture with a difference.

Scandinavian Design

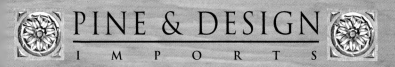

Trianon/Lamplighte

LIVING WITH COMFORT

756 WEST
NORTHWEST
HIGHWAY,

BARRINGTON,
ILLINOIS 60010

TELEPHONE:
847.381.0739

FACSIMILE:
847.381.4859

Custom Furniture

Vintage Pieces

Painted Lines

Area Rugs

Lamps

Chandeliers

Florals

Accessories

Giftables

"Their expertise in manufacturing is invaluable to my creative process"

Nate Berkus,
Nate Berkus
Associates

"Pride in workmanship is increasingly rare. O'Baran (Susan and Doug) truly cares about their finished product."

Thomas Job,
Thomas Job, Inc.

O'BARAN, inc.
Custom Millwork, Cabinetry and Furniture

Mailing Address: 1147 South Wesley Avenue, Oak Park, IL 60304
Shop Address: 743 Circle Avenue, Forest Park, IL 60130
Telephone: (708) 524-8296   Fax: (708) 524-8298
e-mail: obaraninc@yahoo.com

Architecture by Marvin Herman and Assoc.

"If O'Baran is working on something for my firm, I know that my clients will be thrilled with their product."

Daniel DuBay,
Daniel DuBay Interior Design, Inc.

Design by Jeanine Anderson Guncheon

O'BARAN, inc.
Custom Millwork, Cabinetry and Furniture

Mailing Address: 1147 South Wesley Avenue, Oak Park, IL 60304
Shop Address: 743 Circle Avenue, Forest Park, IL 60130
Telephone: (708) 524-8296   Fax: (708) 524-8298
e-mail: obaraninc@yahoo.com

continued from page **648**

MONTAUK ....**(312) 951-5688**
   223 W. Erie, Chicago   Fax: (312) 951-0492
   See Add on Page: 666, 667   800 Extension: 1005
   <u>Website:</u> www.montauksofa.com
MOSAIKO DESIGN ....**(773) 929-9209**
   2150 N. Clybourn St., Chicago   Fax: (773) 929-9217
   See Add on Page: 642, 643   800 Extension: 1078
   <u>Principal/Owner:</u> Kristina Golikova
   <u>Description:</u> Fine furniture can be affordable and shopping doesn't have to be stressful.
O'BARANS ....**(708) 524-8296**
   1147 S. Wesley Avenue, Oak Park   Fax: (708) 524-8298
   See Add on Page: 654, 655   800 Extension: 1185
   <u>Principal/Owner:</u> Susan Barnes
PINE & DESIGN IMPORTS ....**(312) 640-0100**
   511 W. North Avenue, Chicago   Fax: (312) 640-0019
   See Add on Page: 651   800 Extension: 1198
   <u>Principal/Owner:</u> Bill Kowalski, General Manager
   <u>Description:</u> Old wood reproduction furniture, restored european antiques, personalized and custom made pine furniture- eclectic accessories.
SCANDINAVIAN DESIGN ....**(847) 568-0500**
   4028 Dempster Street, Skokie
   See Add on Page: 649   800 Extension: 1187
   <u>Principal/Owner:</u> Tonje Kilen
   <u>Website:</u> www.scandesignfurniture.com
STRAWFLOWER SHOP ....**(630) 232-7141**
   210 W. State Street, Geneva   Fax: (630) 232-4461
   See Add on Page: 650   800 Extension: 6308
   <u>Principal/Owner:</u> Mike Haas/ Susan Haas
   <u>Website:</u> www.strawflowershop.com
TABULA TUA ....**(773) 525-3500**
   1015 W. Armitage, Chicago   Fax: (773) 525-3510
   See Add on Page: 659   800 Extension: 1106
   <u>Principal/Owner:</u> Grace Tsao-Wu
   <u>Website:</u> tabulatua.com
   <u>Description:</u> Chicago's premier tabletop store, featuring handcrafted dinnerware and other unique home furnishings.
TRIANON ....**(847) 381-0739**
   756 W. Northwest Highway, Barrington   Fax: (847) 381-4859
   See Add on Page: 652, 653   800 Extension: 1189
   <u>Principal/Owner:</u> Shirley Irwin

"Spreading out on the *dining room table*, or *kitchen table*, is no longer anywhere near efficient."

Arvin Designs

offers custom creations, which are hand-painted on natural fiber textiles for home furnishings. Designs range from the historically correct for period furniture to the whimsical for the adventurous at heart. Each unique piece is rendered to meet clients' tastes and design requirements.

Arvin Designs

1003 NORTH RANDOLPH STREET
GARRETT, INDIANA 46738
(219) 357-4450   CHI. (773) 871-3185
FAX (219) 357-0947

Shop www.tabulatua.com

TABULA TUA
B E A U T I F U L   W A R E S

1015 W. ARMITAGE AVE.   CHICAGO, ILLINOIS 60614   773.525.3500
Ceramic Dinnerware • Serving Bowls • Linens, Glassware & Silverware • Unique Tabletop Accessories

Darleen's

INTERIORS

2852 West Ogden Avenue
Naperville, IL 60540
630-357-3719
www.darleensinteriors.com

Premium Fabrics from Paris and the French Countryside in widths up to 110 inches.

Custom pillows, duvet covers, upholstered furniture and accent pieces.

Charming Antique Furniture and Accessories from England, Belgium and France.

Les Tissus Colbert

Fabrics • Antiques • Furniture • Design

Downtown Geneva
207 West State Street • Geneva, Illinois 60134 • 630.232.9940

SHOWROOM HOURS

Monday & Thursday - 8:30 a.m. to 7:00 p.m.
Tuesday, Wednesday & Friday - 8:30 a.m. to 5:30 p.m.
Saturday - 9:30 a.m. to 3:30 p.m.
Free Parking on Saturdays — Call store for details.

VARIED TREASURE ....**(847) 202-0509**
117 W. Slade Street, Palatine   Fax: (847) 202-0569
See Add on Page: 671   800 Extension: 1253
<u>Principal/Owner:</u> Marilyn and Dan Kathrn
<u>Website:</u> variedtreasure.com   <u>e-mail:</u> varietreasure@home .com

"Lighting is a critical design element;
it can be the focal point of a
room, or it can be so subtle that it's
almost invisible."

MONTAUK

"the
most important
skills
I bring to the design process
are the skills of
listening
and observing.
My goal is to identify
the client's personal style and
celebrate
life's everyday rituals."

Eric Mullendore
Eric Mullendore, Architect - Interior Design
Chicago

Oriental Rugs International

"**each person**
and
each project is unique.
My goal for **every** client
is to create an
exceptional environment
reflecting
his or her **taste,**
personality
and lifestyle."

Lois Gries, ASID
Lois Gries Interior Design
Chicago

photo: Jason Penney

Holly Hunt

Custom
Furniture

ALCHEMIST WOODWORKS ....**(608) 987-4554**
711 Center Street, Mineral Point
See Add on Page: 673   800 Extension: 1235
Principal/Owner: David Bancroft

HARDWOOD FURNITURE & DESIGN ....**(630) 543-2022**
230 Laura Drive, Addison
See Add on Page: 674   800 Extension: 1051
Description: Specializing in hand-crafted, authentic hardwood furniture, wall
units, bookcases, home office, home theater, audio cabinetry and entertainment
centers.

SAWBRIDGE STUDIOS ....**(847) 441-2441**
1015 Tower Court, Winnetka   Fax: (847) 441-2442
See Add on Page: 675   800 Extension: 1211
Principal/Owner: Paul Zurowski
Description: Handcrafted furniture and home accessories made by artisans from
across the country.

SAWBRIDGE STUDIOS ....**(312) 828-0055**
153 West Ohio Street, Chicago   Fax: (312) 828-0066
See Add on Page: 675   800 Extension: 1212
Principal/Owner: Paul Zurowski
Description: Handcarfted furniture and home accessories made by artisans from
across the country.

SWARTZENDRUBER HARDWOOD CREATIONS, INC. ....**(219) 534-2502**
1100 Chicago Avenue, Goshen   Fax: (219) 534-2504
See Add on Page: 622, 623, 676   800 Extension: 6314
Principal/Owner: Larion Swartzendruber
Website: www.swartzendruber.com e-mail: sales@swartzendruber.com
Description: Custom hardwood furniture. Specializing in the Prarie, Arts &
Crafts, French, Country and Contemporary styles.

672

Contemporary Hardwood Furniture

Offered in a full range of intelligent sizes and configurations

We make the only furniture ever
"Highly Recommended"
by *Stereophile* Magazine

B uy our world-renowned, hand-crafted natural hardwood
furniture direct from our studio showroom and save 50%
• Wall Units • Bookcases • Home Office Systems •
• Home Theater • Audio Cabinetry • Entertainment Centers •

HARDWOOD
FURNITURE & DESIGN
• CHERRY • OAK • MAPLE • WALNUT •

Sat. 10-5, Sun. 12-5, Tue. Wed. Thu. Fri. 10-5
230 Laura Drive • Addison, Illinois 630 543-2022

**Furniture Made Here Has Been Chosen for More Magazine
Front Covers Than Any Other Contemporary Wood Furniture in America**

MADE BY HAND
NOT A FACTORY.

ALL FURNITURE IS NOT CREATED EQUAL.

FINE HANDCRAFTED FURNITURE STANDS APART. ADMIRE THE SELECT

WOOD GRAINS. NOTICE THE PRECISION JOINERY. SAVOR THE HAND-

RUBBED SURFACES. EXPLORE COLLECTIONS FROM SOME OF THE FINEST

INDEPENDENT FURNITURE MAKERS IN AMERICA. CRAFTED IN A BROAD

RANGE OF STYLES, EACH PIECE IS BUILT TO YOUR SPECIFICATIONS

WITH EXTRAORDINARY PRIDE AND SKILL.

CARPET COURTESY OF OSCAR ISBERIAN RUGS, EVANSTON AND CHICAGO

SAWBRIDGE STUDIOS

HANDCRAFTED FURNITURE & ACCESSORIES

CHICAGO: 153 WEST OHIO STREET 312/828-0055
WINNETKA: 1015 TOWER COURT 847/441-2441

Lighting

ACTIVE ELECTRICAL SUPPLY.......................................**(773) 282-6300**
4240 W. Lawrence Ave., Chicago   Fax: (773) 282-5206
See Add on Page: 440, 678, 679   800 Extension: 1010
<u>Principal/Owner:</u> Skip Leigh

BRASS LIGHT GALLEY ....**(414) 271-8300**
131 S. First Street, Milwaukee   Fax: (414) 271-7755
See Add on Page: 680, 681   800 Extension: 1047
<u>Principal/Owner:</u> Stephen Kaniewski
<u>Website:</u> www.brasslight.com   <u>e-mail:</u> showroom@brasslight.com
<u>Description:</u> Brass Light Gallery designs and manufactures better quality decorative lighting for residential and commercial use.

TECH LIGHTING GALLERIES ....**(312) 642-1586**
300 W. Superior, Suite 101, Chicago   Fax: (312) 642-6605
See Add on Page: 682   800 Extension: 1177
<u>Principal/Owner:</u> Peter Pechianu
<u>Website:</u> www.tlgalleries.com   <u>e-mail:</u> tlight@aol.com
<u>Description:</u> Midwest's premier lighting showroom specializing in monorail twin rail, kable lights & other exquisite hand blown murano glass fixtures.

From Contemporary

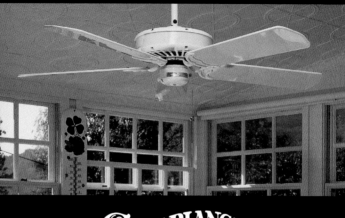

To Traditional

SCHONBEK
BEYOND LIGHTING™

✦PROGRESS
LIGHTING

At *Fox Lighting Galleries*, we don't just improve atmosphere, we create it. Since 1953, value, selection and personal service have made us Chicagoland's leading single supplier of lighting. Stop in or call and see why.

Pianos

FMAR-COLE MUSIC ....**(630) 980-3200**
400 West Army Trail Road, Bloomingdale
See Add on Page: 684, 685   800 Extension: 1061
HENDRICKS PIANOS ....**(630) 969-5082**
421 Maple Avenue, Downers Grove
See Add on Page: 684, 685   800 Extension: 1007
KARNES MUSIC CO. ....**(312) 663-4111**
333 South State Street, Chicago
See Add on Page: 684, 685   800 Extension: 1015
ORTIGARA'S MUSICVILLE ....**(708) 423-7910**
10830 South Central Avenue, Chicago Ridge
See Add on Page: 684, 685   800 Extension: 1066

"When we remember a place as cozy,
elegant, or dramatic, or cold and
uncomfortable, we're feeling the emotional
power of illumination."

Window
Coverings

H&R CUSTOM DESIGNS ....**(847) 562-0487**
300 Skokie Blvd., Northbrook   Fax: (847) 562-9487
See Add on Page: 690   800 Extension: 1176
Principal/Owner: Helene Weiner
Website: www.H&Rdesigns.com   e-mail: Helene315@aol.com

KIRSCH CO. ....**(800) 817-6344**
524 W. Stephenson Street, Freeport   Fax: (815) 266-8750
See Add on Page: 688, 689   800 Extension: 1092
Principal/Owner: Linda Busch
Website: www.kirsch.com
Description: Worldwide manufacturer and distributor of decorative hardware, curtain rods, traverse rods, specialty rods and drapery track systems.

NATIONAL WINDOW SHADE COMPANY ....**(630) 920-1919**
667 Executive Drive, Willowbrook   Fax: (630) 920-1934
See Add on Page: 687   800 Extension: 1076
e-mail: natwinshad@aol.com
Description: Servicing the Chicagoland area since 1900 with the finest aluminum and hardwood shutters.

SHUTTER HUT, INC...**(847) 740-6790**
31632 N. Ellis Drive, Suite 101, Volo   Fax: (847) 740-1369
See Add on Page: 692   800 Extension: 6297
Principal/Owner: Michael Ready

SUNBURST SHUTTERS ....**(847) 640-6622**
1315 Howard Street, Elk Grove Village   Fax: (847) 640-6742
See Add on Page: 691

National Window Shade Co.

667 Executive Drive
Willowbrook, IL 60521
630.920.1919
FAX 630.920.1934

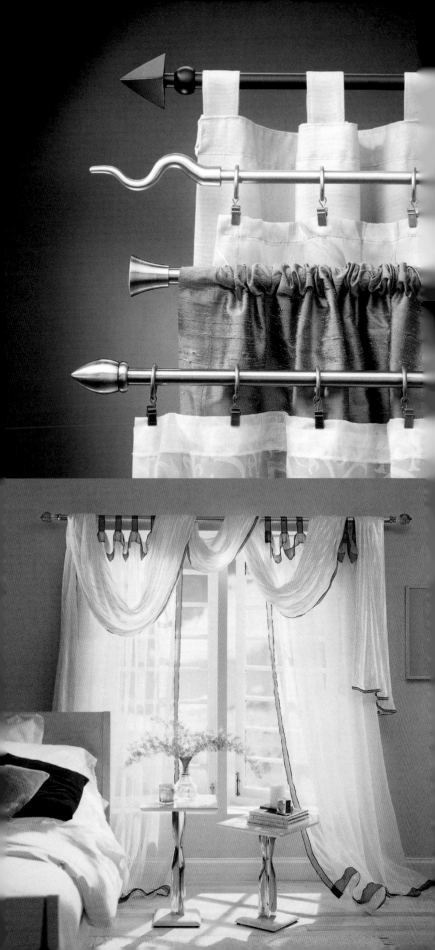

Kirsch

k ...decorating your life

Freeport, IL 61032
1-800-817-6344 • www.kirsch.com

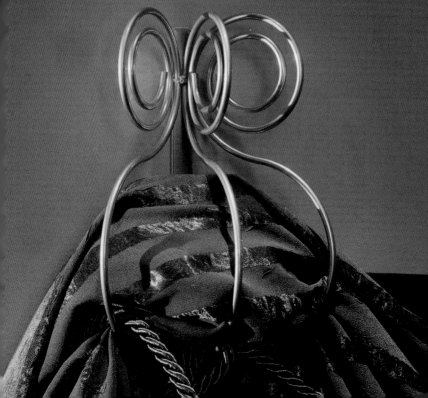

Create more than beautiful windows with
H&R Custom Designs

Specializing in: **HunterDouglas**
WINDOW FASHIONS

- Duette® Honeycomb Shades • Silhouette® Window Shadings
- Luminette Privacy Sheers® • Country Woods®
- Plantation Shutters • Vertical & Mini Blinds • Cornices
- Fabrics • Bedspreads • Headboards • Pillows • Wallpaper
- Faux Texturing • Draperies • Specialty Valances • And More!

H&R Custom Designs
Commercial • Residential
300 Skokie Blvd • Northbrook Illinois
847.562.0487 • 630.323.6800
Hours M - F 10-4
www.handrdesigns.com

Shutter Hut INC.

CUSTOM SHUTTER SPECIALISTS

PLANTATION SHUTTERS

Beautify your windows with custom shutters from Shutter Hut. Manufactured in the finest quality cedar or basswood, shutters are made in $1\frac{1}{4}$, $1\frac{7}{8}$, $2\frac{1}{2}$, $3\frac{1}{2}$, $4\frac{1}{2}$ or $5\frac{1}{2}$-inch width louvers. Custom stained or painted to match your decor. Come see full size displays in our well appointed showroom. Vinyl clad shutters, wood blinds and Silhouette® are also available.

Owned and operated by the Ready family for 26 years.

Located at the Volo Commerce Center, Route 120 just east of Route 12 in Volo, IL
Daily 8:30 to 5:00 • Saturday 10:00 to 4:00 • Closed Sunday

847-740-6790

Shown below 8' sliding door

Specialty
Wall Finishes

CHICAGO PLASTERING INSTITUTE ....**(773) 774-4500**
6547 N. Avondale, Chicago   Fax: (773) 774-5828
See Add on Page: 694   800 Extension: 6057
Principal/Owner: Gerald Holdway
Description: Providing information and specifications to Architects and Builders
on all phases of plastering.

HESTER DECORATING ....**(847) 677-5130**
7340 N. Monticello, Skokie   Fax: (847) 677-5139
See Add on Page: 695   800 Extension: 1130
Principal/Owner: Tom Hester
Website: www.hesterdecorating.com   e-mail: info@hesterdecorating.com
Description: With over 30 years of experience, Hester Decorating provides fine
residential printing, paperhanging, faux and specialty finishes throughout
Chicagoland.

"As more homeowners opt
for a *casual, yet elegant ambience,*
furnishings continue to
in popularity."

The Art of Plastering

Class that Lasts!

It's a fact! No wall finish provides better fire protection, sound control, or design flexibility than plaster.

Chicago Plastering Institute

6547 N. Avondale Ave.
Chicago, IL 60631
773-774-4500
Fax. 773-774-5828

Today's plaster walls may be made with conventional plaster and lath, or a faster and more cost-efficient veneer plaster system. Either way, plaster's tougher surface means that it stands up to abuse better than any other interior finish.

And only plaster can offer detailed ornamental treatments, and mouldings that look better, install faster and actually cost less than wood alternatives.

For more information about plaster systems and the best professionals to apply them, call us.

Home Office,
Closet & Garage

CALIFORNIA CLOSETS ....**(847) 541-8666**
339 Egidi Drive, Wheeling   Fax: (847) 541-8974
See Add on Page: 699   800 Extension: 1028
<u>Principal/Owner:</u> Ray Reddi

CALIFORNIA CLOSETS ....**(630) 916-7393**
123 Eisenhower Lane S., Lombard   Fax: (630) 916-7420
See Add on Page: 699   800 Extension: 6045

CLASSIC CLOSETS ....**(630) 355-7850**
560 W. Fifth Avenue, Naperville   Fax: (630) 355-6770
See Add on Page: 700   800 Extension: 1251
<u>Principal/Owner:</u> Bob Callaghan

CLOSET WORKS ....**(630) 832-3322**
953 N. Larch, Elmhurst   Fax: (630) 832-6878
See Add on Page: 697   800 Extension: 6064
<u>Principal/Owner:</u> Mike Carson
<u>Website:</u> www.closetworks.com <u>e-mail:</u> closetworks@hotmail.com
<u>Description:</u> Closet Works is an independantly owned company with an in-house manufacturing facility. A proud member of, "The National Closet Group".

HOME OFFICE SOLUTIONS ....**(847) 299-3911**
4348 Regency Drive, Glenview   Fax: (847) 299-3709
See Add on Page: 698   800 Extension: 1039
<u>Principal/Owner:</u> Marc Levin
<u>Website:</u> officedesigns.com

KARLSON KITCHENS ....**(847) 491-1300**
1815 Central Street, Evanston   Fax: (847) 491-0100
See Add on Page: 458, 459, 701   800 Extension: 1225
<u>Principal/Owner:</u> David Karlson
<u>Website:</u> www.karlsonkitchens.com <u>e-mail:</u> karlkit@wwa.com
<u>Description:</u> We have been designing and installing finer kitchens and master bathrooms for over 30 years.

life   stuff   storage

California Closets has been organizing homes and simplify lives **since 1978**, when we founded the industry. We are still the inovators today, pushing ourselves to deliver the best possible product and customer service in the industry.

We create custom solutions for your closet, home office, garage, pantry, kid's rooms and utility areas.

Where do you put the stuff that you're about? All that you are? Tell us. We're listening.

Call for a complimentary design consultation in your home.

800.2SIMPLIFY (274-6754) • www.calclosets.com

CALIFORNIA CLOSETS®

Classic Closets, Inc.

Custom Storage Cabinetry

We do more than just closets!

Garage • Pantry • Laundry Room • Basement
Home Office • Media Center • Study

Once you own a custom closet, you will wonder how you got by before. Having a place for all your belongings makes your life more organized and less confusing. In today's fast paced life, being able to get ready faster can mean the difference in spending more time with loved ones or a moment for yourself.

We invite you to setup an appointment at our factory showroom or a free in-home consultation.

560 W. 5th Ave
Naperville, IL
630-355-7850 Tel
630-355-6770 Fax

Finally...
Chicago's Own
Home & Design
Sourcebook

The CHICAGO HOME BOOK, a comprehensive hands-on
design sourcebook to building, remodeling, decorating, furnishing
and landscaping a luxury home in Chicago and its suburbs,
is a "must-have" reference for the Chicagoland homeowner.
At over 700 pages, this beautiful, full-color hard cover
volume is quite simply the most complete, well-organized
reference to the Chicagoland home industry. It covers all aspects
of the process, with hundreds of listings of local home industry
professionals, accompanied by hundreds of inspiring photographs.
You will also find articles to assist in planning and completing a
project. The CHICAGO HOME BOOK tells you how to
find what you need when you need it.

Order your copy today!

Published by
The Ashley Group
1350 E. Touhy Avenue • Des Plaines, IL 60018
888-458-1750
E-mail: ashleybooksales@cahners.com

Photo courtesy of:
Gallery Northwest

ART&
ANTIQUES

CALEDONIAN

Fine English Antiques and Furnishings

820 Frontage Road Northfield, Illinois 60093
847.446.6566   Fax 847.446.6569   www.caledonianinc.com

Invest in the Past

INVEST IN BEAUTY, HANDCRAFTED QUALITY AND TIMELESS
VALUE. CALEDONIAN IS AN INTERNATIONALLY RECOGNIZED
GALLERY FOR FINE PERIOD ANTIQUES FROM EIGHTEENTH
AND NINETEENTH CENTURY ENGLAND. ESTABLISHED IN 1941,
AND NOW IN ITS THIRD GENERATION, CALEDONIAN INVITES
YOU TO BROWSE THEIR ELEGANT 10,000 SQUARE FOOT
GALLERIES IN NORTHFIELD.

"**Art**
does not
reproduce the
visible;
it makes visible. "

Paul Klee

Something Old Something New

photo courtesy of:
**Penny & Gentle
Fine Art Studio**

707

The fine art and antiques scene is as dynamic as ever. From cutting-edge modern galleries to showrooms of stately antiques, few places in the world offer more choice for bringing truly unique works of art into the home.

Beloved one-of-a-kind items give a home personality in a way that other purchases can't match. Fine art must speak to the soul of the owner. Antique furnishings tell their story through the generations.

Art and antiques, unlike so many other pieces purchased for the home, have the potential to become a family's heirlooms. Even an inexpensive "find" may someday become a most treasured item because of the warm memories it rekindles. Truly, these choices should be made with the care and the guidance of an experienced professional who understands their significance in your home.

LEARN ABOUT ART & ANTIQUES

Part of the pleasure of collecting art or antiques is learning about them. Many homeowners buy a particular painting or sculpture they love, and find that following the art form or the artists becomes a lifetime passion.

The best place to start to familiarize yourself with art is at one of the many wonderful museums in the Chicago area. Wander through historic homes in the different historic neighborhoods of the city and get an idea of what the art feels like in a home environment. Go to auctions. Buy the catalog and attend the viewing. At the sale, you'll begin to get an idea of the values of different types of items. Finally, get to know a dealer. Most are pleased to help you learn and want to see more people develop a lifetime love affair with art, similar to their own. If a dealer seems too busy or isn't genuinely interested in helping you, then go to another dealer.

Haunt the local bookstores and newsstands. There are many publications dedicated to these fields.

THE WORLD OF ANTIQUES

Homeowners find their way to antiques by many different paths. Some are adding to an inherited collection that connects them with past generations of family or with the location of their birth. Some are passionate about pottery or porcelain, clocks or dolls, and want to expand their knowledge while building a life-time collection.

Antique furniture, artwork and collectibles also can be used to make a singular statement in an interior. Through a 19th Century English chest, or an American Arts & Crafts table, homeowners put a personal signature stamp on their interior design.

Making the right selection is as much a matter of taste and personal aesthetic as it is knowledge and experience. An interior designer or gallery owner will be a good guide to making a choice.

As top quality antique paintings, photographs and other desirable items become more and more difficult to find, getting expert guidance in identifying good and worthwhile investments is crucial. Top galleries in the area are operated and staffed by knowledgeable professionals who will do just that.

When you enter a store or gallery, be prepared to seriously consider what type of investment you wish to make and how it will work in a given interior. If someone besides yourself will be involved in the final decision-making process, try to have them with you.

If you're pursuing pieces to add to an existing collection, do your research to determine which galleries in town cater to your interests. Or, check with a favorite gallery for information.

Be open to ideas and suggestions, especially when you're just beginning a collection, or a search for a special antique. The best galleries are gold mines of information and ideas. There is so much to know about so many different objects, time periods, and design, that it truly does take a lifetime to develop an expertise. The owners of these establishments are first and foremost interested in finding you an antique that will impress and delight today, and in the future, and usually prefer to have you invest in one or two good pieces, than in a handful of items that won't bring you as much pleasure in the long run.

VISITING THE GALLERIES

More than anything else, choosing to make beautiful and distinctive art objects a part of your home brings the joy of living with beautiful things into the daily life of yourself, your family and your guests.

The most important rule to know as your begin or continue to add art to your home is that there truly are no "rights or wrongs." Find what reaches you on an emotional level, and then begin to learn about it.

Use your eyes and react with your heart. Look at art magazines and books. There are many, many beautiful periodicals, and just as many books published on artists and art genres. Visit the museums in town, and those in other cities as you travel. Go to the galleries. Visit many of them for the widest exposure to different possibilities. Let only your sense of beauty and aesthetics guide you at this point. Consider other constraints after you've identified the objects of your desire.

When you've found what really speaks to you on a personal level, start learning more about who creates art in that style, where it's available locally, and if it's within your budget. The more information you can take with you when you begin your shopping, the more help a gallery can be to you in your search.

EXPERT ADVICE

The most reputable art gallery owners and dealers have earned their reputation by establishing an expertise in their field, and serving their clients well.

Buying from these established and respected professionals offers many benefits. Their considerable knowledge of and exposure to art translates into opinions that mean a great deal. You can put stock in the advice and education they offer you. They've done considerable research and evaluation before any item gets placed in their gallery, and determined that it's a good quality item, both in terms of artistic merit and market value. You'll also enjoy a sense of security when you patronize these businesses. They will stand behind the authenticity of what they present in their galleries. Most offer free consultations, trade-back arrangements, and installation, and will help you with selling your art at some point in the future as your collection grows, you change residences, or your tastes change.

Don't expect a gallery to be an expert in categories outside of those they specialize in.

VALUE JUDGEMENTS

Buy for love, not money. This is the advice we heard time and again from the best art galleries. Not all art appreciates financially – often it fluctuates over the years according to the artist's career, consumer tastes, and the state of the overall economy. If you love what you own and have been advised well by a knowledgeable professional, you'll be happiest with your investment.

THE FALL SEASON

Fall signals the beginning of the art season. Galleries will open exhibits and the excitement is contagious. Ask to get on gallery mailing lists to stay informed of fall openings.

SEE THE SHOWS

The Chicago area abounds with arts, antiques, and collectibles shows and festivals. These are great places to browse for and learn about thousands of items – from jewelry to pop culture collectibles. Local newspapers and magazines run announcements for these kinds of events, or ask your favorite gallery owner for information.

709

MATCHING ART TO ARCHITECTURE

If you're renovating an historic or old home of distinction, ask your favorite gallery owner or renovation specialist for guidance in choosing art that will fit your home.

There is no upper limit on what you can spend on an art collection, or a single artwork, and there are no set standards for pricing. Gallery owners set prices according to their own standards, evaluations and experience, to represent a fair market value. Set a working budget (possibly a per-piece budget) and let the gallery know upfront what the guidelines are. This saves both you and the gallery time and energy. You'll be able to focus on items that are comfortably within the range of your budget. Buy the best quality possible in whatever category you like. You will appreciate the quality for years. Don't hesitate to do some comparison shopping. Although each art object is unique in itself, you may find another piece in the same style that you enjoy equally as well.

The best dealers understand budgets, and respect your desire to get good quality at a fair price. They are happy to work with enthusiastic clients who want to incorporate beautiful art into their lives. Ask if the dealer offers terms, if you're interested in making your purchases on a payment plan. Also inquire about return or exchange policies, consignment plans, consultations and trade-up policies.

Only deal with dealers who are helpful and present their art fairly. If you feel intimidated in a gallery, or feel the dealer isn't giving you the time and information you deserve to make intelligent choices, visit another gallery. Never buy art under pressure from a dealer, or to meet an imposed deadline in your home interior timetable.

GO TO AN AUCTION HOUSE

Attending an auction is an excellent way to learn about decorative arts, develop and add to a collection, and simply have a good time. Whether you attend as a buyer, seller, or observer, an auction is an experience that will enrich your understanding and enjoyment of the art and antiques world.

If you're a novice, it's important to choose a well established auction house with a reputation for reliability. Try to be a patient observer and learn about the process as well as the value of items you may be interested in later on.

Buy a copy of the catalog and attend the viewing prior to the beginning of the auction itself. Each item, or "lot," that will be available for sale at the auction will be listed, and a professional estimate of selling price will be included. Professionals will be available during the viewing to answer questions and help you become familiar with the art objects as well as the process. Once bidding starts, it is done by "paddle," small numbered placards used to signal a bid, which are obtained before or during the auction.

CHOOSING AN AUCTION

Find out about interesting auctions from the proprietors of galleries you like, or ask to be added to the mailing list of a reputable auction house. With these sources of information, you'll be informed of events that will feature quality items that interest you. Local newspapers and magazines also print upcoming auction dates and locations. The established auction houses that have earned a reputation for reliability and expertise generally have a single location where they hold their auctions. Sometimes an auction will be held at an estate site, or a seller's location.

Before attending the auction, spend some time researching the art or antique you're interested in bidding on, so you'll be informed about its value and can make an informed decision. Talk to people at the galleries. There also are books available that publish recent auction sales to help you get an idea of price and availability. Check your library or book seller for publications like Gordon's Price Annual.

There is an air of mystery and sophistication that surrounds the auction experience, but don't let that discourage you from discovering the auction experience. Auctions are enjoyable and educational for anyone who is interested in obtaining or learning about art and antiques.

BE REALISTIC

For many of us, an auction might seem an opportunity to pick up an item at a bargain price. Realize that there may be bargains to be found, but in general, auctioned items are sold for a fair price. There may be a "reserve price," which is a private agreement between the seller and the auctioneer on a minimum bid.

If you educate yourself about the category you're interested in, you'll be in better stead at an auction. It's equally important to research the market value of any lot you may be considering. Remember that there is an auctioneer's commission of 10 to 15 percent of the hammer price, to be paid on top of the purchase price, as well as applicable sales taxes.

Auctions are essentially competitive in nature, with potential buyers bidding against one another. Until you've attended enough auctions to feel confident in your own knowledge, as well as in your understanding of the auction process, don't become an active participant. It's easy to get swept up in the fast pace and excitement. While you won't end up making the top bid simply by tugging your ear, it's important to pay attention when you're bidding. Be aware of the way the auctioneer communicates with the bidders and always listen for the auctioneer's "fair warning" announcement just before the gavel falls. ■

Antiques

CALEDONIAN, INC. ....**(847) 446-6566**
820 Frontage Road, Northfield   Fax: (847) 466-6569
See Ad on Page: 704, 705, 716, 717   800 Extension: 6044
<u>Principal/Owner:</u> Barrie Heath
<u>Website:</u> www.caledonianinc.com

GURNEE ANTIQUE CENTER ....**(847) 782-9094**
5742 Northridge Drive, Gurnee   Fax: (847) 782-9095
See Ad on Page: 718   800 Extension: 6137
<u>Principal/Owner:</u> Luan Watkins
<u>Website:</u> www.gurneeantiquecenter.com <u>email:</u> watkins@flash.net
<u>Additional:</u> Over 200 dealers specializing in fine 18th, 19th and early 20th century furniture and accessories. Open M-Sat 10-5,12-5. Open Thursday evenings until 8pm.

ROUZATI RUGS..**(847) 328-0000**
1907 Central Street, Evanston   Fax: (847) 328-2306
See Ad on Page: 586, 587, 719   800 Extension: 1207
<u>Principal/Owner:</u> Jafam Rouzati

BERNARD BARUCH STEINITZ ....**(014) 289-4050**
9, rue du Cirque, Paris   Fax: (014) 289-4060
See Ad on Page: 714, 715   800 Extension: 1247
<u>Principal/Owner:</u> Bernard Baruch Steinitz

TROWBRIDGE GALLERY ....**(312) 587-9575**
703 N. Wells Street, Chicago   Fax: (312) 587-9742
See Ad on Page: 713   800 Extension: 6324
<u>Principal/Owner:</u> Cecily Brainard McAfee
<u>Additional:</u> Trowbridge Gallery specializes in 16th - 19th century prints. A lively array of Botanical Natural History and Architectural prints can be found framed in European hand crafted frames at the Trowbridge Gallery.

BERNARD & BENJAMIN
STEINITZ
Antique Dealers

invite you to visit
their gallery

16, avenue Natignon

9, rue du Cirque

Paris 75008

NEW YORK

PALM BEACH

CHICAGO

For Inquiries in the USA

773-348-2376

Tel (33) 1.42.89.40.50 Fax (33) 01.42.89.40.60

An impressive reproduction of an English Regency mahogany sideboard incorporating dramatic shaping, rosewood inlays and well-modeled legs.

The Caledonian Collection is an exclusive range of 18th century English furniture reproductions. Replicas and custom commissions are of the highest quality, handcrafted in small workshops throughout England.

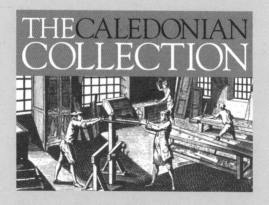

Handcrafted Reproductions
of 18th Century English Furniture

Rouzati Oriental Rugs, Inc.

1907 Central Street
Evanston, IL 60201
847 328 0000 Fax 328 2306

Art Galleries

THE CRYSTAL CAVE ....**(847) 251-1160**
1141 Central Ave., Wilmette
See Ad on Page: 727
Principal/Owner: Josef Puehringer
email: allerystall1141@acl.com
Additional: Custom engraving on crystal giftware - crystal blocks - vases -
bowles etc. Send us a picture of your home and we can create an heirloom.
Fax: (847) 251-1172
800 Extension: 1063

FRAMED CLASSICS/PURSUING THE PAST ....**(773) 871-1790**
2227 West Belmont, Chicago
See Ad on Page: 726
Principal/Owner: Brian McCarty
email: frmdclcs@aol.com
Fax: (773) 248-7749
800 Extension: 1158

GALLERY NORTHWEST ....**(847) 391-0014**
234 N. Northwest Highway, Palatine
See Ad on Page: 723
Principal/Owner: Brent Willers
Website: www.artnframing.com
Additional: Unique design with emphasis on conservation framing- originals,
limited editions and posters.
Fax: (847) 356-1538
800 Extension: 1244

MARSH ....**(561) 994-9119**
6560 W. Rogers Circle, Suite 25, Boca Raton
See Ad on Page: 721
Fax: (561) 994-8811
800 Extension: 1143

PENNY & GENTLE FINE ART STUDIO ....**(312) 467-0273**
900 West Lake Street (at Peoria), Chicago
See Ad on Page: 726
Principal/Owner: Mary Jane Maher / Marilyn M.
Additional: This studio offers a vast assortment of original oil paintings as well
as old master "re-creations" - all in museum reproduction frames. Excellent
commission works and beautifully framed mirrors are a specialty.
Fax: (312) 467-0274
800 Extension: 1125

PRINCETON LTD. ....**(847) 432-1930**
1844 First Street, Highland Park
See Ad on Page: 727
Principal/Owner: Joan Schnadig/ Richard Schnadig
Fax: (847) 432-2009
800 Extension: 1132

THE STUDIO OF LONG GROVE ....**(847) 634-4244**
360 Historical Lane, Long Grove
See Ad on Page: 724, 725
Principal/Owner: Thomas Hilligoss
Fax: (847) 634-4722
800 Extension: 1195

VINTAGE POSTERS INTERNATIONAL, LTD. ....**(312) 951-6681**
1551 N. Wells, Chicago
See Ad on Page: 722
Principal/Owner: Susan Cutler
Fax: (312) 951-6681
800 Extension: 1191

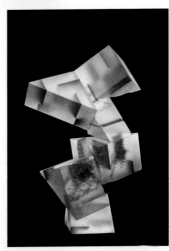

Marsh

6560 W. Rogers Circle, Ste. 25
Boca Raton, FL 33487
561.994.9119
fax 561.994.8811
www.rgarrettdesigns.com

Photography: Rich Sistos Photography/Oak Brook

$\mathcal{G}$ allery Northwest is a truly unique destination for anyone looking for a broad selection of traditional to contemporary art. Add to this an impressive selection of over 2,000 frame choices and a wide array of mats, fillets and liners and you begin to get a feel for the unlimited possibilities of acquiring great pieces of art and making them everything they can be through custom framing. All of this can be done at Gallery Northwest – a wonderful taste of Chicago in the suburbs. Particular attention is paid to quality materials with an emphasis on conservation framing. No detail is too small to make your art look its best throughout the millennium. This even includes wonderful visions of custom mirrors. So come surprise your artful senses at Gallery Northwest. You'll be glad you made the trip.

Gallery Northwest

Fine Art & Custom Framing

234 North Northwest Highway • Palatine, IL 60067
(847) 991-0014 Fax (847) 358-1538 Web www.artNframing.com

HILLIGOSS GALLERIES
*In the Shops
at North Bridge
520 N. Michigan Ave.
(312) 755-0300
(in the Nordstrom Complex)*

Alan Wolton

Tuan

Michael Gerry

Mersad Berber

PENNY & GENTLE

MERCANTILE COMPANY

900 West Lake Street, Chicago IL 60607 312/467-0273

Framed Classics

WHEN QUALITY COUNTS.

2227 West Belmont Avenue

(773) 871-1790 Mon-Sat **11-6,** Sunday **12-5**

Evening hours are available by appointment

Visit our Gallery of Chicagoland's
Largest Selection of Antique Prints,
Maps & Vintage Graphics.

Museum Quality Custom Framing.
The largest selection
of choices to choose from.

- Chicagoland's Biggest variety of antique
  prints & maps
- Vintage graphics and paintings
- Frame and art restoration services available

BRING IN THIS INVITATION TO RECEIVE

$50 OFF

your purchase of $250 of more

$100 OFF

your purchase of $ 500 or more

PRINCETON ART GALLERY

VINTAGE POSTER & PRINTS

Imaginative Custom Framing & Custom Acrylic Display

1844 First St. Highland Park, Illinois Phone 847.432.1930

THE

CRYSTAL CAVE

Crystal Repair
Glass Engraving

OF
WILMETTE

1141 Central Ave.· Wilmette, IL 60091
(847) 251-1160 · Fax (847) 251-1172
allcrystall1141@aol.com

**EVERY TIME
WE SAY LET THERE BE!
IN ANY FORM,
SOMETHING HAPPENS.**
Stella Terrill Mann

The
Ashley
Group

Publishers of Fine Visual Reference for the Discerning Connoisseur

1350 Touhy Ave. • Des Plaines, Illinois 60018
888.458.1750 • FAX 847.390.2902
ashleygroup@cahners.com

Finally...
Chicago's Own
Home & Design
Sourcebook

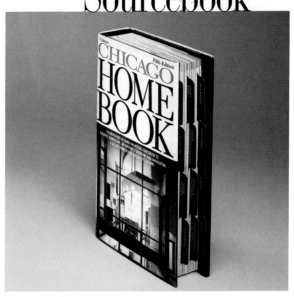

Call Toll Free at 888-458-1750

The Chicago Home Book, www.chicagohomebook.com, is your
final destination when searching for home improvement services.
This comprehensive, hands-on-guide to building, remodeling,
decorating, furnishing, and landscaping a home, is required
reading for the serious and discriminating homeowner. With over
700 full-color, beautiful pages, this hard cover volume is the most
complete and well-organized reference to the home industry. The
Home Book covers all aspects of the process, including listings of
hundreds of industry professionals, accompanied by informative
and valuable editorial discussing the most recent trends. Ordering
your copy of ***The Chicago Home Book,*** now, can ensure that
you have the blueprints to your dream home, in your hand, today.

Order your copy today!

O R D E R   F O R M

THE CHICAGO HOME BOOK

☐ YES, please send me _____ copies of the CHICAGO HOME BOOK at $39.95 per book, plus $3 postage & handling per book.

Total amount sent: $_____   Please charge my: ☐ VISA   ☐ MasterCard   ☐ American Express

Card # _____ Exp. Date_____

Signature _____

Name _____ Phone ( ) _____

Address _____

City _____ State _____ Zip Code _____

Send order to: Attn: Book Sales–Marketing Dept., The Ashley Group, 1350 E. Touhy Ave., Suite 1E, Des Plaines, Illinois 60018
Or Call Toll Free at: 1-888-458-1750   Or E-mail ashleybooksales@cahners.com

All orders must be accompanied by check, money order or credit card # for full amount.

Photo courtesy of:
Columbia Audio/Video

HOME
THEATER

&

TECHNOLOGY

KASS
ELECTRONICS

- Structured Wiring
- Kass Electronics designs and installs systems to meet a wide range of price levels
- Showroom with state of the art technology
- Complete documentation and simple instruction cards for all systems that we install
- Our installers and sales representatives are trained on all products that we use
- Work coordinated with other subcontractors
- Advanced engineering background
- Exhaustive attention to detail
- All systems designed to be easy to use

KASS
ELECTRONICS

Home Theater Installations

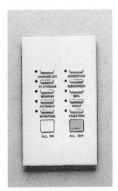

Lighting Systems

Whole House Audio Systems

• Custom Design
• Installation
• System Integration

HOME ELECTRONICS NETWORK

- Systems That Blend into Any Decor
- Designs To Fit Your Lifestyle & Budget
- Exhaustive Attention to Detail to
  Insure Ease of Use and Reliability

CEDIA

LUCASFILM
THX

FOR MORE INFORMATION,
CALL OR VISIT OUR SHOWROOM
THX is a registered trademark of Lucasfilms Ltd.
26W515 St. Charles Road
Carol Stream, IL 60188

(630)221-8480   Fax (630)221-8430
www.kasselectronics.com

"There is
music
wherever there is

*harmony,
order and
proportion.* "
Sir Thomas Browne

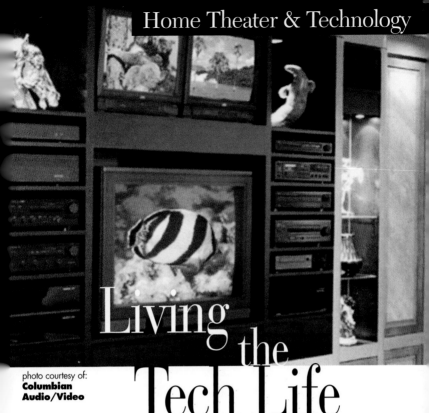

Living the Tech Life

733

Home theaters just keep getting better and better. Technology wizards continue to deliver bigger and better products less obtrusively, and more affordably, into our homes. What was once a rare home luxury has become a top priority item in new custom homes, and in home additions and renovations.

Sophisticated Chicago area homeowners have had their level of appreciation for quality in sight and sound elevated through years of experience in concert halls, movie theaters and sports arenas. As they gravitate toward making the home the focus of their lifestyle, and strive to incorporate that high level of performance into their leisure time at home, home theater becomes a more desirable and practical investment. Systems are used for viewing commercial movies, home videos, live concerts and sport events, playing games, and accessing interactive technology. Media or entertainment rooms, custom-sized and designed to deliver concert hall sound and a big, sharp picture, are frequently specified in new construction and remodeling projects. Interest in upscale prefabricated home theaters, which are far more luxurious than some of today's movie theaters, continues to increase. "Hey, kids, let's go to the movies!"

THE IMPORTANCE OF A
HOME THEATER DESIGN SPECIALIST

Home theater is widely specified as a custom home feature today. The sophisticated homeowner with a well-developed eye (and ear) for quality demands the latest technology in a home entertainment system that will provide pleasure for many years. Because of the fluid marketplace, the vast possibilities of the future, and the complexity of the products, it's crucial to employ an established professional to design and install your home theater.

The experts presented on the following pages can advise you on the best system for your home. They can find an appropriate cabinet (or direct you to expert custom cabinet makers), expertly install your system, and teach you to use it. Their expertise will make the difference.

THE HOME THEATER DESIGN PROCESS

Tell your builder or remodeling specialist early if you want a home theater, especially if built-in speakers, a large screen or a ceiling-mounted video projection unit are part of the plan.

Inform the interior designer so proper design elements can be incorporated. Window treatments to block out light and help boost sound quality, furnishings or fabrics to hide or drape speakers, and comfortable seating to enhance the media experience should be considered. If you plan to control the window treatments by remote control, these decisions will have to be coordinated.

Visit one of the following showrroms. Be ready to answer these questions:

• What is your budget? There is no upper limit on what you can spend.

• Do you want a television tube or projection video system? A DVD player or hi-fi VCR? Built-in or free-standing speakers?

• Do you want Internet access?

• What style of cabinetry and lighting do you want? Do you want lighting or a built-in bar? How much storage is needed?

• What are the seating requirements? Seating should be at least seven feet from the screen.

• Do you want whole-house control capability so you can distribute and control the system from different rooms of the house?

• How will you incorporate the system with the rest of the room? Must the home theater room meet other needs?

• Do you want extra luxuries, like multiple screens, or a remote control system that allows you to dim the lights and close the draperies? Ask your salesperson for ideas.

• Will this room function in the future? As technology continues to change our lifestyle, plan for this room to grow and change as well. Ask your salesperson for advice.

Take your blueprints or pictures to a specialty store where an "experience room" is set up for firsthand testing of different components and knowledgeable consultants can answer your questions. Electronics is a complex subject, but a good consultant will educate, not mystify you.

An in-home consultation with the designer should take place early in the planning stages. You can discuss issues like speaker placement and location of wall control panels.

Before hiring a designer, make sure your service needs will be met in a timely and expert manner. Ask for the names of former and repeat clients for references.

Experienced audio-video or media consultants can astutely determine your needs. They can design and install an end product that is properly sized for your room, satisfies your desire for quality, and meets the terms of your budget. They respect cabinetry requirements and the decorating elements that must be addressed in the deliverance of a top quality home theater.

The media consultant should be willing to work with the architect, builder and interior designer to make sure your requirements will be met.

Home theaters are installed at the same time as the security and phone systems, before insulation and drywall. In new construction or remodeling, start making decisions at least two months before the drywall is hung. Allow four weeks for delivery and installation scheduling.

CREATING A HOME THEATER

For the best seat in the house, you'll need:

• A large screen television and/or projection video system (from 32-inch direct view up to 200-inches, depending on the size of the room). New, compact products are available now.

• A surround-sound receiver to direct sound to the appropriate speaker with proper channel separation

• A surround-sound speaker system, with front, rear, and center channel speakers and a sub-woofer for powerful bass response

• A hi-fi stereo VCR or DVD (digital video) player for ultimate audio and video quality

• Appropriate cabinetry, properly vented

• A comfortable environment, ideally a rectangular room with extra drywall to block out distractions.

PLAN AHEAD

Even if you aren't installing a home theater system right away, have a room designed to serve that purpose later. Get the wiring done and build the room an appropriate shape and size. Get the right antenna. Ask for double drywall for noise control.

THE FUTURE'S HERE

Smart homes, those with whole-house integrated control systems and computerized automation, even voice-activated automation, are a reality in the late 1990s.

Many professionals believe it will one day be as standard as central air conditioning. It will be commonplace for a system to start your morning coffee, crank up the furnace, close drapes during a downpour, or send a fax.

BEST TIP:

Have phone lines pulled to every TV outlet in the house for Internet access and satellite reception.

Home Theater
Designers

AUDIO CONSULTANTS..**(847) 864-9565**
   1014 Davis Street, Evanston   Fax: (847) 864-9570
   See Add on Page: 740   800 Extension: 6016
   <u>Principal/Owner:</u> Simon Zreczny

COLUMBIA AUDIO/VIDEO..**(847) 433-6010**
   1741 Second Street, Highland Park   Fax: (847) 433-9332
   See Add on Page: 737   800 Extension: 1136
   <u>Principal/Owner:</u> Gary Rozak
   <u>Website:</u> www.columbiaaudiovideo.com

CUSTOM HOME THEATERS, LTD. ....**(847) 836-8197**
   514 Regan Drive, East Dundee   Fax: (847) 836-8198
   See Add on Page: 738   800 Extension: 1085
   <u>Principal/Owner:</u> Ray Finato
   <u>Description:</u> Specializing in state of the art, dedicated movie viewing environments and whole house audio/video distribution systems.

KASS ELECTRONICS, INC...**(630) 221-8480**
   26W515 St. Charles Road, Carol Stream   Fax: (630) 221-8430
   See Add on Page: 730, 731, 741   800 Extension: 1036
   <u>Principal/Owner:</u> Bill Dwyer
   <u>Website:</u> www.kasselectronics.com   <u>e-mail:</u> kasswjd@aol.com

SOUND & VISION ....**(708) 403-2500**
   14474 S. LaGrange Road, Orland Park   Fax: (708) 403-2428
   See Add on Page: 739   800 Extension: 1180
   <u>Website:</u> www.soundandvisionusa.com

**Design/Build
Custom
Environment**

**Multi-Room
Audio/Video
Distribution
Systems**

Custom Home Theaters integrates
the disciplines of architectural design,
interior design, general contracting
and audio/video engineering.

Each individual design achieves
the highest level of technological
performance while maximizing
available space.

**Structured
Wiring**

**Customized
Control
Systems**

**C
H
T** **Custom Home Theaters, Ltd.**
Phone: 847-836-8197 Fax: 847-836-8198

PUT A BREATHTAKING ADDITION IN YOUR HOME.

If you're thinking of adding a home theatre, think Audio Consultants.
Whether your budget is lavish or modest, our approach is simple... when it's
perfect, we're done. This uncommon dedication to customer satisfaction is just
one of the reasons why Audio/Video International Magazine perennially lists us
as one of the top 30 A/V retailers in the U.S. Experience why individuals who
demand unparalleled quality in audio and video become lifelong customers.

Since 1967

audio consultants

Evanston	Hinsdale	Libertyville	Chicago
847.864.9565	630.789.1990	847.362.5594	312.642.5950

"THE BEAUTIFUL RESTS ON THE FOUNDATIONS OF THE NECESSARY "

Emerson

The
Ashley
Group

Publishers of Fine Visual Reference for the Discerning Connoisseur

1350 Touhy Ave. • Des Plaines, Illinois 60018
888.458.1750 • FAX 847.390.2902
ashleygroup@cahners.com

KASS
ELECTRONICS

- Custom Design
- Installation
- Systems Integration

FOR MORE INFORMATION,
CALL OR VISIT OUR SHOWROOM
26W515 St. Charles Road
Carol Stream, IL 60188

(630)221-8480   Fax (630)221-8430
www.kasselectronics.com

Intergrated Home Systems

AUDIO IMAGE...**(773) 334-2400**
5810 N. Lincoln Avenue, Chicago   Fax: (773) 334-2444
See Add on Page: 743   800 Extension: 1257
Principal/Owner: Kevin In

BAUMEISTER AUDIO VIDEO INTERIORS, INC. ....**(773) 774-9080**
5342 North Northwest Highway, Chicago   Fax: (773) 774-9039
See Add on Page: 744   800 Extension: 1249
Principal/Owner: John Baumeister
e-mail: bavi@bavi.net

DIGITAL HOME TECHNOLOGIES ....**(847) 776-5063**
346 N. Northwest Highway, Palatine   Fax: (847) 776-1297
See Add on Page: 745   800 Extension: 1069
Principal/Owner: John Goldenne
Website: www.adigitalhome.com   e-mail: info@adigitalhome.com

KASS ELECTRONICS, INC....**(630) 221-8480**
25W515 St. Charles Road, Carol Stream   Fax: (630) 221-8430
See Add on Page: 730, 731, 741   800 Extension: 1040
Principal/Owner: Bill Dwyer
Website: www.kasselectronics.com   e-mail: kasswjd@aol.com

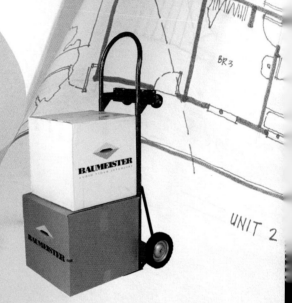

 ome Theater

 Security Systems

 Fiber Optic Cabling

 ome Automation

 Installation

 Phone Systems

 mart Lighting

 Audio/Video

 Satellite TV

Computer Networks

 Smart Monitoring

DIGITAL HOME
TECHNOLOGIES

Integrating Your Home's Communications, Entertainment, Security, and Automation.

Visit Our Showroom At:
346 N. Northwest Highway - Palatine, IL 60067
(847) 776-5063 - http://www.adigitalhome.com

Security System
Contractors

KEYTH TECHNOLOGIES, INC ....**(847) 433-0000**
1575 Oakwood Avenue - Sun Valley Plaza, Highland Park   Fax: (847) 998-0000
See Add on Page: 747   800 Extension: 1004
<u>Principal/Owner:</u> Keith Fisher
<u>Website:</u> www.Keyth.com   <u>e-mail:</u> Keith@keyth.com
<u>Description:</u> Keyth established in 1975 provides custom solutions for any security and communication need. Locksmiths, safes, CCTV, automation.

"Nowhere in the home is the *rapid pace of technology* more evident than in the field of home theater and technology."

LOCATION

We'd Love To Sha

Photo courtesy of:
Wynstone Realty

LOCATION

LOCATION

ur Views With You!

CONWAY FARMS

Homesites from 0.5 to 1.5 acres
Homes from approximately $560,000 to $1,300,000

Located 1 mile west of Waukegan Road and 1/4 mile south of Rt. 60 on
Conway Farms Dr. in Lake Forest. Open daily 11:00 a.m. to 5:00 p.m., or by appointment.
Call 847-615-9515 for more information.

Golf Course Architect: Tom Fazio   *Henebry Photography*

"Must I leave thee, *Paradise?* Thus leave thee, *native soil,* *these happy walks* & *shades.*"

John Milton

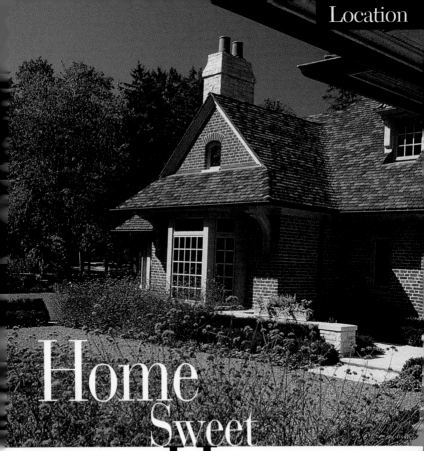

Home
Sweet
Home

photo courtesy of:
Poulton Group, Ltd.

 One of the most endearing charms of this area is the wide diversity and individuality of its neighborhoods. Whether your fantasy is to live in a stately, traditional home surrounded by lush sweeping lawns, or an ultra-modern custom built home overlooking a golf course, you are sure to find a neighborhood to call you home. To savvy homeowners, location is the most valuable of assets, and has long been their mantra.

Today's state-of-the-art homebuilders have given life to new communities in masterfully planned environments. Visually delightful and diverse, yet cohesive in architectural style and landscape, these communities address with impeccable taste the needs of their residents: proximity to excellent schools, shops, restaurants, favored leisure pursuits, the workplace. Safe havens, often in country or golf course settings, these developments cater to the homeowners' active lifestyles. Artistically designed for ease, these gracious homes welcome family and guests; they are sanctuaries in which to entertain, relax and nourish the spirit.

Location

THE COMMUNITY SPIRIT

Enclave neighborhoods built in luxury locations have the benefit of being part of two communities. The neighborhood identity is strong and so is the larger community spirit. It's the best of both worlds.

THE MASTER PLAN

Homes and landscapes in "master plan" locations are as unique and customized as anywhere in the Chicago area. However, they are established according to a well-defined overall plan, which gives the homeowners the security of knowing that the high quality look of their neighborhood will be rigorously upheld.

THE ULTIMATE IN LUXURY LIVING

The builders and developers of custom homes in upscale locations throughout the city and the suburbs realize the value of simplicity and strive to deliver it.

Simplicity is one of the qualities we most desire in our lives. By offering a community designed and built on the philosophy that homeowners deserve a beautiful environment, peaceful surroundings and luxurious amenities to enhance their lives, locations like those featured in the following pages deliver simplicity on a luxury scale.

Homeowners who live in these kinds of communities and locations know what they want. They want an environment where architecture and nature exist in harmony. Where builders have proven dedication to protecting the natural surroundings. They want recreation, like golf, swimming, lakes, walk and biking paths, or tennis courts. They want to live where there is a sense of community, and the convenience of close-by shopping and transportation. Finally, they want the conveniences of a well-planned community – guidelines on buildings and landscaping, strong community identity, and commitment to quality.

FINDING THE PERFECT LOCATION

Think about what kind of location would enhance the lifestyle of yourself and your family:

Do you need to be near transportation?

Do you want the security of a gated community?

What kind of recreational amenities do you want? Golf, tennis or pool? Paths, fishing lakes, or horse trails? Party facilities, restaurants?

What kind of natural environment do you prefer? Wildlife sanctuary, urban elegance, club luxury?

What kind of home do you want to build? Determine if your dream house fits the overall essence of a particular community. Some planned communities allow only certain builders at their locations. Find out if these builders create homes that would satisfy your desires.

THE VALUE OF A LUXURY LOCATION

The availability of building sites diminishes with every passing year, and the builders and developers of our finest residential locations know that quality must be established to attract custom home owners. Their commitment to building top quality homes is apparent in the designs and materials used in their projects and in the reputations their locations enjoy.

The demand for homes built in these locations is growing. Their benefits, plus the unique opportunity to build a new custom home in a totally fresh, and new environment, are very enticing. ■

CONWAY FARMS ....(847) 615-9515
Conway Farms Drive, Lake Forest
See Add on Page: 750, 751, 758   800 Extension: 1091
Website: www.conwayfarms.com
WYNSTONE REALTY ....(847) 381-7100
101 S. Wynstone Drive, North Barrington   Fax: (847) 304-2880
See Add on Page: 756, 757   800 Extension: 6337
Principal/Owner: Ron Sever/Christie Baines
Website: www.wynstone.com e-mail: contact@wynstone.com
Description: Exclusive agents for Wynstone, a limited access Jack Nicklaus golf
community in North Barrington selling luxury residences.

"Homeowners want an
environment where
nature and harmony
exist in *harmony.*"

Dream it – Play it – Live

Good friends and good times await you

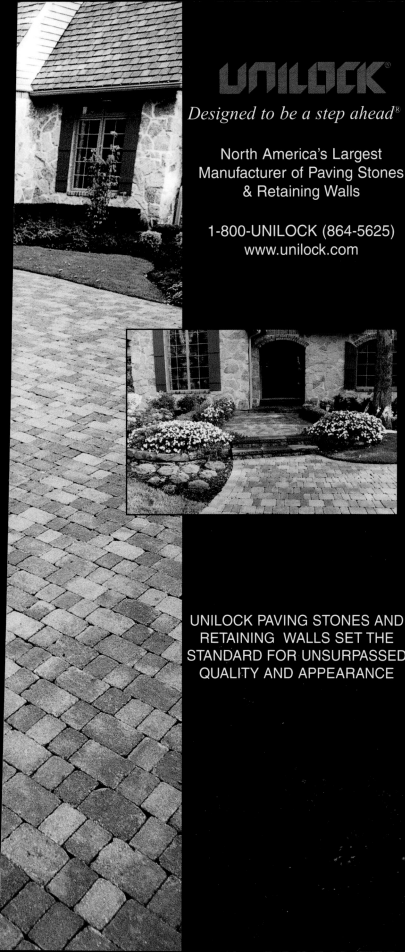

"If eyes were Made for seeing, Then Beauty is its own excuse. "

Ralph Waldo Emerson

Alphabetical Index

Alphabetical Index

Professional Index

ARCHITECTS

Professional Index

769

CUSTOM WOODWORKING, METAL, HARDWARE & GLASS

Professional Index

FLOORING & COUNTERTOPS

HOME FURNISHING & DECORATING

Professional Index

775

Professional Index

Specialty Wall Finishes

Traditional

Transitional

Wall Coverings

Window Coverings

HOME THEATER & SOUND

Audio/Video Retailers

Audio/Video, Custom

Home Theater Design

Integrated Home Systems

Lighting

Modular A/V Furniture

Security System Contractors

Telecom Systems

INTERIOR DESIGNERS

American Traditional

Art Deco

KITCHEN & BATH

783

Notes

785

786

787

789

Notes